ALPHA BRAVO DELTA
GUIDE TO
AMERICAN AIRBORNE FORCES

ALPHA BRAVO DELTA
GUIDE TO
AMERICAN AIRBORNE FORCES

W. THOMAS SMITH JR.

ALPHA

A member of Penguin Group (USA) Inc.

International Standard Book Number: 1-59257-166-2
Library of Congress Catalog Card Number: 2003115222

06   05   04   8   7   6   5   4   3   2   1

Interpretation of the printing code: The rightmost number of the first series of numbers is the year of the book's printing; the rightmost number of the second series of numbers is the number of the book's printing. For example, a printing code of 04-1 shows that the first printing occurred in 2004.

Printed in the United States of America

This book is dedicated to those American soldiers, sailors, airmen, and Marines who wear or have worn silver or gold parachute wings over their left breast pockets.

It is also for Dad, the late William Thomas "Bill" Smith; my brother, the late Michael Robert Smith; and for the late U.S. Senator James Strom Thurmond, a former glider-infantry officer with the 82nd Airborne Division at Normandy, who years later was instrumental in my winning a slot to jump school.

CONTENTS

FOREWORD

PARATROOPER! The very name conjures up the image of a heavily armed, swiftly moving, face-painted demon who comes out of the night to wreak his havoc on the enemy and then just as quickly disappear. That's not an altogether false image.

Since the inception of airborne forces, military parachutists have largely come from volunteers whose main desire was to be considered among the elite of their services. These warriors were all required to pass more stringent physical requirements than their fellow soldiers. They endured tough training preparing them for something wholly unnatural: flinging themselves from a swiftly moving aircraft, sometimes at night, trusting their lives to their training, to a few pounds of nylon fabric and cord, and to someone else's expertise in packing a parachute. It has always taken someone of incredible bravery to "jump." It's a testament to the strength of character of young Americans and to our training methods that literally hundreds of thousands have been so successful at it since 1940.

W. Thomas Smith Jr. has captured the mystique and the history of all of America's airborne forces from their inception to the present. His descriptions of early airborne training and forces, as well as how equipment, techniques, and tactics have evolved up to today's elite airborne units, are inspiring and entertaining.

So why is it that every year thousands of young people volunteer for the arduous training and dangerous business of military parachuting? What is it that drives soldiers, sailors, airmen, and Marines to sign up to do something so inherently dangerous? When I was a young Marine officer, we would literally fight each other to get a "quota" to jump school. Everybody wanted to do it. We wanted to do it for the same reasons we joined the Marine Corps. To serve our country, surely, but even more we wanted to test ourselves against an unyielding standard that demanded more than we might be able to give. After all, when the green light goes on that first time and the jumpmaster says "Go," you either jump or you don't. There isn't any equivocation. We would have endured most anything, any tough, dirty, exhausting training necessary just to earn the right to take the test.

It's that willingness to go the extra mile, to run farther than you have to, do more push-ups than necessary, to take death-defying chances, to strive to meet the challenge that distinguishes military parachutists, divers, mountaineers, Marines, and Special Forces from "ordinary" military men and women. We all knew it would be tough going and yet no one shied away. All of us were willing to risk failure, even death, to prove, mostly to ourselves, that we had what it takes to be considered among the elite. Some would say it's foolish. But when your business is to be successful in the most chaotic, demanding, and dangerous of human endeavors—combat— well, the more you know about your weaknesses and strengths, the more you understand your own motivations, the better for you and everyone who counts on your judgments.

The willingness to take the risk most wouldn't is the distinguishing characteristic of an "elite" warrior. It's also the primary reason America's elite forces are so successful. Whether the measure is the fabled 82nd and 101st Airborne of World War II fame, the Marines who made the Inchon landing and fought the Chosin Reservoir campaigns in Korea, the Special Forces, SEALs, or Rangers of Vietnam, those who were forged in the hottest fire have the steel to win over any odds.

Perhaps Thucydides said it best in about 400 B.C.E. when he described the Spartan warriors during the Greek Peloponnesian Wars. He wrote, "We must remember that one man is much the same as another, and that he is best who is trained in the severest school."

I can tell you from experience that today's armed forces are fully up to the challenge and legacy of those who pioneered and perfected airborne operations. Over the past 2 years, I've been privileged to help train nearly 40,000 young men and women to be United States Marines. They are superb, the best I've seen in 28 years of service. Their average age is 19.7 years. When you put this book down in the evening before you go to bed, think about what George Orwell said more than 60 years ago. He wrote,

"We sleep safe in our beds because rough men stand ready in the night to visit violence on those who would do us harm." Then remember those steely eyed warriors who stand on freedom's borders and who carry the legacy of the "devils in baggy pants" are mostly less than 25 years old.

Col. Jeff Bearor, USMC

Col. Bearor is a career Marine officer and paratrooper who served as an operations officer with the CIA's Counterterrorism Center. A graduate of Great Britain's famed Royal Marine Commando course, he is currently the commanding officer of the Recruit Training Regiment at the U.S. Marine Corps Recruit Depot, Parris Island, South Carolina.

INTRODUCTION

Where is the Prince who can afford so to cover this country with troops for its defense, as that 10,000 men descending from the clouds, might not, in many places, do an infinite deal of mischief before a force could be brought together to repel them.
—Benjamin Franklin, 1784

The thing that distinguished us most from other soldiers was our willingness to take chances and risks in a branch of the army that provided a great, new, almost unexplored frontier. In other days, paratroopers would have been the type of men to sail with Columbus, or the first to seek out the West and fight the Indians.
—Ross S. Carter, a paratrooper with the 82nd Airborne Division during World War II

When I attended "jump school" more than two decades ago, there was a saying among nonparatroopers that ground week separated the men from the boys. Tower week separated the fools from the men. And during the third and final week, the fools jumped. Of course, we knew it was all light-hearted jabbing and a bit of sincere professional jealously.

Every member of the U.S. armed forces was aware then, as they are today, that there was something special about a paratrooper, something that set him apart from the ordinary "leg" infantryman. In fact, the initial perception of most anyone gazing upon a uniformed soldier or sailor from any nation wearing some form of a badge, medal, or patch with a parachute on it might be that that soldier or sailor is "specially trained." The second thought might be "he knows how to fight." Gen. William C. Westmoreland, the senior American military commander in Vietnam until 1968, was often photographed inspecting and addressing the rank and file wearing his trademark sateen cap. Pinned on the cap's crown above his four stars was the silver-winged badge of a master parachutist: It was obviously the general's most important personal decoration.

In his book, *Airborne: A Guided Tour of an Airborne Task Force*, best-selling author Tom Clancy writes, "Most special forces claim a unique ethos. Many other branches of military service have tried to claim their own code: One that is special to them. Trust me: In most cases, the people doing the claiming are full of crap. In the whole of the American military, only a handful of groups are truly worthy of such a distinction—the Marine Corps, certain special forces units, and of course, Airborne."

Indeed, Clancy was right: The American paratrooper is the epitome of the modern warrior. In order to be an airborne soldier, one has to be athletically fit and able to endure physical hardship beyond that required of an ordinary soldier. He must be able to fight with a variety of personal weapons as well as his bare hands. He must have physical courage, and he must have a reasonable capacity to think on his own, outside the box, and during periods of extreme stress.

In fact, the very basic requirement of any "special operations" combatant is that he be first and foremost a sky soldier. There are three primary reasons for this: First, the very nature of a parachutist's mission is special. Dropping behind enemy lines is essentially an unconventional, thus, "special," operation. Second, the levels of personal commitment and athleticism required of a paratrooper are, at a minimum, a prerequisite for joining the ranks of special operations or special operations-capable forces. Last, a paratrooper is not likely to be the kind of soldier who would fold under fire. The "airborne spirit" is a kind of ethos that, when integrated with a soldier's psyche, practically ensures he will fight well. And that is not some hollow *rah-rah* statement.

"The intangible but very real end product that stems from an individual's evaluation of himself is perhaps the most precious result of the process that produces parachute soldiers," wrote Lt. Gen. William Pelham "Bill" Yarborough in the foreword to *Airborne* by Edward M. Flanagan Jr.

Yarborough should certainly know. A celebrated combat paratrooper, he is considered one of the "founding fathers" of both American airborne and special operations forces. (Yarborough is also the designer of the famous silver parachute wings, the first commander to order his Special Forces soldiers to don green berets, and one of the earliest proponents of airborne soldiers wearing red berets.) "A warrior who will bail out at night onto a battlefield deep in enemy country while carrying fifty pounds of equipment, weapons, and ammunition is not likely to perform poorly in combat," Yarborough adds.

Brig. Gen. David L. Grange agrees but adds, "it's a cultural phenomenon within a unit based on solid training and leadership, and the resulting pride from both."

Grange, a CNN national security analyst and senior executive with the Robert R. McCormick Tribune Foundation, commanded myriad combat units—Special Forces, Ranger, aviation, and infantry—while on active duty in the Army. And with extensive airborne experience, including High Altitude/Low Opening (HALO) parachute jumps, he concedes that airborne units make up some of the world's finest military organizations, but they do not hold exclusive rights to combat efficiency. "The 1st Infantry Division, the 'Big Red One' for example, is as fine a division as has ever been fielded," Grange says.

No one could argue with that. After all, the Army's 3rd Infantry Division—known as the "Rock of the Marne" for its stalwart defense of France's Marne River in 1918—performed magnificently during the recent war with Iraq. The division's soldiers, along with leathernecks from the 1st Marine Division, were the first American forces to smash their way into Baghdad. Both divisions had trained paratroopers in their ranks (the Army more so than the Marines). But for the most part, the rank and file were conventional soldiers infused with a warrior's mindset. The difference between airborne and nonairborne units, however, is that *all* airborne units are products of this same warrior's mindset or esprit de corps, what Grange refers to as "culture" and Clancy as "ethos."

During the American military's darkest days, the Vietnam War, it was this same airborne ethos that the Army found to be most dependable. Only one mass jump was made by the Americans (the 173rd Airborne Brigade) over Vietnam, but U.S. paratroopers often bore the brunt of much of the toughest fighting.

"After Tet '68 the war was so unpopular the paratrooper probably did not initially volunteer for military service," said John Temple Ligon, an airborne/Ranger-trained artillery officer in Vietnam. "Once in, however, he went to jump school only as a volunteer with the full understanding that he was training as a shock trooper, a soldier the brass would always send first in its order for combat while the leg infantry followed. Once occupation settled in, such as with the 173rd Airborne in the Central Highlands, the paratroopers were still sent on tougher assignments and longer patrols than the leg infantry. With the 173rd, we humped the hills on combat ambush patrols for 15 days and nights each mission, while the leg infantry tended to operate from artillery stationed firebases on simple overnight assignments, returning each morning for a hot breakfast and a behind-the-wire rest."

Soldiers before and since Vietnam have joined the airborne ranks for reasons as simple as knowing that the man on one's left or right could be depended upon in combat because he was a paratrooper. One often-shared tale among sky soldiers is the story of a conversation between Gen. Maxwell Taylor, who commanded the 101st Airborne Division during World War II, and one of his paratroopers. During inspections, Taylor used to ask his men if they enjoyed jumping out of airplanes. In nearly all cases, the response was, "Yes, sir, airborne, sir!" In one instance, however, a paratrooper matter-of-factly responded, "No, sir." When Taylor asked him why he had joined the 101st, the young man responded, "Because I like to be with people who do like to jump."

Parachuting by nature is a dangerous pursuit. A free-falling paratrooper exiting an airplane can reach speeds of up to 120 to 125 miles per hour (mph) before pulling his rip cord. If his chute fails to function, his body will reach the earth at that same speed.

The average terminal velocity of a free-falling human with arms and legs outstretched is 120 to 125 mph. Higher speeds can be achieved by free-falling skydivers who streamline their bodies by bringing their arms and legs together as they fall. Experienced jumpers can reach speeds of 160 to 180 mph. A human body in a tight ball can reach terminal speeds of around 200 mph. The record speed of a free-falling human is 714 mph. Naturally, the body must be falling at a far slower rate before attempting to deploy the parachute. The maximum safe speed for chute deployment is between 110 and 120 mph.

Most military parachutists making mass-unit jumps use a static line, a long steel cable above the parachutist's head that runs lengthwise through the cargo compartment of an airplane. Prior to jumping, the parachutist stands up and connects a webbed line from his main parachute to the static line. On the end of the webbed line is a closing spring-loaded steel hook that clasps onto the static line but runs freely down the line as the parachutist shuffles with his fellow jumpers toward the exit door. When the jumper leaps from the airplane, the webbed line automatically begins to pull and deploys the parachute canopy from the parachute pack. The jumper falls for about 300 feet before feeling the "jerk" of his blossoming canopy.

With his chute fully deployed, the paratrooper descends to the earth at a rate of approximately 12 to 17 mph, but his forward directional speed is between 7 and 14 mph. The rate of descent and the rate of forward directional movement vary according to the actual wind speed and the combined weight of the jumper and his equipment. The higher the wind speed, the greater the forward directional movement of the paratrooper. The heavier the individual and the battle load, the greater the rate of descent.

Modern parafoil or ram-air parachutes used by sport jumpers (and some military special operations forces) are highly maneuverable. They can reach forward directional speeds of 20 to 30 mph and can be slowed to near 0 mph upon landing. Standard U.S. military parachutes, however, such as the T-10C and MCI-1B/C, do not allow the combat paratrooper as much speed control or maneuverability. The reasoning is simple. In a mass jump environment, parachutists traveling at forward directional rates of 20-plus mph would pose a danger to other jumpers in the area. Additionally, combat jumps are usually made in darkness and at very low altitudes, thus eliminating the need for highly maneuverable parachutes.

Of course, high-performance parachute rigs, modern extreme sports such as base jumping (parachuting from a fixed point such as a tower, building, or cliff), and even tandem jumping (a novice jumper strapped to an experienced skydiver) have stripped away much of the paratrooper's mystique. No longer is jumping out of a perfectly good airplane considered to be a military function conducted by only a very few pioneering warriors. Even female soldiers attend jump school, though their physical fitness training standards are not the same as those of the males and they are barred by federal policy from serving in direct combat action roles. They cannot make "true" combat jumps, and they are not allowed to serve in special operations forces. But they are allowed to serve as riggers (parachute packers) and in noncombatant supporting roles. Consequently, and to the dismay of many old sky soldiers, parachuting is no longer the exclusive military men's club it once was.

So what is it that sets the contemporary paratrooper apart from his "leg" infantry brothers and his civilian "sport-parachuting" counterparts? It is the physical courage required to jump out of fast-moving, propeller-driven, and jet aircraft with hundreds of others doing the same thing in an environment that is dangerous in more ways than one. Unlike civilian parachutists, combat-trained paratroopers carry a heavy equipment load. They often jump at night with no artificial lighting. They sometimes jump at dangerously low altitudes and usually with many other jumpers and planes in the air and with troopers on the ground. If a paratrooper is jumping at a low altitude and his main chute fails, there will be no time to use his reserve chute. He will simply die.

"At 600 feet we were in the air only about 25 to 30 seconds," writes former 82nd Airborne Division officer T. Moffat Burris of his training jumps prior to being deployed in World War II. "In combat even that short amount of time can seem like an eternity."

If the paratrooper is jumping at a high altitude and his main chute fails, he must keep his wits about him and employ his reserve chute within an ultra-brief window of time or, again, he will be killed. On top of all that, the paratrooper has to face all the inherent dangers associated with any type of flying or sport jumping.

Because it is usually dark when a paratrooper jumps, he can only hope the pilot drops him safely over the preselected drop zone. If the pilot misjudges, the paratrooper might land in unseen trees that could disembowel him, electrical wires that could electrocute him, or water that could drown him. And that's just for training purposes. In combat, the difference between paratroopers and regular soldiers is the combination of both the jump and the mission.

En route, the paratrooper is in just as much danger as any combat aircrewman who has to brave antiaircraft fire, missiles, enemy planes, and unseen small arms fire from the ground. When he exits the aircraft, the paratrooper is a drifting target silhouetted against the sky and unable to adequately defend himself until he lands. On the ground, he is in unfamiliar territory, behind enemy lines, temporarily cut off from his unit. He could be landing on top of an enemy platoon or a pitchfork-wielding farmer, either of which could kill him before he unhooks himself from his parachute harness.

Airborne units have always had to be ready on a moment's notice. The 82nd Airborne Division, for example, "is on tab to go anywhere in the world in eighteen hours," says Brig. Gen. Marvin E. "Mitch" Mitchiner, a former battalion commander with the 82nd. A remarkable feat, considering the fact that most infantry units can take up to two weeks to ship out.

Two schools of thought have arisen regarding the function of large division and brigade-size airborne forces: One regards them as hybrid "special" forces—half-conventional infantry/half-commando. The other school contends that the unit's parachute capability is just one of several delivery options available to senior military commanders. If a problem flares up anywhere in the world that requires a U.S. ground combat presence (beyond small special operations teams), America's two immediate options are forward-deployed amphibious assault ships with Marines or on-call Army airborne forces. "A parachute is merely a means of delivery, but not a way of fighting," writes Bernard B. Fall in *Street Without Joy*, a history of France's own military debacle in Indochina (Vietnam).

Nevertheless, airborne delivery is a unique concept in military history. As such, it has become an element in the evolution of shock warfare, which has existed for centuries in the form of horse cavalry. Striking behind enemy lines with thunderclap surprise and operating as highly mobile, protective screens or anchoring units on the flanks of friendly forces, American paratroopers are indeed the reincarnation of U.S. cavalry troopers, as are helicopter-borne, fixed-wing aircraft-landed (troops transported in conventional troop-carrying airplanes and landed on a forward airfield), amphibious, and some light mechanized forces. In the eighteenth and nineteenth centuries, it was always the cavalry "on the way to the rescue." In the twentieth century, more often than not, it has been the sky soldier who has "jumped" to the rescue.

Nowhere was this more evident than during Operation Urgent Fury, the invasion of the Caribbean island nation of Grenada. On the morning of October 25, 1983, American medical students attending St. George's Medical College on Grenada were awakened by the sounds of distant gunfire and aircraft. Jumping out of bed and peering through their dormitory windows, they saw two planes circling the Point Salinas airport. Minutes later, they watched as helicopters roared in from the sea and flew through antiaircraft fire. Then there were the blossoming parachutes—hundreds of them. The students became frightened when the heavily armed, blackened-faced paratroopers landed, rushed toward their complex, and began cutting through the school's chain-link fence. Believing the sky soldiers to be enemy commandos coming to take them prisoner or worse, many of the students began to panic, and some cried. But tears were soon replaced with cries of joy when they discovered that the tough-looking paratroopers were actually U.S. Army Rangers coming to their rescue.

Paratroopers also serve as the basic element of modern American special operations forces. All services—Army, Navy, Marine Corps, Air Force, and even the Central Intelligence Agency—maintain airborne units or elements, though the Army maintains the only remaining "division" of paratroopers, the 82nd Airborne Division (the 101st is also referred to as "airborne," but it is, in fact, air assault). And all paratroopers, regardless of service branch, are initially trained at the U.S. Army's "jump school" at Fort Benning, Georgia.

The colorful history of American paratroopers spans a period of less than a century. The idea of parachuting armed men into battle wasn't conceived until the end of World War I, and the concept was not put into practice until the beginning of World War II. Since then, U.S. airborne forces—including the short-lived glider forces—have played a major role in every American military action, including the current war against terrorism and the recent invasion of Iraq. And with an increasing dependence on fast, flexible conventional and special operating forces, the scope of the airborne soldier's responsibilities will only increase.

So perhaps the *fools* do jump during the final week of parachute training. But it is the threat of those same fools that keeps America's enemies wide awake at night … while the rest of us soundly sleep.

Acknowledgments

There are far too many to thank for their assistance in the research and the writing of this book. However, I am particularly indebted to my agent, James C. Vines in New York, my editors at Alpha Books—Gary Goldstein in New York; Michael Hall in Portland, Oregon; Christy Wagner in

Indianapolis, Indiana—and my publicist, Dawn Werk, also in Indy. Special thanks also to Marie Butler-Knight, vice president and publisher of Alpha Books, who also took time to work with me in an editorial capacity.

Others deserving special recognition include Lt. Gen. John Bruce Blount (U.S. Army, ret.), former chief of staff of Allied Forces Southern Europe; Lt. Gen. Charles W. Bagnal (U.S. Army, ret.), former commanding general of the 101st Airborne Division (Air Assault); Brig. Gen. David L. Grange (U.S. Army, ret.), CNN national security analyst and former commanding general of the 1st Infantry Division; Brig. Gen. Marvin E. "Mitch" Mitchiner (U.S. Army, ret.), former battalion commander with the 82nd Airborne Division; the late Dr. Richard Walker, former U.S. ambassador to South Korea; Col. Jeffery W. Bearor (U.S. Marine Corps), former CIA counterterrorism officer and current chief of staff of the Marine Corps Training and Education Command at Quantico, Virginia; Col. Gary S. Supnick (U.S. Marine Corps), former Air Naval Gunfire Liaison Company commander and current commanding officer of the Headquarters and Service Battalion, Parris Island, South Carolina; executive news editor Gordon Witkin and senior writer Linda Robinson, both with *U.S. News & World Report* in Washington, D.C.; Lt. Cmdr. Mark "Cy" Divine (U.S. Naval Reserve), SEAL Team One and president of Special Operations Group, Inc., San Diego, CA; 1st Lt. Tamarra L. "Tammy" Megow (U.S. Marine Corps), public affairs officer for the 6th Marine Recruiting District, Parris Island, SC; Dan Crawford and Annette Amerson of the Marine Corps Historical Center in Washington, D.C.; Jim Crouch, director of safety and training with the United States Parachute Association in Alexandria, VA; Gilbert Bagnell, former U.S. Army interrogator with the 173rd Airborne Brigade in Vietnam; John Temple Ligon, former U.S. Army artillery officer and Airborne Ranger in Vietnam; Brian Mitchell, former U.S. Army airborne officer, intelligence operative, author, and the current bureau chief of *Investors Business Daily* in Washington, D.C.; Marie Hope Lipton, wife of the late 1st Sgt. Carwood Lipton of the 506th Parachute Infantry Regiment; Bob Mayer, novelist, lecturer, and former U.S. Army Special Forces (Green Beret) officer with the 10th Special Forces Group; Master Gunnery Sgt. Mike Ressler, U.S. Marine Band in Washington, D.C.; Gunnery Sgt. Kevin R. Helms (U.S. Marine Corps), schools coordinator for the 2nd Reconnaissance Battalion at Camp Lejeune, NC; Sgt. Spencer Harris

(U.S. Marine Corps), public affairs specialist at Camp Lejeune, NC; Chief Petty Officer Randy Bagoly, public affairs officer U.S. Navy Recruiting District Atlanta, Georgia; Elsie Jackson at the U.S. Army Infantry School Public Affairs Office, Fort Benning, Georgia; Luquita N. McDonald at the Donovan Research Library at Fort Benning, Georgia; Mark Henry with the Marine Corps Museum at Marine Corps Base, Quantico, Virginia; and Rebecca Hirsch at PhotoAssist, Inc., in Bethesda, Maryland.

Additional support was received from Brett Harvey, Zeleika Raboy, and all my other friends and colleagues at the American Society of Journalists and Authors in New York; Delacey Skinner with the Southern Literature Council of Charleston (South Carolina); the Southeastern Writers Association on St. Simons Island, Georgia; the Columbia (South Carolina) World Affairs Council; and the incredibly helpful librarians and library assistants at the University of South Carolina's Thomas Cooper Library, the Richland County Public Library, and the South Carolina State Library in Columbia.

Battle perspectives were gleaned from far too many individuals to list by name. However, a few include the above-mentioned officers and noncommissioned officers from the various branches of service. The book is also a reflection of my previous interviews and conversations with former paratroopers and airborne commanders, including Gen. William C. Westmoreland, former U.S. Army chief of staff; the countless U.S. Marines, sailors, and paratroopers with whom I was privileged to serve years ago; and many others.

I would like to thank my immediate family, including Mom, Alba Antoinette "Tita" Smith Rowell; Lt. Col. Howard Tobias Rowell (U.S. Air Force Reserve, ret., and a former U.S. Marine); Annette Smith Fowler; James David Smith; Michael Paul Fowler; and William Maxwell Fowler; as well as so many in my extended family for their unwavering support on all fronts. I would also like to thank my eternally patient magazine and newspaper editors for hanging tough with me despite months of manuscript work, which kept me out of the news fray.

Beyond that, there is an army of friends and supporters who in some way assisted with the work or deserve special recognition for simply keeping my spirits from flagging, sometimes unwittingly. A few of those include

INTRODUCTION

Mary Ann Bagnell, Edmund Bagnell, Debbie Jones Hart, Daniel Patrick "Danny" Smith, Kirby Wilbur, Kelly Minnis, F. Reid Buckley, Bill McDonald, Patricia McNeely, Aida Rogers, Dean DuBois, Bill Webber, Michael and Jennifer Graham, Candy Rikert, Dickie Anderson, Donna Bunting, Eugene Germino, Danelle Germino Haakenson, and Uncle Woody and Aunt Sandy's girls.

Although it would be almost an independent work to recognize everyone, special thanks to all those not named in Columbia, Charleston, Aiken, and Myrtle Beach, South Carolina; Raleigh and Durham, North Carolina; Omaha, Nebraska; Chicago, Illinois; Washington, D.C.; New York; and New Jersey, who in some way contributed to the completion of this book.

I would also like to thank those magnificent devils in baggy pants—American paratroopers—whose deeds and sacrifices on the battlefield have not only provided me with so much grist for the word mill, but allowed all American authors the freedom to write with accuracy and without fear of political or ideological persecution. Few scribes in history have been so fortunate. And finally and most important, thanks to God, for without him, this work would not have been possible.

W. Thomas Smith Jr.
Columbia, South Carolina

PART 1

AMERICAN PARATROOPERS

CHAPTER 1

"GERONIMO!"

Geronimo!

—Jump or battle cry of American airborne forces, first
shouted by Pvt. Aubrey Eberhardt as he leapt from an airplane over Fort Benning, Georgia, August 1940

MEN WHO MIGHT DO "AN INFINITE DEAL OF MISCHIEF"

Few divisions in American military history have a reputation as
stellar as the U.S. Army's 1st Infantry Division.

Known as the "Big Red One" for its red numeral "1" on the
uniform shoulder patch, the 1st was the first regular U.S. Army
division organized for combat action in France during World War I.
In the spring of 1918, elements of the division attacked the German
defenders at the French town of Cantigny. The fighting was brutal,
characterized by frontally assaulting the German positions, cracking
the line, storming the town, fighting house to house, and repelling
several fierce enemy counterattacks.

The battle for Cantigny was not the largest battle of the war,
but it was the first for the American Expeditionary Force (AEF). It
was a victory for the Americans, and the *fighting* 1st became world
renowned. For that reason alone, the division came very close to
becoming the first division of American paratroopers in history.

U.S. Army Air Corps Brig. Gen. William P. "Billy" Mitchell, an air warfare visionary and the senior air officer in the AEF, proposed a plan wherein American soldiers would be parachuted behind enemy lines. His soldiers of choice would be the men of the "Big Red One."

Parachutes and airborne warfare were not new concepts. In Ancient Greece, stories were told of "flying men" who attacked their enemies from the rear. Chinese acrobats in the fourteenth century were said to have performed aerial stunts with parachutelike devices. The first known parachute design was sketched in the fifteenth century by the famous Renaissance artist and inventor Leonardo da Vinci. In 1759, English poet Samuel Johnson suggested that an airborne army might well change the face of future wars. "What would be the security of the good, if the bad could at pleasure invade them from the sky?" Johnson wrote in his *History of Rasselas, Prince of Abyssinia*, "Against an army sailing through the clouds neither walls, nor mountains, nor seas, could afford any security."

Echoing Johnson's words 25 years later, American statesman Benjamin Franklin rhetorically asked, "Where is the Prince who can afford so to cover this country with troops for its defense, as that 10,000 men descending from the clouds, might not, in many places, do an infinite deal of mischief before a force could be brought together to repel them."

Parachute, originally a French word, was first used in the late 1700s. It was taken from the words *parare,* a Latin-rooted word meaning "to shield, defend, or protect" (for example, *parasol* literally means "to shelter from the sun"), and *chute,* which means "fall." Thus, *parachute* means to "shield from a fall" or "protect from falling," which is exactly what the device is designed to do.

Credit for actually considering the possibility of landing an airborne force in the enemy's rear goes to French emperor and military leader Napoleon Bonaparte. Just after the turn of the century, Napoleon in fact toyed with the idea of invading England from the air. The emperor's plan called for 2,500 balloons, each loaded with 4 French soldiers. The balloons would be launched from the continent, sail on the wind across the English Channel, reform at a point above the British Isles, and land behind the British army.

The balloon attack would coincide with an amphibious landing by regular ground forces, the latter being the primary invasion element, but Napoleon's plan never left the drawing room.

MILITARY BALLOONISTS AND CARNIVAL DAREDEVILS

For the next 100 years, the passenger-carrying balloon came into its own as a military conveyance. The craft was simple: An enormous container (the balloon itself) made of impermeable fabric was filled with heated air or a gas (usually hydrogen). Suspended beneath the container was a large wicker basket capable of carrying one or more passengers. The lighter-than-air gas enabled the balloon to rise above the surface of the earth. The early balloons had no forward control; they were simply guided up and down by a series of long tethers controlled by men on the ground. The passenger, known as a balloonist, could raise the craft skyward by dropping weighted sandbags attached to the basket. By turning a release valve that would allow some of the gas to escape from the container, the passenger could lower the balloon back to the earth.

The balloon was far too large, slow, unmaneuverable, and thus vulnerable for attacking purposes. But from a reconnaissance standpoint, the balloon changed the nature of warfare. No longer were armies concealed from their foes by simple rises or draws in the terrain. From his lofty perch high above the ground, the balloonist—usually a signal officer—could observe the fixed works, disposition, or movement of enemy forces. He could then report what he saw by wire or wait and report when he landed.

Throughout the nineteenth century, balloons were commonplace as carnival attractions. By the late nineteenth and early twentieth centuries, civilian daredevils were thrilling carnival-goers by leaping out of balloons with crude parachutes. During that same period, the heavier-than-air, engine-powered flying machine—the airplane—was invented.

As to who made the first parachute jump from an airplane is debatable. Most histories and official documents credit U.S. Army Capt. Albert Berry as being the first. Some sources contend it was made by a civilian, Grant Morton.

Berry's jump took place over Jefferson Army Barracks near St. Louis, Missouri, in 1912. His canopy deployed when it was pulled free of a bell-shape metal case beneath the aircraft fuselage, making it the first static-line–type jump. Morton allegedly jumped from a plane over Venice Beach, California, the previous year. Jumping with his parachute folded in his arms, Morton cleared the aircraft, tossed the folded chute away from his body, and it blossomed.

WORLD WAR I AND THE FIRST MILITARY PARACHUTISTS

In 1914, World War I erupted in Europe. It was the first war to herald a military application for the parachute. Soon balloonists of both the western allies and the Germans were using parachutes to escape from their hydrogen gas-filled death traps when attacked by enemy planes. By 1918, German pilots were regularly using them to bail out of doomed airplanes. But the Allies initially believed that outfitting pilots with parachutes was impractical. It was argued that pilots might opt to vacate their damaged aircraft when in fact those machines could be safely crash-landed. It was also feared that, when leaping from a speeding airplane, a parachute canopy might be ripped apart in the windblast and be snagged on the tail of the plane. Parachutes might become entangled in the aircraft propellers, or the out-of-control airplane might collide with the parachuting pilot. Beyond that was the issue of combat dignity for pilots who saw themselves as modern-day knights of the air. Many of them believed it was their duty to either crash-land their crippled airplanes or perish with them, much as a seagoing captain would go down with his ship. Nevertheless, aviators from both sides used parachutes to airdrop supplies to isolated units.

The French, Italians, and Russians actually began parachuting small reconnaissance teams and saboteurs behind enemy lines as early as 1916. But such missions were rare, and little attention was paid to them by American military leaders.

One man, Gen. Mitchell, took notice and began drawing plans for what might have been history's first airborne assault operation. On October 17, 1918, he presented his idea to Gen. John J. "Black Jack" Pershing, commanding general of the AEF. Mitchell's proposal included strapping parachutes onto 12,000 select infantrymen of the "Big Red One" and loading them onto 1,200 British-built Handley-Page biwinged bombers. Each plane would carry 10 men and 2 machine guns, and the paratroopers would be dropped on the French city of Metz, a German stronghold deep behind enemy lines.

En route to the drop zone, the entire air fleet would be escorted by fighters that would fly above, below, and on both flanks of the formation. Once they were safely on the ground, the paratroopers would assemble their weapons, reform into infantry units, and dig in. Overhead, Mitchell's fighters would provide close air support until the paratroopers were sufficiently positioned behind their newly dug works and ready for action. With the paratroopers spreading panic and confusion in the German rear areas, the primary ground elements of the Pershing's AEF would leave their trenches and attack along the front. Mitchell further proposed that his new "vertical envelopment" concept be launched in the spring of 1919.

> A vertical envelopment is a tactical maneuver wherein troops striking from the air attack the rear and/or flanks of an opposing force, in effect cutting off or encircling the force. First considered during the early years of military ballooning, the tactic was not successfully employed until World War II, when both sides vertically enveloped opposing forces with armed parachutists, gliderborne forces, troops landed by transport aircraft, or combinations thereof. Today a vertical envelopment can also be employed with helicopters.

Pershing—an old-school cavalry trooper—was naturally skeptical but gave Mitchell the green light to flesh out his plan. Mitchell put his staff to work. Senior among Mitchell's staff was Maj. Lewis Hyde Brereton who, a quarter-century later, would command an entire airborne army at the rank of lieutenant general. But Mitchell's airborne operation was not to be. The war ended in November 1918, several months before Mitchell would have been able to carry out his daring operation.

"It is conceivable that all would not have landed safely, that not every platoon could have been reformed behind those German lines," Mitchell would later say. "But remember, we should have had a potential strength of 2,400 machine guns. If we could have only got 10 percent in action against the enemy's rear we should have been successful."

Post-War Development of the Airborne Concept

Parachute experimentation continued after the war. At McCook Airfield in Ohio on April 28, 1919, Leslie L. "Sky High" Irvin—a circus acrobat—made history when he became the first man to make a free-fall descent from an airplane before deploying his parachute. Later asked if he was apprehensive before the jump, he said, "I would have been all right if everyone around me had not acted as though they were going to be my pallbearers."

Irvin blazed a new trail not only for future aviators who would be able to safely escape doomed aircraft before pulling their ripcords, but for future small teams of paratroopers who would find themselves making special operations jumps.

Gen. Mitchell himself refused to give up on his idea of a parachute force. In the spring of 1928, he arranged for an airborne demonstration at Kelly Field (the future Kelly Air Force Base) in San Antonio, Texas, and invited a number of dignitaries, including foreign military observers. There on April 29, six armed soldiers leapt from a U.S.-built Glenn Martin biwinged bomber, parachuted to the earth, landed, disengaged from their parachute harnesses, assembled their weapons, and deployed to attack positions. The entire demonstration—from the point of exiting the airplane to being ready to fight on the ground—took all of three minutes.

The jump, though wholly dramatic, failed to impress American military observers as a practical use of force. The Germans and Russians, however, took it to heart.

AIRBORNE IN WORLD WAR II: GERMANY AND RUSSIA LEAD THE WAY

Soon thereafter the Russians began developing military and civilian sport parachute teams and encouraged young men to join the paratroopers. In August and September 1930, Soviet paratroopers participated in military maneuvers.

The Germans, restricted by the postwar Versailles Peace Treaty from rebuilding any semblance of an offensive military force, established civilian sport parachute clubs and even police parachute squads. Both were the thinly veiled germinations of future German airborne forces.

The opening shots of World War II were fired when German leader Adolf Hitler's Nazi army invaded Poland in September 1939. In December, the Soviets launched the first of several small-scale airborne assaults during their early attempts to take Finland. But in all cases, the Red Army paratroopers—mostly lightly armed partisan forces—failed to achieve the necessary element of surprise and shock, and met with disaster.

The following spring, Hitler focused his attention westward. In April of 1940, large numbers of German *fallschirmjäger* (translated as "parachuting hunters") jumped over Norway and Denmark, seizing key bridges and military installations. Surprisingly, the attacks received little attention. This has since been attributed to the fact that a series of more dramatic Naval clashes took place off the Norwegian coast around the same time.

On May 10, 1940, the German army crossed the borders of Holland, Belgium, and Luxembourg. The Nazis spearheaded their combined-arms *Blitzkrieg* (translated as "lightning war") attacks with surprise airborne and gliderborne assaults that both confused and overwhelmed their enemies and shocked the world.

The effectiveness of the German fallschirmjäger compelled the U.S. War Department to immediately begin planning and building their own airborne forces.

AMERICA'S FIRST SKY SOLDIERS

Interservice bickering—primarily between the sub-branches of the Army—began over which branch would get the largest slice of the parachute pie and its accompanying funding. The Navy, which maintained a small parachute test program at the Lakehurst Naval Air Station in New Jersey, had no real interest or need for paratroopers in the late 1930s to early 1940s. The Navy's program was strictly for the purposes of testing and developing parachutes for Navy and Marine Corps aircrew members.

The Marine Corps was passively interested in the concept of vertical envelopment. In fact, the Marines had conducted two parachute landing demonstrations—one in the Washington, D.C., area in 1927 and another on islands off the California coast in 1937. However, the Marines had spent much of the period between the world wars perfecting the art of amphibious assault. Airborne operations were considered more of a "sideshow" to senior Marine officers. Nevertheless, the Corps would form wartime parachute battalions.

The Army Air Corps was a different matter entirely. The most junior of the Army's combat elements, the Air Corps, had a keen interest in bringing the bulk of all parachute forces under its own domain. After all, it was Mitchell and his doctrinal followers in the Air Corps who first began planning parachute landing operations. Additionally, the Air Corps Test Center had recently developed a steerable parachute, the T-4. Despite its simple design, the T-4 was revolutionary. It was the first parachute in history to have four risers connecting the harness to the canopy lines, a feature that enabled the jumper to have some control over speed and direction. Other nations' parachutes were hooked to the parachutists' harnesses in the back. Thus, the jumper was at the mercy of the wind. The Air Corps had also developed a functional reserve parachute, something other nations had yet to develop.

The Air Corps leadership argued that because paratroopers would be dependent upon aircraft for delivery, airborne forces should fall under Air Corps command, just as Germany's fallschirmjäger were members of the *Luftwaffe* (translated as "air force"). Air Corps leaders, hoping that their branch would eventually become a separate arm of service, believed that possessing the nation's primary airborne forces would give them leverage in Washington. It was believed that paratroopers would be to the Air Corps what Marines were to the Navy. Two of the most interesting, albeit odd-sounding, name proposals put forth by the Air Corps was that paratroopers would be called "Marines of the Air Corps" or "Air Grenadiers."

Competing with the Air Corps for overall control of the Army's airborne arm were the Army Corps of Engineers and the infantry. The engineers argued that airborne soldiers should be engineers first because they would be required to have an extensive knowledge of explosives. The infantry argued that paratroopers would become infantry soldiers as soon as they were on the ground and fighting.

All three presented strong cases for why America's new airborne forces should fall under their respective commands. Ultimately, the engineers and the Air Corps lost. Instead, the Army infantry and the U.S. Marine

Corps would be ordered by their respective heads to create combat-ready paratrooper units.

Over the course of the war, the Army would establish five airborne divisions—the 82nd, the 101st, the 11th, the 13th, the 17th—and a few independent airborne regiments. Five "phantom" airborne divisions—the 6th, the 9th, the 18th, the 21st, and the 135th—were created in order to confuse German spies operating in Great Britain. Postwar downsizing would reduce the Army's airborne forces to two divisions, the 82nd and the 101st.

The Marines would establish the 1st Parachute Regiment, comprised of the 1st, 2nd, 3rd, and 4th Marine Parachute Battalions. Three of the battalions would see action in the Pacific. Marine parachutists would in fact become the first American paratroopers in history to engage in armed combat (the U.S. Army's 509th Parachute Infantry Battalion—also known as the 2nd Battalion of the 503rd Parachute Infantry Regiment—was in fact the first American airborne force to *jump* into combat). A shortage of airplanes and an overwhelming need for amphibious troops, however, prevented the Marine battalions from ever jumping into battle. In the end, the "Paramarines"—as they were unofficially known—were absorbed into regular Marine infantry regiments.

THE PARACHUTE TEST PLATOON

In the predawn hours of May 10, 1940, a force of nine German Luftwaffe gliders appeared out of the darkness and landed silently on the grassy rooftop that covered the subterranean fortress of Eben Emael in Belgium. Within seconds, crack teams of German parachute engineers streamed from the gliders and began placing shaped, explosive charges over the fort's cupolas housing the machine guns and artillery pieces. Blowing the cupolas, the 60-something-strong German force was able to storm the fort and overwhelm the 1,200-man garrison below ground. As the parachute engineers battled the Belgian defenders, German fallschirmjäger seized two nearby bridges with equal surprise and results. Meanwhile, German paratroopers were dropping and seizing key bridges and highway junctions in Holland. The airborne attacks opened the way for German armored forces, which raced into the low countries.

Within days, both the U.S. Army and the Marines began formulating plans for experimental parachute units. Lt. Col. William Carey "Bill" Lee oversaw the Army program. A rawboned North Carolina native, World War I infantry officer, and longtime advocate of airborne warfare, Lee would eventually command America's first parachute division—the 101st Airborne "Screaming Eagles" Division. He would also go down in history as the "father of American airborne."

On the morning of June 26, soldiers of the Fort Benning, Georgia-based 29th Infantry Regiment fell out for the reveille formation and a historic announcement: The army was forming a "parachute test platoon" and needed volunteers.

Officially, the parachute test platoon was known as the Test Platoon, Parachute Troops and Air Infantry, United States Army.

The men were warned that the risks would be high. Married men need not apply, and only fit, "athletically inclined" men between the ages of 21 and 32 would be accepted.

By 8:30 A.M., more than 200 enlisted soldiers had volunteered (an amazing fact considering most soldiers in 1940 had never set foot in an airplane, and flying in those days was considered to be far more dangerous than it is today). Another 17 officers volunteered to serve as platoon leader. Unable to accommodate everyone, Lee made the decision to select four men from each company, and the officers would compete for the position of platoon leader through a written test.

In the end, 48 men were chosen. The standard infantry platoon was comprised of 39 riflemen, but an additional 8 volunteers were selected for the "parachute test platoon." They would serve as reserve paratroopers in the event others were killed or injured during training.

First Lt. Ryder was named platoon leader. Having previously studied German and Soviet methods of parachuting men into battle, Ryder breezed through the 2-hour written test in less than 45 minutes and obtained the highest score. Second-highest marks went to 2nd Lt. James A. Basset, who was named assistant platoon leader.

THE FIRST "JUMP SCHOOL"

Training began immediately. Housed in tents overlooking Fort Benning's Lawson Field, the platoon rose each morning before dawn and took off on a brisk three-mile run. Over time, the run was increased to five miles. Calisthenics were frequent throughout the day, with push-ups meted out for both physical training purposes and punishment for infractions.

Classroom instruction was held in a swelteringly hot, metal aircraft hangar. There students learned not only the fundamentals of parachuting, but how to pack their own chutes. In those days, the only military personnel with any parachute experience served in the Army Air Corps. Consequently, they became the first American airborne instructors.

Parachute landing falls (PLFs) were practiced by leaping off the backs of moving trucks. As if that was not tough enough, the fledgling paratroopers wore only a pair of Army Air Corps mechanics coveralls, a cloth flying helmet, and a pair of leather boots.

After six weeks of training in the Georgia backcountry, the students boarded Douglas B-18 Bombers for a flight north to Hightstown, New Jersey, adjacent to Camp Dix. There the men practiced jumping from two 250-foot towers that had been built for the 1939 World's Fair in New York.

During the 1939 World's Fair, the towers were used for amusement purposes, providing fairgoers with the opportunity to experience the sensation of parachuting from a fixed point. The towers were equipped with motors that would hoist 2 seated passengers up to a height of 250 feet. At the top, an "automatic release" mechanism would drop the parachute and the passengers suspended below it. They would then harmlessly float to the earth. Several safety features were incorporated into the tower "jump" ride. A metal ring kept the parachute canopy open at all times, "umbrellalike," as a period greeting card described it. Vertical guide wires prevented the parachute from drifting and its passengers from swinging outward from the tower. Additionally, shock absorbers were fixed to the bottom of the ride so the passengers would land smoothly and without any possibility of injury.

The parachute-tower training for soldiers was far more realistic. Like the World's Fair ride, the soldier was hoisted to the top of the tower, and a metal ring around the outer edge kept the canopy open. Unlike the amusement ride, the soldier was not seated. Once released at the top, the canopy was free of the metal ring. There were no guide wires to prevent the parachute student from either drifting away from the tower or crashing into it. Nor were there any shock absorbers at the bottom, just a lot of hard, unforgiving Earth.

Tower training was tremendously effective in preparing the soldier for the next phase of his training: the actual jump from an airplane. In fact, the Army eventually purchased the two towers from the Safe Parachute Company and moved them to Fort Benning's Eubanks Field. Over time, two duplicate towers were constructed.

Today, three of the four towers are still in use. Nearly every American military parachutist—from the men of the parachute test platoon to the twenty-first-century special operations commando—has trained on either the World's Fair towers or their duplicates.

During tower training, each of the test platoon students made 15 tower jumps. They also practiced parachute landing falls and continued a rigorous program of calisthenics and tumbling exercises. Following Hightstown, the students returned to Fort Benning for their final phase of training.

FIRST JUMPS OVER FORT BENNING

On the morning of August 16, 1940, the airborne hopefuls began leaping from C-33 transports at an altitude of 1,500 feet over a recently cleared drop zone near Lawson Field. Ryder jumped first, making him the first American airborne soldier to jump from a plane. An anonymous enlisted soldier, whose identity has been kept secret for more than 60 years, was second in line. Paralyzed with fear, he was unable to jump. Thus, the honor of being the first enlisted airborne soldier to jump from an airplane fell to the next man in line, Pvt. William N. "Red" King.

Parachutes began to blossom over the Georgia countryside as, one by one, Ryder's men stood in the door of the aircraft and waited for the leg slap and the command "Go" from the Air Corps jump instructor. The platoon made a second jump the next day.

Thanks to one of the test platoon members and a legendary Apache Indian chief, observers of the test platoon's third jump would witness the birth of one of the great traditions of the American paratrooper: the jump cry or battle cry "Geronimo!"

The night prior to the jump, several members of the platoon enjoyed a movie at the base theater. The movie was a western in which the warrior chief Geronimo and a band of his Apache braves were pursued by the U.S. Cavalry. Later, over a few beers, some of the paratroopers began teasing fellow trainee Pvt. Aubrey Eberhardt, saying that during the next day's jump he would be too frightened to speak. Eberhardt boasted that he would not only speak, but shout the name of the great Indian warrior.

The following day, the six-foot-eight-inch Eberhardt leapt from the plane yelling "Geronimo!" He followed the shout with a war whoop so loud soldiers on the ground could hear him. Other jumpers followed, also screaming the famous airborne battle cry.

Over the next several days, four more parachute jumps were made. The final (and fifth) qualifying jump was made on the twenty-second. It was a "mass jump" made by the entire platoon leaping from three transports gliding in over the drop zone in column formation. It was a grand spectacle, witnessed by a number of dignitaries, including U.S. Secretary of War Henry L. Stimson and Gen. George C. Marshall, the Army's Chief of Staff.

On the ground the demonstration was equally impressive. "Moving quicker than they had ever moved in their lives, the men recovered weapons and ammunition from equipment bundles dropped with them," wrote Gerard M. Devlin in his book, *Paratrooper*. "Then they attacked the make-believe enemy, shooting and yelling like a tribe of wild Indians all the while. Hollywood could not have done it better."

Only two glitches occurred in the show. One young private landed on the hangar roof. A ladder was brought up and he somewhat ingloriously climbed down. Another paratrooper's risers slipped over his main chute, creating the first of what has become known as the "Mae West" malfunction. To slow his rapid descent, he deployed his reserve and landed safely.

The test platoon's efforts convinced the Washington decision makers of the value of American airborne forces, but it wasn't without cost. Two men were killed during the Army's experimental training, and a number of others were injured.

COMBAT-READY PARATROOPERS

On September 16, the test platoon was officially expanded and redesignated as the Army's 1st Parachute Battalion. Within 10 days, the designation was changed to the 501st Parachute Infantry Battalion (the first operational airborne unit in American military history). The change was made to create a numerical distinction between Army and Marine parachute forces. All Army units would hence be numbered "in the 500 series." The Marine Corps would begin with "1" and number its units up to 500.

By early October, the 501st Parachute Infantry Battalion had been formed and placed under the command of Maj. William M. Miley (destined to become the commanding general of the 17th Airborne Division). While the Army was busy developing its sky-soldiering skills over the piney woods of Georgia, the Marine Corps was developing its own parachute forces at Lakehurst Naval Air Station in New Jersey. Known as the "parachute school detachment," the Corps' jump training program became operational on October 26.

By January 1941, the Army's 501st Parachute Infantry Battalion was up to strength, trained, and ready for action. Soon thereafter three additional battalions—the 502nd, the 503rd, and the 504th—were organized and placed under a "Provisional Parachute Group" commanded by Lee. The group was essentially a "regiment."

The 502nd was placed under the command of Maj. George P. Howell Jr., the 503rd fell under Maj. Robert F. Sink, and the 504th was under Maj. Richard Chase. Additionally, the 550th Infantry Airborne Battalion, under the command of Lt. Col. Harris M. Melasky, was established. The 550th's soldiers were not parachute trained. Instead they were conventional infantrymen who were to aircraft-land on airfields seized by paratroopers.

The Army's new airborne warfare arm took on a new, albeit short-lived dimension on October 10, 1941. On that day, the first gliderborne infantry battalion was activated. Officially designated the 88th Glider Infantry Battalion, the unit was commanded by Lt. Col. Elbridge G. Chapman Jr., a future major general who would ultimately command the wartime 13th Airborne Division. Glider troops were destined to see action in World War II and would distinguish themselves as members of some of America's most elite forces, but they would be disbanded by the end of the war.

On the morning of December 7, 1941, the Japanese struck the harbor, the main Naval base, and an Army airfield in Pearl Harbor, Hawaii. The attack, which caught the United States completely by surprise, was devastating. America was at war and for the most part militarily unprepared. But American airborne forces were already expanding and making great strides toward operational readiness.

In early 1942, the four existing parachute battalions grew to four parachute infantry regiments. In March, Lee's Provisional Parachute Group was reorganized into an Airborne Command and transferred to Fort Bragg, North Carolina. On May 15, the parachute training program at Fort Benning officially became the "Parachute School."

Like many of the U.S. Army's southern-based installations, Fort Benning, Georgia, and Fort Bragg, North Carolina, are named for Confederate Army generals. The two forts are the primary airborne force bases in North America.

Now buried in nearby Columbus, Georgia, Brig. Gen. Henry Lewis "Old Rock" Benning commanded the 17th Georgia Infantry during the American Civil War.

A North Carolina native, Gen. Braxton Bragg was a storied military commander who led the Army of Tennessee in a number of campaigns from Kentucky to Georgia. His final post was that of overseeing "the conduct of the military operations in the armies of the Confederacy."

Fort Lee, Virginia—where parachute riggers are trained—is named for Confederate Gen. Robert E. Lee.

Meanwhile, the Commandant of the Marine Corps received approval from the Secretary of the Navy to expand the Corps' existing parachute program and open parachute training schools at New River, North Carolina, and the U.S. Marine Base, San Diego, California. The first class at San Diego began on May 6 at nearby Camp Elliot where the Marines were quartered in a tent city. Within a few months, the school was transferred to Camp Gillespie/Gillespie Field (the future auxiliary field of the Marine Corps Air Station in El Toro). By the end of the year, the Marines would field three battalions of combat parachutists.

At Camp Claiborne, Louisiana, on August 15, the Army's 82nd Infantry Division was split up, with the bulk of the division forming the new 82nd Airborne Division. As such, the 82nd became the first airborne division in U.S. Army history (the Army would also be the only branch of service to field a division-size airborne force).

The following day the remaining strength of the old 82nd Infantry Division fleshed out the ranks of the skeletally manned 101st Infantry Division to form the new 101st Airborne Division (see the following sidebar). The new 82nd Airborne Division was under the command of Maj. Gen. Matthew Bunker "Matt" Ridgway, a swarthy, strikingly handsome former member of the War Department's general staff. The 101st was under the command of Bill Lee.

Twenty-two years after Billy Mitchell's wartime proposal was scrapped, America was fielding combat-ready airborne forces. And they were about to make history.

The numerical designation of Army divisions—more so than that of Marine Corps divisions—is often difficult to follow. This fact often prompts the fledgling military-history enthusiast to ask the question: If there is an 82nd Airborne Division and a 101st Airborne Division, what happened to the 83rd, 84th, 85th, ... 99th, 100th, and so on?

The answer is simple: Army divisions are numbered by the order in which they are established. For instance, the famous 1st Infantry Division—also known as the "Big Red One"—was the first division-size unit formed in the U.S. Army. The next division was the 2nd, then the 3rd, and so on.

There are however holes in the sequence. That is because many divisions come and go. The divisions that remain retain their numerical designation.

How does the Army determine which divisions it will keep and which it will dissolve?

"Each unit has its own customs and history, and the Army basically preserves the ones with the most glorious lineage," said Phillip Carter in an article, "How Are Army Divisions Numbered?" (*Slate* magazine, March 28, 2003). "Take the 101st Airborne Division, which has been part of the Army since 1942. During World War II, the 'Screaming Eagles' parachuted into Normandy and fought their way across Europe, making a heroic stand at Bastogne during the Battle of the Bulge. The Army has kept the division on active duty ever since. During the same war, the Army's 100th and 102nd Divisions served no less bravely but somewhat less famously. Both were shuttered for good after the war."

CHAPTER 2

"JUMP SCHOOL"

A soldier who has made a conscious decision to jump out of airplanes is a soldier with a great sense of daring and self-discipline.

—Lt. Gen. Charles W. Bagnal, retired U.S. Army helicopter pilot and former commanding general of the 101st Airborne (Air Assault) Division

"What you wanna be?"

"Airborne, sir!"

"How far?"

"All the way!"

—Typical conversation between "black hat" parachute instructors and jump school students

For more than 60 years, the U.S. Army's basic airborne training center at Fort Benning, Georgia, has been turning out American paratroopers. The center has not been the only military jump school in airborne history, but it was certainly the first. It is the oldest, it is the only one providing basic airborne training today, and the training received by airborne hopefuls in the twenty-first century is not unlike what their forebears experienced in the early

1940s. One of the differences is that jump school today is three weeks long, whereas in the early years during World War II, it lasted for four.

Just as it was during the experimental era of the parachute test platoon, the goals of young warriors today are to obtain a slot in the school (often a competition in itself), attend the program, learn the necessary jump skills, parachute from an airplane, win a pair of silver wings, and earn the title "paratrooper." It's certainly not an easy passage, but it is not impossible if the soldier is committed and prepared.

EARLY JUMP SCHOOL

Although paratroopers began training at Fort Benning in the summer of 1940, a formal jump school was not established until May 1942. Early jump school candidates were selected from the ranks of infantry volunteers. By late 1942, trained Army paratroopers were dispatched to recruiting stations around the country in search of airborne prospects. Young civilian men interested in becoming parachutists were asked to perform various physical exercises, including forward and backward rolls as proof of their agility, a basic and necessary requirement for airborne soldiers.

After a battery of mental and physical tests and upon completion of basic military training, the airborne hopeful was sent to Fort Benning. There he was assigned to a group of fellow soldiers, all of whom were organized to form the nucleus of a brand-new unit in which they would train together, spend off-duty time together, jump together, graduate together, ship overseas together, and eventually share the experience of combat together. In so doing, the paratroopers developed strong bonds with one another, and the Army was able to create cohesive units whose members would fight to the death for one another in combat.

During the first week of jump school, known as "A" stage, physical conditioning far beyond what the soldier had experienced in basic training was the order of the day. Running was constant, even from the barracks to the chow hall and back. The only ones permitted to walk were the injured. The slightest infraction resulted in soldiers being dropped for push-ups or ordered to perform a number of deep knee bends. Obstacle courses were negotiated daily, sometimes several times a day.

In week two, "B" stage, parachute instruction began. Soldiers practiced jumping out of mock airplanes. They mastered parachute landing techniques by leaping from platforms of varying heights, hitting the ground, and rolling. As stated previously, during some of the earliest training cycles, soldiers practiced landing techniques by jumping off the backs of moving trucks. Features of the basic T-4 parachute were also taught, and training was conducted on 35-foot towers (today, 34-foot towers). On the towers, soldiers—connected by parachute harnesses to long steel cables extending horizontally from the towers—practiced jumping off the main platform, dropping several feet, and then sliding down the cables, which gradually descended to the ground.

A major part of the third week of training, or "C" stage, consisted of a course in how to properly pack a parachute. Initially bored, most students quickly became keenly interested when informed that they would be packing their own chutes prior to jumping. Training also began on the famous 250-foot towers.

During "D" stage, also known as jump week, students made five jumps from an airplane at varying altitudes. The fifth jump was a night jump, after which the brand-new paratrooper was awarded silver wings as well as cap and shoulder patches, and was authorized to blouse his trousers in his boots.

PARACHUTE TRAINING IN THE POSTWAR ERA

"You'll double time to and from classes and you'll get the kind of exercises that will put you in top condition," promised an airborne recruiting brochure of the 1950s. "In a short while, you're liable to think you'd have a royal chance against a boxing champ!"

True or not, and regardless of the parachuting skills mastered, jump school has always been a soldier-enhancing experience. Not surprisingly, the school's curriculum has not changed much in more than six decades. The three most important changes are that no instruction on packing parachutes is provided (that is now the domain of trained "riggers"), training is one week shorter, and the physical fitness standards are not quite as high as they once were. But as anyone who has ever attended will attest, jump school is tough, and not all make the cut from one week to the next.

Approximately 2,200 students (just over 12 percent) out of an average 18,000 students who pass through the school each year fail to graduate. Most jump school students, of course, do graduate. They are all volunteers, they want to jump out of airplanes, and they arrive at jump school physically and mentally prepared.

Nongraduates include those who become injured, those who cannot keep up with the physically demanding pace, those who do not have the coordination to perform the proper hit-and-roll techniques required for safe landings, those who cannot overcome their fear of heights, those who are dismissed for excessive infractions or disciplinary problems, or those who simply quit.

To those men who have previously endured or will later suffer through the more grueling experiences of special operations training where the attrition rates are much higher, jump school elimination numbers may seem small. But it is a relatively high failure rate considering that the school is only three weeks long, and most of the all-volunteer student companies arrive motivated and in excellent physical condition.

When it comes to basic airborne skills, soldiers, sailors, airmen, and Marines are all cut from the same cloth—perhaps *silk* might be a better word—because each and every one has to successfully complete the demanding three weeks conducted by the Army before pinning on their silver wings.

Forty-five jump classes are held each year at Fort Benning, with 350 to 450 students in each class. Of those numbers, 80.5 percent are soldiers serving in the regular Army. Three percent are National Guardsmen, and 1.5 percent are Army reservists. Six percent are college students enrolled in the Reserve Officers Training Corps (ROTC), and 2 percent are cadets attending the U.S. Military Academy at West Point. Two percent serve in the Navy (as of this writing, the Navy is considering creating its own basic jump training program which will become a separate phase of SEAL training; see Chapter 12), 3 percent serve in the Marine Corps, and 2 percent serve in the Air Force.

A common misconception among the general public is that American military pilots also must attend jump school. Though they do undergo parachute and ejection seat familiarization training, military pilots are not required to attend basic parachute training. A few attend jump school voluntarily, many of them attending when they are cadets or midshipmen in college. However, most pilots have never jumped from an airplane, and most hope they will never have to do so. Their reasoning is simple: "Why would anyone in their right mind want to jump from a perfectly good airplane?"

FEMALE SKY SOLDIERS

In the modern Army, 3 percent of the students who attend jump school each year are females. Federal policy currently prohibits women from participating in ground combat operations, so consequently female soldiers cannot serve as "combatant" paratroopers. But they can train as such, a fact that has disturbed both those opposed to the idea of women in ground combat (some argue that women do not have the physical strength required for the ground combat environment) as well as number-crunchers who question the cost effectiveness of training personnel for a job they are currently barred from performing.

"I believe it's always been a matter of cost benefit," says Brian Mitchell, author, journalist, former U.S. Army airborne officer, intelligence operative, and an "expert witness" who appeared before the Presidential Commission on the Assignment of Women in the Armed Forces in 1992. "Airborne units are always deployable. Yet women are the least deployable, and for a number of reasons. Females are much more susceptible to injury. They require more medical attention than men. They have less physical strength on average than qualified males, and they have more dependent children issues than males."

Beyond that, Mitchell argues it is "absurd" to field a military force with noncombatant personnel. "You've already given up the game," he says.

Webster's New Universal Unabridged Dictionary defines *paratrooper* as "a member of a military unit trained to attack or land in combat areas by parachuting from airplanes." In one of two U.S. Army Airborne Creeds, the paratrooper is described as "not merely a soldier who arrives by parachute to fight, but is an elite shock trooper and that his country expects him to march farther and faster, to fight harder." The second creed states, "I am an elite trooper—a sky trooper—a shock trooper—a spearhead trooper. I blaze the way to far-flung goals—behind, before, above the foe's front line. I know that I may have to fight without support for days on end." A female soldier can be parachute trained, but no female soldier has ever jumped over a "hot" combat drop zone as a "shock trooper." And with no existing plans to commit them to such, the question arises: Is the term "female paratrooper" an oxymoron?

"No," according to Elsie Jackson, a public affairs spokesperson at Fort Benning. "We don't just train soldiers so they can jump into combat," says Jackson. "Riggers, for example, must be airborne qualified. Soldiers assigned to airborne units are not all assigned to a combat military occupational specialty. They could very easily be combat support or even combat service support, but they have to be airborne qualified."

Jackson also contends that many service personnel, male and female, who graduate from jump school will never be required to jump again.

According to Army Lt. Gen. John Bruce Blount, "That's okay. Those who don't return to airborne units still gain the positive experience of jump school, and America has an extra bank of paratroopers if needed."

"PACKING THE GEAR" TO BE A PARATROOPER

Though it is necessary for airborne students to arrive for jump training in excellent physical condition, surprisingly the minimum fitness prerequisites are not difficult to achieve. All students, regardless of age or service branch, must complete the Army's physical fitness test standards for the 17- to 21-year-old age category. The test includes push-ups (42 repetitions for males, 19 for females in less than 2 minutes), sit-ups (53 for both male and female in less than 2 minutes), and a 2-mile run (15:54 minutes for males, 18:54 minutes for females). That's nearly an eight-minute mile for males and nearly a nine-and-a-half-minute mile for females, hardly the kind of run time one would associate with tough training. But jump school is not easy, and most jump school graduates are quick to say that achieving the minimum fitness requirements will not ensure successful completion of the program. In fact, most agree a minimum score is not enough, but in terms of official physical fitness standards, it is all that is required to walk through the door in 2004.

No maximum age-limit requirement exists, but a jump student cannot be older than 36 years old without an age waiver and a current electrocardiogram (EKG). The age waiver is issued on a case-by-case basis.

Jump school is the responsibility of the 1st Battalion (Airborne) of the 507th Infantry, 11th Infantry Regiment. The battalion is organized into six companies: four line (training) companies, Alpha, Bravo, Charlie, and Delta; one "rigger support" company, Echo; and a headquarters company. The parachute instructors—known as "black hats" because of the color of their caps—are drawn from the noncommissioned officer (NCO) ranks of the Army, the Marine Corps, and the Air Force, although the vast majority are Army NCOs.

Jump school at Fort Benning was officially established as the "U.S. Army Parachute School" on May 15, 1942. Since then, the school has undergone a variety of name changes. In January 1946, it became known as the "Airborne School." In November of that same year, it became the "Airborne Army Aviation Section, the Infantry School." In February 1955, it became the "Airborne Department, the Infantry School." In February 1956, it became the "Airborne-Air Mobility Department." In August 1964, it became the "Airborne Department." In October 1974, it became the "Airborne-Air Mobility Department." In October 1976, it reverted back to the "Airborne Department." In January 1982, it became the "4th Airborne Training Battalion, the School Brigade." In October 1985, it became the 1st Battalion (Airborne), 507th Parachute Infantry, the School Brigade." And in July 1991, the school became the "1st Battalion (Airborne), 507th Infantry, 11th Infantry Regiment."

THE AIRBORNE COURSE

As previously mentioned, jump school today lasts all of three weeks. It is broken down into three distinct phases: Ground Week, Tower Week, and Jump Week.

The first week, Ground Week, is considered by some to be the make-or-break phase of jump school. Ground Week is the period in which airborne students learn the fundamentals that enable them to safely exit an aircraft and land on the ground literally without being killed. In so doing, the students learn to don and adjust their main and reserve parachutes. They learn to identify the basic components inside a propeller-driven C-130 transport aircraft. They learn to respond immediately to commands issued by a jumpmaster in the aircraft. They train in mock aircraft doors, on a 34-foot tower (similar to the 35-foot towers used during the early years of jump training), and on a fast-moving Lateral Drift Apparatus (LDA).

The LDA simulates the last few seconds of a paratrooper's glide to the earth so that fledging parachutists learn how to hit the ground, roll, and recover safely. An improper landing might result in injuries. Thus, those who are initially lacking the coordination required to hit and roll spend more time on the LDA than others. A student who is unable to hit and roll properly from the LDA will be dropped from the program. As paratroopers say, better to be dropped than to "crash and burn" during a real jump.

In order to proceed to the next phase, Tower Week, the students must pass Ground Week without incapacitating injuries, they must keep up on all the physical conditioning runs, and they must meet the specific physical coordination performance standards on both the 34-foot tower and the LDA.

Ground Week may be the make-or-break phase, but Tower Week is by far the most physically demanding. During Tower Week, students learn to respond to commands given inside both C-130 and C-141 (a four-engined, jet transport) aircraft. The students practice making "mass jump" exits from a mock aircraft door on the ground. They continue training on the 34-foot tower, but during Tower Week they are wearing combat equipment.

Students develop and must demonstrate the proper techniques for deploying the reserve chute in the event of a malfunctioning main canopy. They are then strapped into two types of parachute harnesses—the T-10 and the MCI-1—and are suspended above the ground. In that position, they must learn and demonstrate the means by which they will control their parachutes once airborne. They also practice parachute landing falls, or PLFs, from the swing landing trainer, which teaches them to manage their oscillation beneath the canopy on approach to the ground and to hit and roll safely. In this contraption, the student is suspended above the ground and dropped unexpectedly.

The big event during Tower Week is a free drop from one of the famous 250-foot towers. This is done with a modified MC1-1 parachute.

CHAPTER 2: "JUMP SCHOOL"

The third week, Jump Week, is the most important phase of basic airborne training. It is during this week that the students' skills are proven in the skies over Georgia. To qualify as a parachutist, the student is required to make five jumps: two from 1,250 feet, two from 1,500 feet, and one from 2,000 feet. Two of the jumps are made with equipment, and one jump is conducted at night.

It all may sound frightening to the uninitiated, but the students are ready. By the beginning of the third week, they have overcome much of their inherent fear of heights. Physically, most of them are far tougher than they were when they arrived at Fort Benning two weeks earlier. With the exception of the Marines and some of the special operations forces such as the SEa, Air, Land (SEAL) teams who attend jump school later in their combat instruction cycles, the training has been more intense that what many of the students have ever experienced. They have been running four miles each day in combat boots; doing countless push-ups, pull-ups, and deep knee bends for every imaginable infraction; leaping from towers and platforms of varying heights; and hitting the ground, tumbling, and rolling.

"Their bodies are becoming like rocks," writes Tom Clancy in *Airborne: A Guided Tour of an Airborne Task Force*. "It is amazing what just 14 days of heavy physical activity can do to a person."

U.S. Marine Col. Jeffrey Bearor, commanding officer of the Marine Recruit Training Regiment at Parris Island, South Carolina, agrees. "Three weeks at jump school may not sound like a lot," says Bearor. "But it's physically punishing." This is from a leatherneck commander who has endured some of the world's toughest special operations training, including scuba school and the fiercely demanding Royal Marine Commando Course in the United Kingdom.

Though death or life-threatening injuries are rare, few leave jump school unscathed. Students may wind up nursing broken bones, torn ligaments, twisted knees or backs, or lots of pulled muscles. It is not an uncommon sight to see several students with slight limps when they leave Fort Benning.

"I doubt if anyone has gone through the basic airborne course without sustaining some kind of minor injury," says Elsie Jackson. "But for the most part, serious injuries requiring hospitalization are few and far between, and I can't remember when a student sustained a life-threatening injury." The lack of real injuries, she contends, are attributed to superior training and an uncompromising focus on safety.

THE MOMENT OF TRUTH

During Jump Week, airborne hopefuls leap from both high-performance propeller and jet aircraft. Jumping from a propeller-driven C-130 is different than jumping from a C-141 jet.

In the C-130, the first paratrooper in the "stick" stands in the door, hands braced against the doorframe, knees slightly bent. Given the slap on the back of the thigh and the command "Go," he leaps up and out. In a C-141, he simply walks toward the door until he is sucked out. In both cases, the jumper has to maintain a good body position: chin tucked in toward the chest, elbows tucked with upper arms tight along the upper torso, hands and forearms holding each side of the forward-positioned reserve chute, knees slightly bent and together, and feet together. "One thousand!" the jumper shouts. "Two thousand. Three thousand. Four thous ..."

> Though actual numbers vary, the U.S. Army defines a "stick" as the "number of paratroopers who jump from one aperture or door of an aircraft during one run over the DZ [Drop Zone]." Similar to a "stick" is a "chalk," which is usually a dozen or so—a squad of soldiers—assigned to a helicopter.

At the count of "four thousand," the jumper should feel a sharp jerk as the canopy blossoms above him and immediately slows his descent. He then looks up to ensure that his chute has opened completely and is functioning properly. If the parachutist notices twists in the lines—a common occurrence—he must reach up, grab a set of risers with each hand, pull the risers apart, and begin a kicking motion. This action will almost always spin out the tangles. This situation is not considered an emergency.

Jump emergencies are classified as total malfunctions, partial malfunctions, and incidents. The first two require immediate action or the jumper may be killed or seriously injured.

A total malfunction is really a no-brainer, characterized by a total failure of the canopy to deploy. If, after the four-second count, the jumper realizes he has a total malfunction, he must immediately deploy his reserve parachute or, as paratroopers say, "bounce." (As grisly as it sounds, human bodies plummeting at speeds of 120 to 125 mph usually bounce upon striking the earth.)

A partial malfunction is simply a deployed canopy that fails to function properly. This situation can be as dangerous as a total malfunction. Partial malfunctions include everything from a streamer or a cigarette roll—a dangerous malfunction requiring immediate action on the part of the parachutist—to a "Mae West."

A streamer (cigarette roll) is a malfunction wherein the canopy fails to "blossom." The canopy instead slips between two or more suspension lines and begins rolling with the opposite fabric. This causes little to no lift. During the parachutist's rapid descent, the canopy streams overhead.

In a Mae West situation, one or more of the lines ends up being looped over the top of the canopy after the parachute has opened. The weight of the jumper then pulls the improperly deployed lines down over the canopy, thus forming two large bulges in the parachute. Unlike a cigarette roll, a Mae West can often be corrected by an experienced parachutist, but if left uncorrected the jumper may be killed or seriously injured.

Famous for her curvaceous figure and sexually suggestive one-liners, Mae West was a popular American stage and screen star of the 1930s and 1940s. Not surprisingly, during the early days of airborne forces, U.S. paratroopers christened the double-bulging canopy malfunction a "Mae West." British pilots in the Royal Air Force also nicknamed their inflatable life preservers Mae Wests. American air crews later adopted the same nickname for their own life preservers.

Today the term *Mae West* is still widely used in the English-speaking world to describe both the double-bulging parachute malfunction and the life preserver.

Jump school, for all its importance, accomplishes much more than providing young soldiers with the skills needed to jump from low-flying airplanes onto battlefields. The experience builds self-confidence and a special sense of identity required of soldiers and sailors who work in elite conventional or special operations forces. Additionally, the courage required of a novice paratrooper in some ways mirrors that required of a soldier in combat for the first time (experienced soldiers know that combat is far more dangerous than parachuting, though parachuting into combat dramatically increases the risk of death or injury). Consequently, the vast majority of paratroopers perform very well in battle. Those who would not perform well in battle would also not have the guts to jump out of an airplane.

The very act of strapping on a parachute and leaping from a loud, fast-moving airplane 1,000 feet above the earth demands that a student overcome his instinctive fear of heights and, to a certain degree, defy death. Statistically speaking, parachuting is not exceedingly dangerous, but death or serious injury can occur if the student's equipment fails to function properly or if he fails to perform the jump correctly. The student is certainly aware of that fact.

Upon completion of the fifth and final jump, the brand-new parachutist is awarded a pair of silver jump wings: a coveted award for successfully completing a demanding rite of passage.

PART 2

ARMY AIRBORNE FORCES

CHAPTER 3

FIRST COMBAT JUMPS

Most of the men felt secure in the fact that they would eventually be dropped somewhere in the north of France or Holland. One of the really wild rumors had the battalion jumping on Berlin to kill Hitler. It really didn't matter to Raff's men where they'd be dropped, as long as it was right in the middle of the enemy, and the sooner the better.

—Former U.S. Army Airborne Ranger officer Gerard M. Devlin in his book, *Paratrooper!*

The first American airborne unit in military history to make a true combat jump was the 509th Parachute Infantry Battalion. Although it is often referred to as the 2nd Battalion of the 503rd Parachute Infantry Regiment, the paratroopers who leapt first under fire were members of the 509th.

The confusion over the battalion's designation stems from the fact that both the first-ever combat jump and the numerical redesignation of the battalion in question took place within weeks of one another. Some histories contend it was the 2nd Battalion of the 503rd Regiment that made the first combat jump as a unit. Others say it was the 509th Battalion. Either way, it was indeed the same battalion, which held both designations. For our purposes, we will refer to the battalion as the 509th.

The 509th Parachute Infantry Battalion, under the command of Lt. Col. Edson Duncan Raff, was the spearhead of the Allied invasion of North Africa in late 1942, but the airborne phase of the invasion almost never occurred. The enormous distance from England to the African continent through skies patrolled by Luftwaffe fighters was considered far too dangerous by certain U.S. military authorities. These leaders included Gen. Dwight D. Eisenhower, destined to become the supreme Allied commander in Europe, and Col. Hoyt S. Vandenberg, a future Air Force chief of staff and director of the yet-to-be-established Central Intelligence Agency. The strongest proponent of the operation, and the man who may well have been the convincing voice, was Brig. Gen. Jimmy Doolittle, best known for his command of the famous bombing raid over Tokyo the previous April.

According to Maj. William P. "Bill" Yarborough, who was responsible for planning and logistics, it was Doolittle who convinced the operation's chief planner that the airborne phase was doable. The chief planner, Maj. Gen. Mark W. Clark, gave the airborne element the green light, although Ike himself felt it was a bit "harebrained."

The U.S. strategic objective was to capture and occupy French Northwest Africa. The tactical objective for the 509th was the seizure of two French airfields south of Oran, Algeria, the largest and most important being the Tafaraoui Airport. The other was nearby La Senia.

Yarborough had prepared two plans for two scenarios. The first was the "Peace Plan," which called for a daytime, nonparachute air landing at La Senia, the smaller of the two fields. This plan was to be implemented only if Allied sympathizers within the French officer corps convinced their leaders and their charges not to resist the Americans.

> Following the German army's defeat and subsequent occupation of France in 1940, a Nazi-collaborating French "Vichy" government was established, which controlled a small part of France and its global territories. The Vichy did so in order to preserve some measure of French sovereignty. Meanwhile, the anti-Nazi "Free French" resistance forces rose up both within France and in exile.

> Thus, when America entered the war, allegiances among French military units were sometimes mixed and often confused. A number of French military officers chose to serve the Vichy government; others were loyal to the "Free French."
> France was liberated in 1944 by the Allied forces, including the forces of the "Free French."

Yarborough's second plan, or "War Plan," called for a nighttime combat airborne assault over Tafaraoui. There Raff's men would destroy all French aircraft on the ground that might be used against the primary American (seaborne) invasion force during daylight hours. Once the planes at Tafaraoui were knocked out of action, one company of the 509th would march to La Senia and destroy the planes there.

The transport planes, which would be running on near-empty tanks, would meanwhile land on the rock-hard mud flats in the desert near Oran. There they would be met by the advancing seaborne force and refueled for the journey home.

MAKING AIRBORNE HISTORY

On Saturday evening, November 7, 1942, exactly 11 months to the day after the Japanese attack on Pearl Harbor, 556 American paratroopers boarded a fleet of 39 C-47 transport airplanes and prepared for an all-night flight. They were equipped with their parachute rigs, weapons, as much ammunition as they could carry, food, water, and everything else they would need to sustain themselves on the ground (or what the planners believed they would need). Enough equipment was never available for the airborne soldiers once they were on the ground, particularly during the early years of airborne warfare.

"The basic tactic used by all countries employing parachutists and gliderborne troops in World War II was the strike-hold concept, which the initial air assault quickly devolved into a static defense of the objective," wrote John R. Galvin in *Air Assault: The Development of Airmobile Warfare*. "Parachute and glider assaults from their earliest beginnings were characterized by this lack of flexibility. The airborne forces traveled light, without much firepower and with very few ground vehicles, and for this reason were like ducks out of water when they got on the ground."

Lifting off just after 9 P.M., the airborne force flew some 1,600 miles— 11 hours total—from England, over Spain, and across the western Mediterranean Sea toward the North African coastline. By twenty-first-century standards and with current technologies, the mission would rank just above ordinary, but in the early 1940s, the combination of the distant flight and the jump was considered to be an incredible military feat. Nothing of that scope had ever been accomplished before, and although successful, it was fraught with problems. Navigation was difficult. The aircrews were relying on old charts, crude compasses, and a bit of dead reckoning when the cloud cover broke.

A British radar guidance device had been smuggled onto the African continent and a British homing ship had been prepositioned in the Mediterranean, but the airborne force was never able to make contact with either.

Inside the aircraft, the men tried to sleep, but temperatures soon plummeted, and the combination of the cold and their own anxiety and excitement had them shivering under thin blankets. Increasing the pucker factor, the paratroopers were aware they were vulnerable to roving Luftwaffe aircraft, particularly over the Mediterranean. Once on the ground, however, there would be no opposition. Or so they thought.

Prior to the 509th's launch, Ike received word from a few dissenting Vichy French officers that the Vichy would not resist the American landings. Unfortunately, Vichy forces went on full combat alert soon after the American force lifted off. Despite the few dissenters, the bulk of the Vichy army and air force were planning to fight.

Over the target, there were no advance-jumping pathfinders or ground controllers (pathfinder teams would prove to be invaluable later in the war). As they approached their destination, some of the planes running on nearly dry fuel tanks landed in the desert before their passengers had a chance to jump. Other transports were pounced on by French fighters and were quickly shot down, but not without a fight. In almost every case, the attacking planes were met with virtually ineffective rifle, pistol, and submachine-gun fire from the paratroopers inside the transports who were blasting away through the portholes.

"The scene was reminiscent of the typical western movie where the frontiersmen placed the barrels of their long rifles through firing ports of their log forts during attacks by hostile Indians," wrote Gerard M. Devlin in *Paratrooper!* Indeed, the stark difference was that frontiersmen often had a chance of surviving their engagement, whereas paratroopers in the vulnerable transports had virtually no chance when attacked by highly maneuverable fighters.

The French fighter pilots themselves were merciless. In one instance, three crippled C-47s made belly-landings onto the desert floor as the pursuing fighters strafed them all the way to the earth. As the planes slid to a halt, those paratroopers who were able leapt out and began blasting away at the French fighters roaring overhead.

A few paratroopers were given the green light to jump too early after their pilots strayed off course and became lost. Those men were subsequently captured in Spanish or French Morocco. Raff himself jumped 35 miles from the target airfields when he spotted a group of his planes on the ground and under fire. Determined to save them, Raff leapt from his plane, followed by his men and those from other craft. The colonel unfortunately cracked several ribs when he landed in a cluster of jagged rocks. In tremendous pain, staggering, spitting blood, and shouting commands, he led his men forward.

Battalion surgeon Carlos C. "Doc" Alden from Buffalo, New York, also jumped with the paratroopers. Inscribed in his personal diary was the following prayer: "Dear God, in Thy wisdom help me to come back. But if I do not, then help me to do my duty as an American and as a man."

Overall, the battalion found itself scattered over a vast area. Good men were lost along with much-needed combat equipment. Nevertheless, the bloodied Americans—in isolated groups—moved toward their primary objective. Along the way, they offered k-rations and other personal items to nomads who in turn gave them water.

REACHING THE OBJECTIVE

By the time Raff and his surviving force reached Tafaraoui on November 9, American tank forces had taken both airfields. Within two days, Oran itself was under total Allied control.

The paratroopers made history (the first-ever combat jump) and performed heroically (a continuous 24-hour period in which they shivered in the cold of a dangerous 11-hour flight, jumped into action or crash-landed after being attacked by enemy planes, fought on the ground, and then marched across a formidable stretch of unfamiliar desert with little water). However, it was a disappointing first mission in terms of achieving objectives. Nevertheless, the 509th would have numerous opportunities to prove itself, and it did. A second opportunity came within a few days.

The British First Army was preparing for its forthcoming push into Italian- and German-controlled Tunisia. Raff was advised by his British army superiors that American paratroopers were needed to capture Tebessa, Algeria, a strategically vital airfield that the Allies needed to deny the Axis forces. While planning the operation, Raff discovered that a larger air base, Youks-les-Bains, was located just 10 miles north of the Tebessa field. French bombers had, in fact, used it as a launching base during raids against the port city of Tripoli in 1939 and 1940.

Raff acquainted the British with his discovery, and it was then agreed that the 509th would take both airfields. But like the mission to seize Tafaraoui and La Senia, Raff was faced with numerous operational obstacles. He had very few up-to-date maps of the region, his equipment was marginal, intelligence was poor, and accurate meteorological information was virtually nonexistent. On top of that, the airborne leader was still nursing painful injuries suffered during the jump. Raff, however, was not an ordinary man. Known to his troopers as "Little Caesar," Raff was a tough disciplinarian and a fearless leader with great intuitive abilities. He realized the new mission was doable and his men were up to the task. And despite his injuries, he would lead them.

THE TUNISIAN JUMP

Three hundred paratroopers hunkered down in 33 C-47 transport aircraft were sent to seize the Youks-les-Bains airfield in central Tunisia. Among them was reporter John H. "Jack" Thompson—also known as "Beaver" Thompson—of the *Chicago Tribune*. Jumping with the 509th, Thompson was about to make history as the first civilian war correspondent to jump into combat.

On the morning of November 15, 1942, Raff and his paratroopers, many still bandaged from the previous mission, began jumping over the enemy-held airfield at Youks-les-Bains. The paratroopers, now calling themselves "Raff's Ruffians," landed in a vast clearing adjacent to the airfield. In less than 20 minutes, the Americans formed for battle, raced toward the airfield, and accepted the surrender of a supposedly elite French Algerian Zouave Regiment. No shots were fired.

Once Youks-les-Bains was firmly in American control, Raff ordered one company to dig in. A second company was ordered to "speed-march" toward Tebessa. There the paratroopers seized the airfield and soon shot down a German transport plane. The pilot, unaware that the Americans held the ground, attempted to land and was shot down by point-blank rifle fire from Raff's men entrenched along the runway. The shooting marked the first time that U.S. paratroopers saw action against the Germans.

As a token of their respect for the American paratroopers, the Zouave unit, 3rd Regiment, presented their regimental crest to Raff. The 3rd Zouaves also pledged to fight alongside the 509th. Over several bottles of red wine, the French regimental commander promised to help drive the Axis forces from Tunisia and then liberate France from the Germans. "From this day forward, my regiment is your regiment," the French commander told Raff. The regimental crest presented to Raff has since been worn by all members of the first-to-jump 509th.

CHAPTER 4

DEVILS IN BAGGY PANTS: 82ND AIRBORNE DIVISION

American parachutists—devils in baggy pants [of the 82nd Airborne Division's 504th Parachute Infantry Regiment]— are less than 100 meters from my outpost line. I can't sleep at night; they pop up from nowhere and we never know when or how they will strike next. Seems like the black-hearted devils are everywhere.

—Diary entry of a dead German officer

Those young guys up at Fort Bragg have a swaggering confidence about them; there is a good reason for that.

—Col. Jeff Bearor, a U.S. Marine parachutist and Royal Marine Commando, referring to the paratroopers of the Army's 82nd Airborne Division

The U.S. Army's famous 82nd Airborne Division has the distinction of being the first airborne division in American military history. It is the only division-size "true" airborne force in the U.S. armed forces today, and it is the largest single force of paratroopers in the free world.

The division, often referred to as "America's Guard of Honor," is trained and equipped to deploy anywhere on the planet within 18 hours. As such, every member of the 82nd—from cooks to computer programmers to combat infantrymen—are airborne qualified. Depending upon the operation, the division deploys with only 3 to 15 days' worth of food, water, gasoline, and ammunition. Practically every piece of equipment is designed to be parachute dropped onto the battlefield as well.

Although it is almost always associated with its "airborne" laurels, the 82nd has a rich history extending back to the First World War. In the summer of 1917, the 82nd Infantry Division was formed at Camp (later Fort) Gordon, Georgia.

The following spring, the division sailed to France and was soon deployed on the grim "Western Front." By the end of the war in late 1918, the 82nd's accomplishments were legion.

THE TALE OF SERGEANT YORK

Sgt. Alvin C. York will forever be one of the 82nd's most famous soldiers. During the Meuse-Argonne Offensive, September through November, 1918, when the 82nd found itself slugging it out with the Imperial German Army, then-Pvt. First Class York made division history. York, a Tennessee backwoodsman and one-time conscientious objector, became the ranking man in his platoon after the unit suffered heavy casualties. Seizing the initiative, the strapping private led a 7-man team of the 82nd's soldiers against a strong German position. The team killed at least 25 Germans and captured 4 officers, 128 soldiers, and more than 30 machine guns. York, an expert rifleman, later described the action as something akin to a Tennessee turkey shoot. "Every time one of them raised his head, I just teched him off," he said.

For his actions, York was permitted to bypass the rank of corporal and was instead promoted to sergeant. He was awarded both the American Congressional Medal of Honor and the French Croix de Guerre. Personally decorating York with the latter, French Marshall Ferdinand Foch said, "[W]hat you did was the greatest thing accomplished by any private soldier of all the armies of Europe."

The 82nd was disbanded after the war. Twenty years later, when war again erupted in Europe, the American army began outlining plans for a rapid mobilization of its forces. It also began training men for airborne warfare.

WORLD WAR II

On December 7, 1941, the Japanese attacked Pearl Harbor and America quickly declared war on Japan, Germany, and Italy. Less than four months later, on March 25, 1942, the 82nd Infantry Division was reactivated at Camp Claiborne, Louisiana, under the command of Maj. Gen. Omar Nelson Bradley (Bradley was destined to lead the largest "exclusively American" ground combat force in history).

On August 15, the 82nd was split up at Camp Claiborne. The bulk of the division was redesignated the 82nd "Airborne" Division. Thus, it became the first airborne division in U.S. Army history. (That honor might have gone to the 1st Infantry Division, the famous "Big Red One," had World War I ended a few months later than it did—see Chapter 1). The new division's commanding general—and thus the first-ever commander of an American Airborne division—was Maj. Gen. Matthew Bunker Ridgway, destined to command an entire corps of airborne soldiers.

> The distinctive shoulder patch of the 82nd Airborne Division consists of a red square with a blue disk in the center. Inside the disk are the double letters "AA," which refer to the 82nd's nickname, the "All-American division." The nickname was adopted by the division during World War I because its soldiers hailed from what was then all 48 states.
> Arcing above the red square is a blue tab with the inscription "AIRBORNE" in white letters.

The day following the divisional split, the remaining elements of the old 82nd Infantry Division were transferred to the old 101st Infantry Division to form the new 101st Airborne Division, also at Camp Claiborne.

The 82nd's soldiers obediently accepted their transfers without question, but they were not happy with the new orders. Little did they know that most of them would make what the 101st's new commander, Maj. Gen. William C. "Bill" Lee, referred to as a "rendezvous with destiny." Indeed, the 82nd *also* was destined for glory.

In his wartime memoir, *Strike and Hold*, former Army Airborne officer T. Moffat Burris recalled being wholly impressed by the paratroopers he saw jumping in the distance as he plodded across an open field with his regular infantry unit during training at Fort Benning, Georgia. It was 1942, World War II was in full swing, and Burris knew he was destined for the front. When he asked an old college buddy-turned-paratrooper what airborne forces were good for, his buddy replied, "You jump, capture the objective. Then the infantry relieves you, and you go on to the next mission. You never have to dig a foxhole and live in it for three months."

Perhaps in a perfect world. But as Burris and countless other future sky soldiers would discover, paratroopers not only served as the vanguard of attacking forces. They raided and withdrew like commandos. They attacked on the ground and dug in like regular "leg" infantry. They relieved other forces on the line. They were also sometimes broken into units and dispersed throughout the regular Army in order to instill the airborne spirit in regular soldiers.

> The term *leg* or *straight leg* used by paratroopers to describe their non-parachuting infantry brothers is a holdover from the days of horse cavalry and dragoons (horse-mounted infantry). In the nineteenth century, soldiers who rode horses into combat viewed foot soldiers with a condescending eye. Horsemen, believing themselves to be superior to footmen, referred to the latter as "legs." Paratroopers, in many respects the reincarnation of horsemen, continue using the term *leg* to describe their fellow soldiers who do, indeed, walk to the battlefield.

In October, the "All-Americans" moved into garrison at Fort Bragg, North Carolina, their official home for the next 60-plus years. That same month, the recently formed 504th Parachute Infantry Regiment became part of the division.

For the next several months, the division's soldiers perfected their skills in ground combat tactics. They also trained rigorously for airborne insertions. The paratroopers practiced jumping out of C-47 transport aircraft, and the glider infantry trained in their airplane-towed WACO-CG4A gliders.

By the time the 82nd was ready to ship overseas, the division included the 504th Parachute Infantry Regiment, the 505th Parachute Infantry Regiment, and the 325th Glider Infantry Regiment.

NORTH AFRICA TO SICILY

In the spring of 1943, the 82nd became the first division-size airborne unit to be deployed overseas. On May 10, the All-Americans—hunkered down in troop ships that had steamed from New England across the Atlantic and into the Mediterranean—eased into the harbor at Casablanca, Morocco. From there, the division traveled by train and truck toward their final North African destination, Kairouan, Tunisia. Kairouan was to be the division's staging area for the forthcoming airborne assault on Sicily.

While in Tunisia, the airborne soldiers trained, readied their equipment, and shared a drink or two with their free French comrades. One Saturday afternoon, Ross Carter, a paratrooper with the 82nd, shared a bottle of cognac with two battle-scarred veterans of the French Foreign Legion. He considered the fate of his drinking partners … and himself.

One of the Legionnaires was "a murderer from Holland," Carter later wrote in his book, *Devils in Baggy Pants.* "The other an embezzler from France. Their lives were behind them; their future was to die for causes and for a country which meant nothing to them. I too belonged to a legion of doomed men [the 504th Parachute Infantry Regiment of the 82nd Airborne Division], but death is less bitter when the alternative is slavery."

Carter added, "Most of us knew what we were fighting for, and we knew how to fight." Indeed they did, and they were about to prove it. In early July, the All-Americans began saddling up for the Sicilian drops—the first such operation for an airborne division.

American airborne divisions initially consisted of one parachute infantry regiment and two glider infantry regiments. The single parachute infantry regiment was comprised of three battalions of paratroopers. The two glider infantry regiments were comprised of two battalions each.

> In addition to the three regiments (one parachute, two glider), the division maintained an airborne engineer battalion, an antiaircraft/antitank battalion, three artillery battalions, and supporting services.
>
> By the end of the war, the standard American airborne division was comprised of three parachute infantry regiments and one glider infantry regiment.

Code-named "Husky," the Sicily operation was comprised of four airborne assaults. Two were conducted by British paratroopers, and two were conducted by the 82nd.

The first of the assaults—Husky 1—began on the moonlit evening of July 9, 1943. Then, an American regimental combat team led by Col. James Maurice "Slim Jim" Gavin jumped over an area just behind the southern Sicilian coastline near Gela. Comprised of the 505th Parachute Infantry Regiment and a battalion from the 504th, the RCT's paratroopers found themselves scattered over a wide area and temporarily separated from their units. Still, they were able to regroup and attack the enemy along a wide front, killing defenders and seizing highway junctions. The assaults were described by British prime minister Winston Churchill as, "not the beginning of the end, but the end of the beginning."

The following day, Gavin's RCT made contact with the U.S. 1st Infantry Division, the famed "Big Red One."

On July 11, elements of the remaining two battalions of the 504th, under the command of Col. Reuben Henry Tucker III, left their Tunisian staging area, bound for Sicily.

Known as Husky II, the mission nearly failed before it crossed the enemy-held coastline. Over the Mediterranean, an Allied warship, believing the American transport planes were German, opened fire on Tucker's force. Almost at once, other ships and shore batteries began shooting at the airborne formation. The result was one of the war's near disasters. Twenty-three of the 144 transport planes were shot down, killing or wounding nearly 320 American sky soldiers.

By the time Tucker's plane roared over the drop zone, more than 2,000 holes had been punched through the fuselage by bullets and chunks of flak.

However, the force stayed the course. Over the drop zone, the surviving paratroopers stood up, hooked up, leapt, landed, assembled, and attacked. As soon as they landed, Tucker's men begin cutting the major inland roads, knocking out a series of concrete-reinforced bunkers, and seizing the high ground near the Ponte Olivo airfield. The ferocity of their attacks compelled the Germans to send panicked radio messages that suggested the Americans were attacking with 10 times their actual numerical strength.

By late July, a large stretch of Sicily's coastline had been captured by the paratroopers.

SALERNO

Less than two months later, on September 13, the division conducted its second major airborne operation: a nighttime parachute drop onto the beachhead at Salerno. The jump, in support of Gen. Mark Clark's embattled 5th Army, was successful.

The transport pilots ferrying the 504th were guided toward their target drop zones by the flickering light of oil drums along the beach. The drums had been packed with gasoline-soaked sand and were lit every 50 yards. When dawn broke, Clark's weary riflemen were heartened by the presence of reinforcements in the form of U.S. paratroopers.

The following night, the 505th's paratroopers jumped in support (the same night the independent 509th Parachute Infantry Battalion was jumping over nearby Avellino). The 505th was followed the next day by the men of the 325th Glider Infantry Regiment who—instead of using gliders— motored ashore in seaborne landing craft.

On the 16th, the airborne soldiers and Clark's "leg" infantrymen attacked. The 504th struck toward Altavilla, while the other forces battled their way up along the Italian peninsula's west coast toward Naples. On October 1, Naples fell to the Americans.

Soon thereafter, the 504th Parachute Infantry Regiment and its supporting artillery elements were detached from the 82nd Airborne Division and temporarily placed under the U.S. 36th Infantry Division. The regiment's paratroopers then moved into the hills and fought as "leg" infantrymen.

ANZIO

In January 1944, elements of the regiment conducted a landing on the beach at Anzio. From there they fought a series of defensive engagements along the hotly contested Mussolini Canal.

Despite their defensive posture, the paratroopers conducted "aggressive small-unit infiltration patrols" behind enemy lines. This not only terrorized the German rank and file, but frightened and angered their officers. Enemy commanders in fact referred to the American paratroopers as "barbarians" and ex-cons who had been given the option of remaining in prison or serving in the army as frontline combatants.

At Anzio, when an enemy position was overrun by elements of the 504th, a diary was recovered from the personal effects of a dead German officer. The officer's final entry read: "American parachutists—devils in baggy pants—are less than 100 meters from my outpost line. I can't sleep at night; they pop up from nowhere and we never know when or how they will strike next. Seems like the black-hearted devils are everywhere."

On December 27, the weary 504th was relieved by fresh American infantry. Exhausted, the paratroopers trudged down from the hills and regrouped near Pignatoro. Their performance had been magnificent, but it was not without cost. "Half of the 504th's combat strength had been obliterated," said Lt. Gen. E. M. Flanagan Jr. in *Airborne*. Indeed, 54 sky soldiers were dead, 226 were wounded, and 2 were missing. Meanwhile, the remaining elements were withdrawn from Italy and sent to England, where huge plans were in the works.

The 82nd and her fellow sky soldiers in the 101st were going to lead the charge in the greatest air-sea military effort in history: the invasion of the European continent at Normandy.

Code-named "Overlord," the invasion's airborne phase was known as "Neptune." For the mission, the All-Americans were reinforced with two brand-new parachute infantry regiments: the 507th and the 508th. The veteran 504th Parachute Infantry Regiment, still licking its wounds from the fighting on the Italian peninsula, would not participate in Neptune. The division also had an airborne engineer battalion, a glider field artillery battalion, and a parachute field artillery battalion.

Recently promoted Brig. Gen. James Gavin, the deputy division commander, was assigned the task of leading the 82nd's assault elements. The division's primary units included the 505th, 507th, and 508th Parachute Infantry Regiments. The 325th Glider Infantry Regiment followed.

The 82nd's senior commander, Gen. Ridgway, would also participate directly in the landings. He was originally slated to come in by glider, but instead opted for a parachute.

On the eve of the invasion, as the great airborne and seaborne force was preparing to launch, U.S. Gen. Dwight David Eisenhower, commanding general of Supreme Headquarters Allied Expeditionary Force, delivered his now famous "battle message":

Soldiers, Sailors, and Airmen of the Allied Expeditionary Force!

You are about to embark upon the Great Crusade toward which we have striven these many months. The eyes of the world are upon you. The hopes and prayers of liberty loving people everywhere march with you. In company with our brave Allies and brothers-in-arms on other fronts, you will bring about the destruction of the German war machine, the elimination of Nazi tyranny over the oppressed peoples of Europe, and security for ourselves in a free world. Your task will not be an easy one. Your enemy is well trained, well equipped and battle-hardened. He will fight savagely.

But this is the year of 1944! Much has happened since the Nazi triumphs of 1940–41. The United Nations have inflicted upon the Germans great defeats, in open battle, man-to-man. Our air offensive has seriously reduced their strength in the air and their capacity to wage war on the ground. Our Home fronts have given us an overwhelming superiority in weapons and munitions of war, and placed at our disposal great reserves of trained fighting men. The tide has turned! The free men of the world are marching together to Victory!

I have full confidence in your courage, devotion to duty and skill in battle. We will accept nothing less than full Victory!

Good Luck! And let us all beseech the blessing of Almighty God upon this great and noble undertaking.

Despite the grim seriousness, the fears, and the tremendous responsibilities felt by the soldiers, the operation and its scope seemed somewhat surreal to everyone involved.

"My soul was at peace, my heart was light, my spirits almost gay," recalled Gen. Ridgway of his mood on the eve of invasion.

THE INVASION OF NORMANDY

A few minutes into the wee hours of June 6, 1944, D-day began. Some 6,418 paratroopers from the 82nd, their 6,638 airborne brothers from the 101st, and another 4,000 from the British 6th Airborne crossed the English Channel and entered Norman airspace as the vanguard of the invasion. They had been preceded by teams of pathfinders, who marked the target drop zones with lights and electronic homing devices—and they were followed by waves of troop-packed gliders.

The American paratroopers jumped into the darkness along the right flank of the invasion front and behind German lines. Arcing streams of antiaircraft tracers reached toward them as they and their ferrying planes filled the skies. Some of the men were killed by bullets and shrapnel before they exited the doors of the aircraft. Some drowned when they jumped prematurely over the channel. Others were blown to bits when their transporting aircraft took direct hits. Still others died swinging in their harnesses as they descended to the earth.

Over Normandy, the sky looked like "a 4th of July celebration on the Mall in Washington," recalled Gen. Matthew Ridgway in Gerald Astor's *June 6, 1944: The Voices of D-Day*. "The sky was covered with stuff, rockets and tracers were streaking through the air and big explosions were going off everywhere."

On the ground, the surviving paratroopers found themselves off target by as much as 35 miles, dispersed throughout the countryside, or struggling to get through areas that had been deliberately flooded as a defense against airborne landings. In many cases, the sky soldiers discovered that their units had been destroyed or their unit leaders killed. But airborne troops, being the world's most adaptable fighters, quickly regrouped and moved toward their objectives: seizing bridges, roads, and other inland routes of egress for the primary landing forces that would soon be hitting the beaches. They also focused on confusing the enemy, diverting their forces, and protecting the seaborne force's all-important flanks.

In order to differentiate between friendly and enemy forces in the darkness, individual paratroopers in the 82nd relied on whispering the password *flash* and then waiting on the response, *thunder.* Their brothers in the 101st relied on clicking noisemakers found in boxes of Cracker Jack (see Chapter 5).

Gen. Gavin was the officer who made the decision regarding relying on the password as opposed to the noisemaker. His reasoning was simple: One extra pound or a single ounce carried over the beach should be in the form of ammunition. The soul of efficiency, Gavin himself cut the unused fringes off of his maps to make room for 156 rounds of rifle and pistol ammo. Nor did Gavin scrimp when it came to weaponry. A frontline fighting general who would have earned the respect of his nineteenth-century counterparts, Gavin jumped into Normandy with a rifle, a pistol, a knife, and two handfuls of grenades. It was, he said, "in case I had to fight my way through enemy territory, which once I did."

Of the senior airborne commanders at Normandy, Gavin was the only one who had attended and earned his wings at jump school. Other commanders— like Gavin's boss, Ridgway, and the 101st's commander, Maxwell Taylor— had only one or two jumps under their belts.

The British 6th Airborne quickly secured the flanks of Sword Beach on the Allies' extreme left and seized bridges over the Caen Canal and the Orne River.

The American 82nd and 101st did not fare quite as well. Responsible for securing the area behind Utah Beach on the Allied right, they encountered stiff resistance near Sainte-Mere-Eglise and Carentan, and spent much of the first day either fending off attacks or regrouping their scattered numbers.

Jumping with the paratroopers were dummy parachutists, large dolls wired with popping firecrackers that misled the Germans deep in their interior, diverting attention away from the real sky soldiers.

As confusing as it was for the 82nd's men on the ground, the Germans were virtually stymied. The Americans were everywhere. To both Nazi intelligence forces and the German field commanders at ground zero, there seemed to be no developing plan of action, no discernible mission, and no clue as to the numbers of Allied parachutists.

Off course and unable to see where they were landing, paratroopers of the 82nd's 505th Parachute Infantry Regiment began dropping in and around the town of Sainte-Mere-Eglise. Moreover, one of the town's houses was struck by flying incendiaries and quickly caught fire. The ensuing blaze enabled the German garrison to spot the American paratroopers and shoot them as they descended.

One of the sky soldiers, Pvt. John Steele, crashed into the town church's steeple, which he slid down until his parachute snagged. Helpless, hanging in his harness, and suspended above the town square, Pvt. Steele feigned death to avoid being shot by the enemy. He was rescued the following day.

Soon the paratroopers were reinforced by the gliderborne soldiers of the 325th Glider Infantry Regiment. But they, too, were isolated, cut off from the Allied main body, and found themselves immediately under fire. Many of the gliders cracked up upon landing, killing most if not all of the occupants.

Over the next several weeks, the division's parachute and glider elements battled enemy strong points, capturing the French towns of La Fiere, Montebourg Station, Beuzeville-la-Bastille, and Baupt. Moving along the west coast of the Cotentin Peninsula, the All-Americans eventually seized the heights overlooking La Haye-du-Puits.

After 33 days of bitter fighting, the division was withdrawn to Great Britain. "Without relief" and "with replacements," Gavin's after action report read. "Every mission accomplished. No ground gained was ever relinquished."

But it was not without great cost. Casualties among the 82nd's paratroopers were horrendous. In just over a month, some 5,245 paratroopers were killed, wounded, or missing in action.

On August 16, 1944, Gavin was promoted to major general and given command of the 82nd Airborne Division. Nine days later, on August 25, the U.S. XVIII Corps (originally the II Armored Corps) was redesignated the XVIII Airborne Corps. That same day, at the XVIII's headquarters in Orbourne, St. George, England, a blue "airborne" tab was added to the Corps' distinctive "blue dragon" emblem. The 82nd became one of the Corps' divisions.

The XVIII Airborne Corps—including the American 17th, 82nd, and 101st Airborne Divisions (the untested 13th Airborne Division joined the corps near the end of the war)—was one of two corps that together formed the First Allied Airborne Army under the command of U.S. Army Air Forces Lt. Gen. Lewis Hyde Brereton. The second corps-size element in Brereton's airborne army was the British First Airborne Corps, which included the British 1st and 6th Airborne Divisions, and an independent Polish airborne brigade. The establishment of the XVIII Airborne Corps was the result of the Allied commanders' progressive appreciation of airborne power. According to the XVIII Airborne Corps unit history, the fact that airborne tactics had been proven to be a valuable asset to the U.S. Army "was evident by the success of the 82nd Airborne Division and the IX Troop Carrier Command during the Sicily and Italian campaigns. Furthermore, the *esprit de corps* exhibited by the 82nd Airborne and the 101st Airborne Divisions in the critical days following the Normandy invasion ensured that airborne tactics and maneuvers would remain an integral part of U.S. Army operations. By midsummer 1944, it was evident to Supreme Headquarters Allied Expeditionary Force that a unity of command among airborne divisions was necessary in order to fully exploit their unique power. Correspondingly, British airborne and Royal Air Force units found themselves in the same position."

In September, Maj. Gen. Ridgway was named commanding general of the XVIII. The regrouped and healthy 504th Parachute Infantry Regiment returned to the 82nd. The 507th was transferred to the 17th "Thunder from Heaven" Airborne Division, and the 82nd began planning for its fourth combat jump of the war: Operation Market Garden.

THE INVASION OF THE NETHERLANDS

In an attempt to end the war as soon as possible, the Allies conceived a near-brilliant airborne plan to cut off and annihilate the German forces in Holland. But difficult terrain, enemy troop strength, and the enemy's ability to continue fighting were all underestimated. The Germans were certainly on the run in September 1944, but they were far from defeated.

The Allied plan called for three airborne divisions—the American 82nd, the 101st, and the British 1st—a Polish parachute brigade, and other smaller Allied airborne elements to jump into the Netherlands and capture key bridges and highways along a corridor between the towns of Eindhoven and Arnhem. The jumps would all be made deep behind German lines. Meanwhile, British ground forces—specifically XXX Corps—would race straight through the corridor along an open stretch of highway, reinforcing each airborne element at points along the way. The ultimate goal was to cross the Rhine River, smash through Hitler's "West Wall" defenses, destroy the German army, and begin bringing the boys home by Christmas.

> The Allied invasion of the Netherlands in late 1944 was code-named Operation Market Garden. The operation was comprised of two phases: airborne (parachute and glider forces) and ground force (armored). "Market" was the code name for the airborne assault phase. "Garden" was the code name for the ground attack phase.

The mission was doable but dicey. Time was critical. Once the airborne assaults began, the ground forces would have to race against the clock to relieve the paratroopers and glidermen along the main highway. The airborne forces would be landing without the support of artillery and tanks. They would be fully capable of seizing their objectives "with thunderclap surprise," as Gen. Brereton was fond of saying, but they could not be expected to hold out against the Germans—who would surely launch a series of counterattacks—beyond 48 hours.

Market Garden opened with stunning success. The great airborne army lifted off from England just after 10 A.M. on Sunday, September 17, 1944, breaking the morning calm and prompting a temporary break in church services. Worshipers and late sleepers filled the streets and craned their heads skyward. It was one of the most fantastic displays of modern military power anyone had ever seen: 5,000 planes—fighters, bombers, and C-47 transports—followed by 2,500 gliders. In all, some 35,000 American and British paratroopers and glidermen were being hurled against the enemy.

As the force roared across the English Channel, the aircrews were surprised to find themselves virtually unmolested by enemy fighters. But as the transports neared their targets, the pilots could see that they were flying toward a thick wall of flak. The deadly black puffs burst around the planes, but unlike Normandy, the pilots stayed on course. It was an order from

Ike: no evasive action. No breaking of formation. When planes were hit or engines erupted in flame, the pilots held course long enough for the sky soldiers to jump together and land as units.

Scores of American paratroopers descend on Holland during Operation Market Garden, September 1944.

Dropping in daylight, nearly all of the paratroopers landed on target, quickly assembled, and moved toward their objectives. The drops were executed in stark contrast to previous American airborne assaults, which resulted in the scattering of paratroopers over vast areas beyond their target drop zones and leaving many units isolated and vulnerable. In Holland, the drops were textbook.

The glider forces were less fortunate. Many of the gliders crashed hard, killing the crews and the glider soldiers.

The attacks completely surprised the Germans. During the first few hours, they found themselves not only unable to launch a counterattack, but scrambling to organize an adequate defense. That soon changed.

The 82nd's landings were in the area around Veghel, Grave, and Kleve, with the primary objective of seizing Nijmegen (between Eindhoven and Arnhem). The 101st was responsible for capturing Eindhoven farther south. Both divisions became heavily engaged, but the All-Americans, with more widely separated objectives, had it a bit tougher than the 101st. The paratroopers of the British 1st, responsible for capturing the bridges at Arnhem, found themselves in the worst position possible.

Upon landing, elements of the 82nd raced toward their first objectives—the Mass Bridge at Grave, the Maas-Waal Canal Bridge at Heumen, and the Groesbeek Heights—seizing them intact against stiff opposition. The main body of the 82nd's paratroopers, however, encountered impregnable resistance east of Nijmegen. More than one assault was made to take the bridge on the first day, but all attempts failed and as night fell the bridge was still in enemy hands.

Three days later, the 504th conducted a river crossing at the Waal. Casualties were heavy during the crossing and subsequent assault. But by the 21st, the All-Americans had seized the bridge.

In the end, large areas of Holland were liberated, but the invasion as it was planned had fallen far short of achieving one of its primary goals, the capture of Arnhem, and its ultimate goal, that of crossing the Rhine.

Unable to take Arnhem, the British and American paratroopers were taunted by the enemy's propaganda radio broadcasts. "You can listen to our music, but you can't walk in our streets," boasted a female broadcaster the airborne soldiers nicknamed "Arnhem Annie."

British Gen. Montgomery, who supported the operation for the remainder of his life, regarded it as 90 percent successful. "In my prejudiced view, if the operation had been properly backed from its inception, and given the aircraft, ground forces, and administrative resources necessary for the job, it would have succeeded in spite of my mistakes, or the adverse weather, or the presence of the 2nd SS Panzer Corps in the Arnhem area," Montgomery said after the war. "I remain Market Garden's unrepentant advocate."

After Market Garden, the 82nd returned to France for a much-needed rest and refitting, but the respite was short.

BATTLE OF THE BULGE

By mid-December 1944, the German army had been all but defeated, or so it seemed. A bitter cold winter had set in. The weather was poor, and Gen. Eisenhower was regrouping his forces for an upcoming campaign that would surely open in spring.

No one believed the Germans would attack. That fact alone convinced German leader Adolf Hitler that he had one last hope of winning the war. As a result, on December 16, the Germans launched a surprise attack through the Ardennes against American forces in Belgium and northern Luxembourg that penetrated deep into Allied territory and threatened the entire western front.

All the Allied units in the vicinity—those not initially struck by the onslaught—were rushed forward to stem the tide of advancing German armor and infantry. The American paratroopers who raced toward the front were unquestionably some of the most committed soldiers ever fielded by an American army. Although other Americans—mostly inexperienced troops— were retreating and discarding their weapons along the way, the men of the 82nd and 101st were meeting them on the same route and taking their ammunition. The sky soldiers were determined to stop the enemy.

One of the often-told tales of the All-Americans during the Battle of the Bulge is the conversation between a young private first class with the 82nd's 325th Glider Infantry Regiment and a tank sergeant. According to the story, the sergeant, seated on his tank destroyer, part of a force withdrawing in the face of advancing Germans, spotted the PFC digging a foxhole near Belgium's Baraque de Fraiture crossroads.

The young GI looked up from his entrenching work at the sergeant and asked, "You looking for a safe place?"

The sergeant responded, "Yeah."

The PFC started digging again and matter-of-factly said, "Well, buddy, just pull your tank in behind me. I'm the 82nd Airborne and this is as far as the bastards are going."

On December 20, the 82nd reached the Vielsalm-St. Vith region. From there, the division launched a fierce attack against the Germans, beating the enemy back across the Ambleve River. But the Germans counterattacked along the Salm and pushed the paratroopers back near Manhay. On Christmas Day 1944, the 82nd withdrew from the Vielsalm area and soon thereafter renewed its attack northeast of Bra. By January 4, the division had reached the Salm.

Three days later, the famous fighting 508th Parachute Infantry Regiment, also known as the Red Devils, attacked near Thier-du-Mont. After suffering heavy losses, the regiment was pulled back and placed on reserve status until it was relieved by elements of the 2nd Infantry Division. Within days, the Red Devils were back in the fight and inflicting terrible losses on the enemy.

By early February, the German army had all but collapsed. A few hold-outs were fighting fiercely, but most units were falling back en masse.

On February 7, 1945, the 82nd attacked and carried the Roer River town of Bergstein. Ten days later, the division crossed the Roer and secured much of the territory in front of them, including the city of Cologne. They halted briefly to rest and refit.

THE ENEMY IS DEFEATED

In April, the division attacked toward the Elbe River, and Hitler committed suicide on the 30th. On May 2, the entire German 21st Army surrendered to the division's 504th Parachute Infantry Regiment. Germany capitulated that same month. The 82nd Airborne Division was then ordered to serve as the primary occupation force in the new American Sector of Berlin (the British, French, and Soviets also controlled sectors). It was there that the All-Americans earned the title "America's Guard of Honor."

During a dress parade in which the 82nd participated, Gen. George Smith Patton Jr., the famous "blood and guts" commander of the U.S. Third Army, remarked: "In all my years in the Army and of all the Honor Guards I've ever seen, the 82nd Berlin Honor Guard is the best."

POSTWAR PARATROOPERS

On January 3, 1946, the decorated All-Americans returned to the States, but unlike most of its sister divisions, the 82nd was not demobilized. Instead, the division moved into garrison at Fort Bragg, North Carolina (where it remains to this day), and on November 15, 1948, it was desig-nated a permanent regular U.S. Army division. Throughout the 1950s, the division participated in numerous training exercises in all-weather and all-terrain environments throughout the world.

The 1960s proved to be a turbulent decade, with the elements of the division deployed throughout the world in a variety of operations. In 1964, elements of the 82nd deployed to the war-ravaged Congo. In April of the following year, civil unrest swept through the Dominican Republic, and U.S. troops were ordered into the region to protect American lives and prevent a Communist takeover similar to that experienced by Cuba under Fidel Castro.

On April 28, 1965, U.S. Marines landed from the sea, and elements of the 82nd Airborne began moving in—air-landed, not by parachute—a few days later. On the morning of May 3, six battalions of paratroopers linked up with the Marines near the capital of Santo Domingo. By the following day, more than 10,500 soldiers from the 82nd, along with their supporting elements, were on the island.

Additional Army forces, including Special Forces (Green Berets) and psychological warfare teams, reinforced the paratroopers and Marines, increasing the total U.S. combat strength to some 18,500 men. Together, by mid-May, the Americans had effectively shut down the unrest in and around the capital.

By mid-May, the division's primary elements—with the exception of one brigade—returned to Fort Bragg. The remaining paratroopers returned home in September of 1966.

In 1967, paratroopers from the 82nd again returned to the Congo. The division also found itself involved in several civil disturbance operations (anti-Vietnam War protests and race riots) within the United States. Among the protests and riots were major disturbances in Detroit in 1967 and in Washington, D.C., in 1968. Also in 1968, with the Vietnam War in full swing, the 82nd was ordered back into overseas action.

THE TET OFFENSIVE

In late January 1968, during the Vietnamese holiday of *Tet Nguyen Dan* (translated as "lunar new year"), Vietcong (VC) and North Vietnamese Army (NVA) forces launched a series of unexpected attacks. They took place in the South Vietnamese capital of Saigon, the old provincial capital of Hue, and points throughout the countryside. The enemy offensive was timed to kick off during a holiday truce both sides had honored during the previous years of fighting in Vietnam. U.S. and South Vietnamese forces agreed to recognize a 36-hour cease-fire beginning at 6 P.M. on January 29. The VC and NVA forces also agreed to a temporary cease-fire, theirs beginning on the morning of the 27th and lasting seven days. It was a ruse on the part of the North Vietnamese designed to catch U.S. and South Vietnamese military forces off guard.

Almost immediately, the 82nd's 3rd Brigade was placed on full alert, and in less than 24 hours the paratroopers were en route to the American base at Chu Lai.

Once in country, the 3rd Brigade engaged the enemy in the northern I Corps sector, specifically in and around Phu Bai and the nearby provincial capital of Hue. When the upper hand was gained in those areas, the brigade was dispatched south to Saigon. Soon they were engaged in combat along the Mekong Delta, in the Iron Triangle, and along the Cambodian border.

South Vietnam was divided into four primary tactical zones. Each zone was commanded by a South Vietnamese general, but American generals who commanded their own forces also had independent responsibilities within those zones. The I Corps Tactical Zone in the north bordered the Demilitarized Zone in the extreme north, Laos to the west, and the South China Sea to the east. I Corps was the primary responsibility of the U.S. Marine Corps. Below I Corps was II Corps, or the Central Highlands region, which bordered both Laos and Cambodia to the west and the coastline east. III Corps Tactical Zone, the most populated of the four zones, bordered Cambodia to the west, the sea east. Both II Corps and III Corps were the primary responsibilities of the U.S. Army. IV Corps Tactical Zone was located in the far south: The later zone encompassed the storied Mekong River region. The area around Saigon, between III Corps and IV Corps was considered a separate administrative Special Capital Zone.

Combat patrolling and fighting were also conducted along Highway 1—the major north-south transportation artery that runs the length of the country—and at flashpoints along the Song Bo River.

In December 1969, the paratroopers returned to the States and their home base at Fort Bragg.

During the 1970s, the 82nd Airborne Division honed its combat skills and was involved in several training exercises. On more than one occasion, the division was either deployed or placed on combat alert status. An anti-tank TOW missile task force from the 82nd was deployed to Southeast

Asia in the spring of 1972. Combat alerts included possible deployments to the Middle East in 1973, Zaire in 1978, and during the Iranian hostage crisis in 1979. Although the paratroopers were locked and loaded, they were just as quickly ordered to stand down.

In March 1982, the division participated in the "Multinational Force and Observers Peacekeeping Mission" in the Egyptian Sinai. They were the first U.S. Army force to do so. Force rotations to Egypt continued for more than a decade.

GRENADA

If one slightly discolored mark exists on the record of the vaunted All-Americans, it was made on the Caribbean island of Grenada during the American invasion of that country in October of 1983.

On October 13, 1983, the army of Grenada, under the direction of former Deputy Prime Minister Bernard Coard and Grenadian Gen. Hudson Austin, seized power of the tiny island nation in a bloody coup d'état. Martial law was immediately declared and a shoot-on-sight curfew was established. Grenada's prime minister Maurice Bishop, his wife, and most of the government's senior officials were arrested and shot.

Coard was a devout Marxist. Bishop was also a Marxist, but with free-market leanings. Those facts, combined with the rapid and violent ousting of Bishop's government, were unsettling to most of the democratized nations in the Caribbean, as it was to the administration of U.S. President Ronald Reagan. The president, in fact, referred to Coard and his cronies as "a brutal group of leftist thugs," and American troops were ordered in.

A joint service operation, the invasion of Grenada began on the night of October 23 and 24 by Team 6 of the U.S. Navy SEALs (the Navy's elite SEa, Air, Land commandos) and a handful of U.S. Air Force combat controllers. (The latter was an elite Air Force ground combat element trained to set up drop zones and coordinate airborne assaults, among other special operations responsibilities.) They conducted an open-water parachute jump off Point Salinas on the southern tip of Grenada.

The sailors and airmen were responsible for reconnoitering the island's main airfield as well as determining the condition of—and preparing—the runway (which was vital to the forthcoming Army airborne elements). In addition, they had to determine the location and strength of nearby enemy forces. Unfortunately, four SEALs drowned in the heavy seas, and the others were ordered to withdraw before completing the mission. Nevertheless, the operation to seize the island was given a green light.

The first element of the 82nd to arrive was a battalion from the 325th Airborne Infantry Regiment. It was followed by one battalion each from the 505th and 508th. All the paratroopers were airlifted onto the island's Point Salinas airfield, which had been seized earlier by U.S. Army Rangers.

The individual paratroopers of the 82nd performed well on Grenada. All the division's objectives were met, and casualties were light, despite relatively stiff enemy resistance. But obvious problems occurred within the division's leadership at ground zero.

An officer monitoring radio communications from one of the offshore ships later said that it sounded "as if the whole division was on the verge of panic." The speed of movement was also called into question. At one point, Gen. John W. Vessey Jr., then the outspoken chairman of the Joint Chiefs of Staff, telephoned an 82nd commander. Vessey allegedly demanded to know why there were "two companies of Marines running all over the island and thousands of Army troops doing nothing. What the hell is going on?"

Nevertheless, the Grenada operation was successful and command problems were properly ironed out over the next several months.

PANAMA

In late 1989, U.S. forces invaded neighboring Panama in the first major operation with no connection to the Cold War. Code-named "Just Cause," the invasion's objectives were to protect American citizens in what had become a wholly unstable country, neutralize the Panamanian Defense Forces (PDF), and capture Panama's military strongman, Gen. Manuel Antonio Noriega. The invasion was also the largest clash of arms in Panamanian history.

Just after midnight on December 20, a U.S. Air Force combat control team parachuted over Omar Torrijos International Airport and the adjacent Tocumen military airfield. On the ground, the airmen placed aircraft-navigation beacons near the end of the runway.

At 1 A.M., AC-130 Spectre gunships and Cobra helicopters roared in and began pummeling nearby PDF defenses. Within minutes, elements of both the 82nd Airborne Division, under the command of Lt. Gen. Carl W. Stiner, and the 75th Ranger Regiment, under the command of Maj. Gen. Wayne A. Downing, were jumping over both Torrijos Airport and Tocumen airfield.

On the ground, Stiner's 1st Brigade Task Force (of the 82nd), comprised of two battalions of the 504th Parachute Infantry Regiment, linked up with a third battalion that was already stationed in Panama. The Airborne-Ranger force then began attacking various points in and around Panama City. It was the first jump for the famous "devils in baggy pants" since World War II.

Following the jump and subsequent seizure of the two airfields, the paratroopers launched several follow-on combat air assault operations in Panama City and other enemy strongpoints.

"What we saw was fairly determined resistance ..., but [that resistance] doing dumb and stupid things," recalled Maj. Gen. James H. Johnson Jr., commanding general of the 82nd, during an interview with XVIII Airborne Corps historian Dr. Robert K. Wright Jr. "First of all, we encountered nobody in a PDF uniform[;] of course, they were all in civilian clothes— at least half were ... they were wearing [blue] jeans for the most part. But approaching you in a vehicle with AK-47s, firing at you, coming right up to a roadblock. [They d]id not use any kind of tactics that you would normally expect to be able to win a firefight. They were mostly firing to harass."

Johnson stated that the Panamanians lacked leadership and discipline. Still, he said, the enemy was "very determined to make us pay a price. All that disappeared very rapidly when, I think, they saw what the outcome was going to be."

By the end of January 1990, the 82nd's soldiers had returned to Fort Bragg.

THE FIRST GULF WAR

Just over six months later, on the morning of August 2, the 82nd again went on full alert. Without provocation, Iraqi tanks and infantry had swept across the Iraqi-Kuwaiti border and seized Kuwait City. Disregarding Kuwaiti sovereignty, Iraqi leader Saddam Hussein contended that Kuwait was a his-torical province of the Iraqi state, and that the government in Baghdad was simply exerting its authority over what was by tradition Iraqi territory.

Six days later, the 82nd's paratroopers—backed by light tanks, antitank missiles, and Apache helicopters—deployed to Saudi Arabia, moved up to the Saudi-Iraqi border, and essentially "drew a line in the sand." With the division and its supporting elements in place, the Iraqi army was not going to cross the Saudi border, and that army would soon be routed from Kuwait. Over the next several months, the United States assembled a broad multinational coalition of air, naval, and ground forces committed to ousting Hussein's forces from Kuwait. On the night of January 16 and 17, 1991, Operation Desert Storm kicked off with the first in a series of day-night air attacks against Hussein's forces. Just over one month later, on February 24, 1991, the ground-war phase began.

On the left flank—under the XVIII Airborne Corps—the 82nd was tasked with conducting air assault (helicopter-borne) and light armored operations, with the bulk of the division attacking across the desert in light armored vehicles.

The XVIII Airborne Corps, during the 1991 invasion of Iraq, was comprised of the 82nd Airborne Division, the 101st Airborne Division (Air Assault), the 24th Infantry Division (Mechanized), the 3rd Armored Cavalry Regiment, and the attached French 6th Light Armored Division. The XVIIIth's elements quickly isolated the Iraqi army in the Iraqi desert and virtually annihilated the primary elements of Saddam Hussein's elite Republican Guard.

The 82nd, under the command of Gen. Johnson, proved particularly adept at penetrating deep into Iraqi territory, at times pushing through and past other American and allied units. Like all other U.S. and coalition forces, whenever the All-Americans made contact with the enemy it was a lopsided engagement with the Iraqis on the losing end. On February 28, a cease-fire was declared and the war ended.

In early March, the 82nd's elements began a measured return to Fort Bragg. By April, the entire division was home.

In the summer of 1999, elements of the 82nd Airborne were among the first American combat forces on the ground in Kosovo, a war-ravaged nation in the Balkans. A battalion of the 505th Parachute Infantry Regiment was in fact the first of the 82nd's presence. They were soon followed by a battalion of the 504th Parachute Infantry Regiment and then a battalion from the 325th Airborne Infantry Regiment.

Training and global deployments continued throughout the remainder of the twentieth century and into the twenty-first.

Paratroopers of the 82nd Airborne Division jump during a 2001 training exercise/demonstration near Charleston, South Carolina.

THE WAR ON TERROR AND THE SECOND GULF WAR

On September 11, 2001, the unthinkable happened when terrorists commandeered four commercial airliners filled with passengers and used them as giant missiles against American targets. Two planes slammed into New York City's World Trade Center towers, completely destroying them both. A third crashed into the Pentagon in northern Virginia. A fourth crashed into a remote field in Pennsylvania. Thousands were killed, and the hunt was on for the attack mastermind, Osama bin Laden, and the members of his al Qaeda terrorist network.

Almost immediately, the All-Americans were placed on alert. Soon many of the division's paratroopers were deploying to Afghanistan, while others were dispatched to Central Command headquarters at MacDill Air Force Base in Tampa, Florida, and to various staging areas in the Middle East and west Asia.

The war against terror was on, and the 82nd was once again fighting. As part of that war, on March 19, 2003, the United States led an allied force into Iraq to disarm the Iraqi military and oust President Saddam Hussein, who some top U.S. officials believed was in league with al Qaeda terrorists.

Though the details of many of the 82nd's recent combat missions in both the Afghanistan and Iraq theaters remain classified, the paratroopers have been and are indeed currently engaged in ongoing operations against terrorists and the holdouts of Saddam Hussein's regime.

"The 82nd Airborne Division, which helped overwhelm the airport on its way to Baghdad this week, can be viewed as the New York Yankees of the U.S. Army," wrote Bill Straub of the Scripps Howard News Service on April 5, 2003. He would describe them as being "a unit filled with stars."

That they are, and those paratroopers who are not currently overseas earning laurels are constantly preparing for deployment, and predeployment training is still demanding for America's only true remaining airborne division. In a peacetime year, a paratrooper with the 82nd can expect to train for nearly 270 days (including day and night live-fire exercises), run approximately 700 miles, and make a minimum of 12 training jumps. Tough, but necessary, and those are just the minimums.

Speaking from the deck of the aircraft carrier USS *Abraham Lincoln* in early May, President George W. Bush announced the end of major combat operations in Iraq. The president also discussed the ongoing operations in Afghanistan, specifically the work of the 82nd Airborne Division in that country.

"In the Battle of Afghanistan, we destroyed the Taliban, many terrorists, and the camps where they trained," Bush said. "We continue to help the Afghan people lay roads, restore hospitals, and educate all of their children. Yet we also have dangerous work to complete. As I speak, a special operations task force, led by the 82nd Airborne, is on the trail of the terrorists, and those who seek to undermine the free government of Afghanistan. America and our coalition will finish what we have begun."

As the war against terror progresses and potential hot spots threaten to flare up around the world, the 82nd Airborne Division will continue to be one of America's quick-response forces of choice. The division's paratroopers would indeed be some of the first combatants on the ground if general war were to erupt on the troubled Korean peninsula. This fact was highlighted in a *USA Today* news feature published on August 27, 2003. According to the article:

The Defense Department will not officially comment on war plans for the Korean peninsula, but people who have read the plans or who have participated in updating them have outlined broad aspects. The main war plan, OPLAN 5027, assumes that North Korea would strike first with artillery and missiles, followed by a ground invasion. South Korean and U.S. forces would be expected to stop the North Koreans just outside Seoul and to hold for up to 30 days. A counter-attack would be led by a Marine expeditionary force and the Army's 82nd Airborne Division.

THE 82ND IN THE NEW CENTURY

According to the Army field manual on light infantry and airborne divisions, the role of the modern 82nd Airborne Division is to "plan, coordinate, and execute a rapid, combined arms, and forced entry operation employed alone or as part of a joint task force across the depth and width of the battlefield."

That is not an easy task, but the 82nd is able to do so by employing its assets methodically in three distinct "echelons."

The first echelon is the assault element. This is the spearhead force responsible for "kicking in the door." It includes combat-ready paratroopers, immediate backup forces, and all of their essential logistics soldiers.

The second or follow-on echelon reinforces the assault element with heavier equipment and greater firepower than the swiftly striking assault element can wield. Like the assault element, this echelon moves in with tremendous speed. They are trained and equipped to do so via a massive parachute drop or movement over land. According to a description of the All-Americans at GlobalSecurity.org, "The airborne forces do not need the follow-on echelon in the objective area during the initial assault but do need it for subsequent operations."

The final or rear echelon is the force responsible for noncombat administrative and service functions. During the initial assault, this echelon remains in the airborne departure area and from there is capable of effectively providing support to the first and second echelons. If the combat operation stretches into weeks rather than days, the rear echelon may be deployed to the initial objective area. In that capacity, they can perform their primary support roles or, if need be, shoulder a weapon and fight.

CHAPTER 5

SCREAMING EAGLES: 101ST AIRBORNE DIVISION

We few, we happy few, we band of brothers;
For he today that sheds his blood with me
Shall be my brother; be he ne'er so lowly,
This day shall ennoble his rank.

—Henry V to his soldiers before the battle of Agincourt,
1415, in William Shakespeare's *The Life of King Henry V*

Death from above.

—Unofficial motto of all Army airborne forces (The motto's
origin is often attributed to the 502nd Parachute Infantry
Regiment of the 101st Airborne Division.)

Of all the Army's airborne divisions, brigades, and regiments, none
has a more evolutionary history than that of the 101st Airborne
Division.

Known as the "Screaming Eagles," the division is today not an
"airborne" division in the true sense of the word. It is a helicopter-
borne air assault division. But military tradition dies hard, and, thus,
the 101st is still officially designated as the 101st Airborne Division.

On August 16, 1942—two years to the day after the first jump was made by the Army's "parachute test platoon"—the 101st Infantry Division was redesignated the 101st Airborne Division at Camp Claiborne, Louisiana. Command of the division was awarded to Maj. Gen. William C. "Bill" Lee, who justifiably came to be known as the "father of United States Airborne."

Lee, a career-long advocate of airborne warfare, had been instrumental in the development of U.S. airborne forces. He would always be known as one of America's first airborne division commanders, but he was knocked out of the first spot by Maj. Gen. Matthew B. Ridgway. The 82nd Airborne Division, under Ridgway's command, had been created the day before. Thus, Ridgway won the honor of being the first-ever commanding general of an American airborne division.

The 101st had previously existed as a nonairborne unit during and after World War I, but it had never been bloodied as a division in combat and had never been fully manned or operational.

The distinctive shoulder patch of the 101st Airborne Division consists of a black shield with a "screaming" bald (or white) eagle head in the center. The black shield is symbolic of the Wisconsin regiment of the old American Civil War "Iron Brigade." Wisconsin was the home state of the original 101st Division after World War I. The eagle is symbolic of "Old Abe," an eagle that was in fact carried into battle by the Iron Brigade's Wisconsin regiment.

According to legend, a Chippewa Indian by the name of Chief Sky had a newly hatched eaglet he swapped with an unknown trader for a sack of corn in 1861. The bird was later bought for $4 and donated to C Company of the 8th Wisconsin Regiment. It was subsequently named "Old Abe" in honor of Abraham Lincoln, then president of the United States. During the Civil War, "Old Abe" was carried forward into battle on a shield and was present at 36 battles. Tradition also has it that the eagle was wounded during two of those battles: Vicksburg and Corinth. Living eagles have since been adopted as mascots by the 101st.

Above the shoulder patch, arcing above the black shield bearing Old Abe's head, is a black tab with the inscription "AIRBORNE" in gold letters.

Originally activated on July 23, 1918, during mobilization for World War I, the 101st was one of several American units lacking weapons, ammunition, and equipment for training. When the war ended in November 1918, the division was disbanded.

In 1921, the 101st was reestablished as the 101st Infantry Division, with its headquarters in Milwaukee, Wisconsin. However, it was considered to be a "paper" division, unmanned and wholly unprepared for combat.

"A RENDEZVOUS WITH DESTINY"

On December 7, 1941, the Japanese struck Pearl Harbor, Hawaii, and soon thereafter the United States declared war on Japan, Germany, and Italy.

In the summer of 1942, following the division's new "Airborne" designation, Lee made his famous "rendezvous with destiny" address to the troops:

> The 101st Airborne Division, activated at Camp Claiborne, Louisiana, has no history, but it has a rendezvous with destiny. Like the early American pioneers whose invincible courage was the foundation stone of this nation, we have broken with the past and its traditions in order to establish our claim to the future.
>
> Due to the nature of our armament, and the tactics in which we shall perfect ourselves, we shall be called upon to carry out operations of far-reaching military importance and we shall habitually go into action when the need is immediate and extreme.
>
> Let me call your attention to the fact that our badge is the great American eagle. This is a fitting emblem for a division that will crush its enemies by falling upon them like a thunderbolt from the skies.
>
> The history we shall make, the record of high achievement we hope to write in the annals of the American Army and the American people, depends wholly and completely on the men of this division. Each individual, each officer and each enlisted man, must therefore regard himself as a necessary part of a complex and powerful instrument for the overcoming of the enemies of the nation. Each, in his own job, must realize that he is not only a means, but an indispensable means for obtaining the goal of victory. It is, therefore, not too much to say that the future itself, in whose molding we expect to have our share, is in the hands of the soldiers of the 101st Airborne Division.

Although the first part of Lee's statement regarding the 101st having "no history" was not quite true, the second part—"a rendezvous with destiny"— certainly was.

In October, the paratroopers and glider infantry soldiers of the 101st moved to Fort Bragg, North Carolina, and began a rigorous program of detailed organization and training for war. Beginning in early 1943, the division conducted maneuvers in the backcountry of North Carolina and Tennessee. It was during one such training exercise that Lee was injured in a glider mishap. "Next time I'll take a parachute," he remarked.

By the summer of 1943, the Screaming Eagles were preparing for an overseas deployment. Soon thereafter, the division was shipped to England. There the airborne soldiers continued to train, but with greater intensity as plans were in the works for the forthcoming invasion of Europe.

THE "FATHER" LOSES HIS COMMAND

In early February 1944, Lee suffered a heart attack while participating in a field exercise with his men. Within days of the attack, Lee's doctors informed him that he would have to be relieved of command for medical reasons and he returned stateside for treatment. It was a serious personal blow to Lee (the general died four years later in his hometown of Dunn, North Carolina).

Command of the 101st was awarded to Gen. Maxwell Davenport Taylor on March 14. For the next several months, the division's paratroopers made a number of training jumps. These included jumping from moving trucks as well as airplanes. Additionally, field exercises were conducted based on what the division's commanders believed the paratroopers and glidermen would encounter when they landed at Normandy.

BAND OF BROTHERS

On the evening of June 4, Gen. Taylor visited with his men. "Give me three days and nights of hard fighting," he told them. "Then you will be relieved." The reality was the 101st would be slugging it out for more than a month before it would be relieved.

"You know you're in the parachute troops. You're going to be jumping behind enemy lines. What do you expect? You have no idea," recalled Maj. Richard Winters, a former paratrooper with the 101st, in a documentary excerpt for the film *Band of Brothers*. "That will make anybody stand and search his soul for a few minutes."

That night, the airborne soldiers ate well: steak, mashed potatoes, green peas, bread, ice cream, and coffee—as much as they could hold. "Fattening us up for the kill," some joked. After supper, the invasion was cancelled due to poor weather.

The following night, Gen. Dwight D. Eisenhower issued the history-making order, "Go." The general then visited the 101st's staging area at Newbury, near Portsmouth, England. There he had dinner with Gen. Taylor and Taylor's staff. Ike then toured the airfields, often stopping and chatting with his paratroopers face to face in a manner that resembled more of a father and his sons than a general and his soldiers. The paratroopers, many with their heads shaved in Mohawk Indian fashion and their faces striped with war paint, gathered around the supreme Allied commander. The general, knowing full well that many of the young men around him would be dead in a few hours, engaged in light conversation and shared thoughts of home.

It was during one such meeting with the sky soldiers of the 502nd Parachute Infantry Regiment that the famous "Ike and the blackened-faced paratroopers" picture was taken.

"Where are you from, son?" the general asked one of the paratroopers as the photo was shot.

"Michigan, sir," was the response.

"Oh yes, Michigan," said Ike. "Great fishing there. I've been there several times and like it."

The general then asked the young man from Michigan if he was ready and had he been briefed well. The soldier responded by stating that he and his buddies were "all set" and that he did not think they would have "too much of a problem."

(National Archives)

Gen. Dwight D. Eisenhower speaks with members of the 101st Airborne Division on June 5, 1944, the eve of the invasion of Normandy.

Eisenhower remained at Newbury until the last transport plane filled with paratroopers was airborne.

Like their American brothers in the 82nd Airborne Division and their British cousins in the 6th Airborne, the paratroopers of the 101st were in the vanguard of the invasion force. The division's primary units included the 501st, 502nd, and 506th Parachute Infantry Regiments. Elements of the 327th and 401st Glider Infantry Regiments followed.

LIKE MEDIEVAL KNIGHTS

Onboard the aircraft, the paratroopers found their surroundings most uncomfortable. They were "weighted down like medieval knights in armor," wrote Clay Blair in *Ridgway's Paratroopers: The American Airborne in World War II*. "In all, the average paratrooper carried between 125 and 150 pounds of gear tightly strapped on his body. This made it difficult—or impossible—to walk upright or climb into the planes. Men helped one another through the plane doors. Inside the cabin, many found they could not sit in the bucket seats. They simply knelt in the aisles in a praying position, with the bulk of the equipment resting in the seat."

Making matters worse, all were nervous and thus many found themselves needing to urinate frequently. This was accomplished with great difficulty by getting to one's feet, maneuvering through the men and equipment, and then standing behind other nervous souls—also loaded up with all manner of parachute and war-fighting gear—who were waiting their turn to be helped down the boarding ladder. Prior to takeoff, a line of men relieving themselves was always present beneath the aircraft wing.

The Screaming Eagles were slated to jump before the 82nd. Consequently, the first American airborne soldiers to land in France were part of the 101st. The first of those jumps was made at 15 minutes past midnight. Capt. Frank L. Lilly, a pathfinder, leapt into the darkness some 450 feet above the surface of the earth, made a hard landing on a previously injured leg, and became the first American paratrooper to land in German-occupied France on D-day.

U.S. Army Air Force Col. Charles H. Young was the commanding officer of the 439th Troop Carrier Group. The 439th was tasked with ferrying the paratroopers of the 101st over their designated drop zone on June 6. Just after 1 A.M., Young, his crew, and passengers were roaring over their target area. The Germans were desperately trying to knock them out of the sky. Young was fortunate. Others were not. An excerpt from his diary follows:

> Machine gun fire with yellow tracers came from the right rear where we crossed the railroad that ran from Cherbourg to Carentan. The tracers went by the nose of my ship so thick at this point that they lit up the inside of the cockpit. Later I found out that much of my No. 2 element had been shot up, though none were shot down by this fire. Tracers of various colors—red, green, blue, and orange—came from guns two to three miles from the north in a head converging on our column and by now tracers were crossing in front of us and around us, and large explosions were occurring along the coastline ahead of us. The combination of these several guns shot down two more ships of our second serial of 36 ships, led by Major Tower. The two that crashed were flown by Lt. Harold Capelluto and Lt. Marvin Muir. Lt. Muir was able to hold his plane in the air long enough to jump their stick of troopers, and he and his crew sacrificed their own lives to do so.

Leaping into the darkness from their transport planes just after 2 A.M., many of the Screaming Eagles shouted "Bill Lee!" as a tribute to their former commander. Others shouted "Currahee!"

> The battle cry and motto of the 506th Parachute Infantry Regiment of the 101st Airborne Division was "Currahee!" The word is a Cherokee Indian term meaning "stands alone," as in "he who stands alone," "we who stand alone," or "it that stands alone."
>
> The 506th adopted the battle cry during its initial combat training at Camp Toccoa, Georgia, during World War II. There the future sky soldiers trained in the shadow of—often running up and down—the camp's legendary Currahee Mountain (so named by the Cherokee), a conical 900-foot-high eminence in the Chattahoochee National Forest.

Seconds after exiting the planes over Normandy, the paratroopers found themselves in a new environment. Aside from the occasional malfunctioning parachute, jumpers were running over the tops of other's canopies, and enemy flak and tracers were reaching up toward their vulnerable bodies. Some of the men, carrying the weightiest loads or jumping from airplanes flying beyond the safe speed for parachute operations, lost vital equipment or had canopy panels blown out during the opening shock of their parachutes. Blown panels often proved fatal to the jumpers if reserve canopies were not deployed in seconds. Many of those surviving the flight and the subsequent jump found themselves landing far off target and separated from their units.

Though he had no formal jump school training and only one training jump under his belt, Gen. Taylor leapt with his men. He too shouted the name of his predecessor, "Bill Lee!" Taylor's deputy division commander, Brig. Gen. Don Pratt, had never jumped from an airplane, so he opted for a glider ride. Unfortunately, he was killed when his glider crashed hard upon landing.

On the ground, Americans and Germans were practically crawling over one another. In order to differentiate between friendly and enemy forces in the darkness, individual paratroopers in the 101st relied on tiny noise-makers called "crickets" found in boxes of Cracker Jacks. The cricket was actually a child's toy, a handheld metal clicker. To the 101st, one click was the challenge. The appropriate response was a double-click. Their brothers in the 82nd relied on the oral password *flash* and the response *thunder* (see Chapter 4).

SAINTE-MARIE-DU-MONT

Fighting was grim, and the Germans gave up ground to the Screaming Eagles grudgingly. Early in the battle, elements of Easy Company, the 506th Parachute Regiment, were ordered to move toward the village of Sainte-Marie-du-Mont. There, on the Brécourt Manor estate, the enemy had set up a battery of four 105-millimeter howitzers (small cannon). The guns employed in the hedgerows were interconnected by an extensive system of well-fortified and camouflaged trenchworks.

Defending the positions was a 50-plus-soldier German force. The guns were ripping into the Allied seaborne elements on Utah Beach and had to be knocked out of action. The assignment fell to 1st Lt. Richard "Dick" Winters and a handful of paratroopers.

In what would become a textbook attack on a fixed position—today studied at military academies across North America—Winters and his men attacked the Germans point by point, killing the defenders, and destroying the 105s. The fighting was intense, characterized by intense rifle and machine-gun fire as well as grenade duels.

"There was German fire right over us," recalled 1st Sgt. Carwood Lipton, a member of Easy Company, during a 2001 newspaper interview with Southern Pines, North Carolina's *The Pilot*. According to Lipton, a warrant officer whom he knew well crawled to him while their unit was being cut to pieces by low, grazing fire. "The officer asked for the location of battalion headquarters. A second officer shouted back the direction of the headquarters. The warrant officer then raised his head for a better look: just 8 or 10 inches—and a bullet hit him right in the forehead," said Lipton. "I was looking straight at him. The bullet entered his forehead and came out the back of his head, killing him instantly."

Lipton added, "The body doesn't die instantly. The body jerks and snorts and twists, and that shook me up. The machine gun fire was cracking right over us, and I was sure they were going to get me too." The warrant officer was the first American whom Lipton had seen killed in action. "That was the time I was probably most afraid," he said.

> The character of 1st Sgt. Carwood Lipton was played by actor Donnie Wahlberg in the HBO miniseries *Band of Brothers* (based on Stephen E. Ambrose's book). Lipton believed that Wahlberg's performance was an accurate portrayal of himself, as were the portrayals of Lipton's fellow paratroopers by other members of the HBO cast. Lipton and Wahlberg became friends.
>
> On December 16, 2001, 1st Sgt. Lipton passed away in his hometown of Southern Pines, North Carolina, but not before addressing a group of U.S. Army Special Forces soldiers who were preparing to deploy to Afghanistan in September 2001 (days after the terrorist attacks of September 11). "The young Special Forces men asked Carwood about fear and how does one handle it," said Carwood's widow, Mrs. Marie Hope Carwood, during an interview with the author. "He told them that the fear would always be there. But to remember that they and their buddies were well trained, that they would be supported by their buddies [during combat], and that they needed to take care of their buddies in turn."

After three hours of fighting—some of which had devolved into a grisly close-quarters action—the surviving Germans retreated toward the Brécourt Manor. The house itself was later secured by U.S. armored forces.

By the afternoon of the first day, the bloodied and exhausted paratroopers had made contact with the U.S. 4th Division, which had pushed inland from Utah Beach. On D+1 (the day following D-day), the 101st received badly needed supplies from the gliders and new orders from headquarters. The sky soldiers were to attack and seize the town of Carentan as well as the nearby villages situated between Utah and Omaha Beach that were key to controlling the entire peninsula. The men of the U.S. V Corps had established a tenuous foothold on Omaha, but the Corps needed the paratroopers to take the town and then link up with them on the beachhead.

CARENTAN

Carentan was a bloody house-to-house slugfest. The Germans were ordered to fight to the last round and the last man. The German commanders realized that losing Normandy would mean an ultimate loss of the continent. As a means of preventing isolated German units from surrendering, the German commanders told their soldiers that the American paratroopers had been recruited from among society's dregs: gangsters, cutthroats, and condemned men. Thus, the American paratroopers would take no prisoners.

True, U.S. airborne soldiers were unable to take prisoners during the first few days of the invasion. They were moving too fast, and they did not have the means to provide care and security for prisoners. But they were certainly not the social miscreants the enemy believed them to be. Most were hardworking young men recruited from farms, small towns, eastern metropolises, and college campuses across America. Many had joined the airborne forces after reading an article in *Life* magazine about paratroopers. All were volunteers looking for adventure and an opportunity to "be the best," and most had never heard a shot fired in anger until Normandy.

There is, however, some debate as to whether or not fast-moving U.S. paratroopers executed prisoners or enemy combatants attempting to surrender. In combat, terrible things happen. In some isolated cases, there may well have been German soldiers killed while trying to surrender. Most were placed under a small guard force and lead to the rear.

At Carentan, the Screaming Eagles proved themselves worthy of the title *paratrooper*. In one instance, Lt. Col. Robert G. Cole, a battalion commander with the 502nd Parachute Infantry Regiment, found his unit pinned down by a strong German position near a farmhouse along the Madeleine River. Artillery was called in on the enemy stronghold, but the shelling was ineffective. Refusing to fall back, Cole ordered his men to fix bayonets and charge. Leaping from the ground, the colonel sprinted toward the enemy. However, not all the paratroopers had received the order when Cole attacked. A quick-thinking subordinate officer hurriedly urged the men to get up and follow their commander, and the Germans were soon routed from their position. For his actions, Cole was awarded the Congressional Medal of Honor. Sadly, he was killed in a later action.

Fighting raged around Carentan, the surrounding hills, hedgerows, and causeways during the first week following D-day. On June 12, the final drive to take the town was launched by several of the division's elements. The following day the Germans launched a fierce counterattack, but the attack was beaten back by the airborne soldiers supported by newly arrived armored forces.

By the middle of June, the work of the 101st at Normandy was over. The Germans were being driven back by Allied tanks and conventional infantry forces, and the American paratroopers were in a defensive posture near Carentan.

By the beginning of July, the division had been moved to Cherbourg. It was there, on July 7, that Gen. Taylor stood before his men and boasted, "You hit the ground running toward the enemy. You have proved the German soldier is no superman. You have beaten him on his own ground, and you can beat him on any ground."

Beaten the enemy indeed, but it was not without cost. One month after jumping into France, one in four soldiers with the 101st Airborne Division was either dead or wounded. Soon thereafter, the Screaming Eagles boarded landing craft bound for England.

On August 25, the U.S. XVIII Corps was redesignated the XVIII Airborne Corps. The 101st became one of the Corps' divisions, as did her sister divisions, the 82nd, the 17th, and, late in the war, the 13th. Within a month of forming, the First Allied Airborne Army was established (see Chapter 4), and Maj. Gen. Matthew B. Ridgway was named commanding general of the XVIII.

While the Screaming Eagles were resting, regrouping, training, and indoctrinating newly arrived green replacements, the Allied leadership was preparing for the invasion of the Netherlands.

OPERATION MARKET GARDEN

On September 17, elements of the First Airborne Army, including the 101st, the 82nd, and the British 1st, crossed into the airspace over Belgium and Holland from the west in broad daylight. Meanwhile, the British XXX Corps raced up an open stretch of road dubbed "Hell's Highway" in hopes of reaching each airborne force at bridges along the way and ultimately reaching the Rhine.

The airborne drops were textbook: parachutes filling the skies in broad daylight with little initial opposition. On the ground, the Screaming Eagles landed on target with their units intact. The men quickly unhooked themselves from their harnesses, checked their weapons, and hurriedly moved toward their objectives.

The 101st was tasked with seizing Eindhoven, the critical front door of the operation, and securing a 15-mile stretch of highway between Eindhoven and Veghel. Essentially the "anchor" of the operation's southernmost flank, the town of Eindhoven was the point at which the British ground forces would make first contact with Allied airborne forces along the corridor. The 101st's brothers in the 82nd were responsible for landing and securing the corridor farther north in the area around Veghel, Grave, and Kleve, with the primary objective of seizing Nijmegen. The British 1st Airborne Division was responsible for capturing the bridges at Arnhem, the most distant of the initial objectives and the point at which the Germans had their strongest positions and largest troop concentrations.

"The progress of the battle gripped the attention of everyone in the theater," Gen. Eisenhower wrote in his memoirs. "We were inordinately proud of our airborne units, but the interest in that battle had its roots in something deeper than pride. We felt it would prove whether or not the Germans could succeed in establishing renewed and effective resistance—on the battle's outcome we would form an estimate of the severity of the fighting still ahead of us. A general impression grew up that the battle was really a full-out attempt to begin, immediately, a drive into the heart of Germany."

The latter impression, Eisenhower added, "gave a great added interest to a battle in which the circumstances were unusually dramatic."

In the end, the 101st achieved its objectives, beat back several enemy counterattacks, and kept its section of highway open. But German strength around Arnhem prevented the Allied force from achieving all of its original goals. By late November, the 101st had been withdrawn to France, where the division's soldiers rested, regrouped, and prepared for the next airborne assault.

THE ARDENNES OFFENSIVE

The division's respite, however, was short-lived when, in mid-December, German forces attacked through the Ardennes and struck the Allied main lines in Belgium. The attack created an enormous salient—or "bulge"—in the lines (thus, it was known as "the Battle of the Bulge") and threatened to cut American and British forces in half.

As the Germans continued deepening the salient, fresh American units were hurriedly trucked forward from France, including the 101st and the 82nd Airborne Divisions from Ridgway's Corps.

The 82nd was the lead division on the road north. The All-Americans were tasked with blunting the enemy's advance along the Salm River, and the 101st followed. En route, the advancing Germans passed between the 82nd and the 101st, separating the two.

BASTOGNE

The 101st, under the acting command of Brig. Gen. Anthony McAuliffe (due to Gen. Taylor being back in the United States on War Department business), was about to make history. The division was rushed toward the strategically vital town of Bastogne.

The Allies believed that by holding Bastogne, they could regroup their forces and launch a counterattack. The Germans also realized the value of the town. It served as a major highway junction in the Ardennes and a potentially important hub for mechanized forces. Control of the roads was critical. The surrounding terrain was rugged and not particularly vehicle-friendly. Thus, the Germans and the 101st raced to the city.

Having been hurried to the front, the division was unable to properly equip itself. It was desperately short of ammunition, food, water, medical supplies, and winter clothing.

On the road, the 101st's paratroopers were shocked to see frightened, fleeing American soldiers. They demanded much-needed ammo from their retreating "leg" brethren. The latter happily complied.

The American paratroopers arrived first on December 18, 1944, and set up defensive positions. The Germans arrived the following day, quickly surrounded the 101st, and laid siege to Bastogne. At that point, 18,000 Americans at Bastogne were facing 45,000 Germans. Worse, the weather was so poor Allied aircraft were not able to provide close air support for forces on the ground, nor were they able to make resupply drops for besieged forces like the 101st. Despite the weather, subzero temperatures, dwindling supplies, and numerous enemy attacks to drive the 101st out of Bastogne, the Screaming Eagles held.

On December 22, German officers under a flag of truce delivered a rather long-winded message from Lt. Gen. Heinrich von Luttwitz to Gen. McAuliffe. The message, which demanded the surrender of Bastogne, appealed to the "well-known American humanity" to save the citizens of Bastogne from further suffering. The Americans were given two hours to reply.

McAuliffe, who had no intention of surrendering, was initially at a loss for words. One of his aides remarked that the General's first comment upon receiving the surrender demand might be wholly appropriate. McAuliffe agreed and penned his now-famous response to the Germans. It read "NUTS."

This message was then delivered by American Col. Joseph Harper to a group of German officers waiting in a nearby woods. Harper handed the note to one of the German officers who read it and then looked at Harper in confusion.

"What does that mean?" the German asked. "Is this affirmative or negative?"

Harper responded, "It means you can all go to hell."

The following day, skies were clear and aircraft were up. Fighters provided close air support for attacking Allied infantry and armored forces, and transports air-dropped much-needed supplies to the 101st.

On Christmas Eve, with the exception of a German air raid, things were relatively quiet at Bastogne. Gen. McAuliffe visited German prisoners of war and wished them well. He shared with his men the story of his response to the surrender demand. He also presented his famous Christmas message to the 101st Airborne, a portion of which read:

> What's merry about all this, you ask? We're fighting. It's cold. We aren't home. All true. But what has the proud Eagle Division accomplished with its worthy comrades ...? Just this: We have stopped cold everything that has been thrown at us from the north, east, south and west. We have identifications from four German panzer divisions, two German infantry divisions and one German parachute division. These units, spearheading the last desperate German lunge, were heading straight west for key points when the Eagle Division was hurriedly ordered to stem the advance. How effectively this was done will be

written in history; not alone in our Division's glorious history but in world history. The Germans actually did surround us, their radios blared our doom. Allied troops are counterattacking in force. We continue to hold Bastogne. By holding Bastogne we assure the success of the Allied armies.

Out on the perimeter, cold, hungry soldiers shook hands with one another and said good-byes. Despite McAuliffe's words, the situation was bleak, and the paratroopers knew it. They were running perilously short of food and ammunition. Frostbite and pneumonia casualties were thinning their ranks almost hourly, and a numerically superior enemy force was surrounding them in the darkness.

On the 26th, Patton's Third Army punched through to Bastogne. The following day Hitler consented to allow his generals to conduct a limited withdrawal from certain sectors.

For its heroic stand at Bastogne, the 101st was awarded a presidential unit citation, the first time a division-size unit had been cited for gallantry. Presenting the award, Eisenhower said the 101st was "hurried forward and told to hold that position. All of the elements of drama, of battle drama were there. You were cut off, you were surrounded. Only valor, complete self-confidence in yourselves and in your leaders, a knowledge that you were well-trained, only the determination to win, could sustain soldiers under those conditions."

Following the relief at Bastogne, the weary airborne soldiers were ordered to seize the Bois Jacques (Jacques Woods), Recogne, Bizory, and the village of Foy, as well as other Belgian towns and hamlets.

In late February 1945, the 101st was withdrawn to France, where it began preparing for an airborne assault on the German capital of Berlin. Instead, it moved overland up into the Bavarian Alps, where it appropriately seized the "Eagle's Nest," Hitler's vacation retreat in the mountains above Berchtesgaden. Strategists believed the paratroopers would face stiff resistance from SS soldiers and other fanatical Nazi holdouts in the mountains. Instead, the Americans were met with only token opposition from fleeing German soldiers, who easily surrendered when contact was made.

Two German Army Corps—XIII SS and LXXXII Corps—surrendered to the 101st while the division was garrisoned at Berchtesgaden. Additionally, the 101st accepted the surrender of several prominent Nazis, including Field Marshal Albert Kesselring; Julius Streicher, the editor of *Der Sturmer* (an anti-Semitic newspaper); SS *Obergruppenfuhrer* Karl Oberg; and armored warfare master Col. Gen. Heinz Guderian.

When Germany surrendered in early May, the 101st remained in Berchtesgaden. The Screaming Eagles were relieved by the 42nd Infantry Division on August 1. The paratroopers then moved into camp at Auxerre, France, where they began training for combat against the Japanese. But Japan soon surrendered and the division was deactivated.

"Its battle record in World War II is without blemish," wrote acclaimed military historian Brig. Gen. S. L. A. Marshall of the division in *Encyclopedia of World War II*. "Its people captured every assigned objective and in defense never yielded."

This is no surprise to historian Stephen Ambrose, author of *Band of Brothers*. Describing one of the 101st's most celebrated units, E Company of the 506th Parachute Infantry Regiment, Ambrose wrote, "the physical fitness of the Easy men was a sine qua non. They put out more energy than a heavyweight boxer in a fifteen-round title match, way more; they put out more energy than a man would playing sixty minutes in three consecutive football games."

He added that the company's communication system was also noteworthy, "with radio messages, runners, and hand signals being used effectively. The leapfrog advances and retreats put into play the training they had undergone at Toccoa [the regiments initial training camp in Georgia] and were carried out in textbook fashion."

In 1948, the 101st was temporarily reactivated, but as a training unit, not a combat division. Shortly thereafter, the division was deactivated, but then was reactivated again in 1950.

LITTLE ROCK

One of the division's first tasks upon being reactivated centered around the growing American Civil Rights Movement. In 1954, the United States

Supreme Court ruled in *Brown v. the Topeka Board of Education* that segregation in the public schools was a violation of the 14th Amendment to the Constitution. Nevertheless, many southern states resisted the ruling.

One of the most widely publicized incidents of state resistance occurred in 1957 when a federal court ordered the integration of public schools in Little Rock, Arkansas. The state's governor, Orval E. Faubus, called up the Arkansas National Guard to prevent nine black children who had previously enrolled in Little Rock's Central High School from attending the school. He also forbade white students from attending the previously all-black Horace Mann High School. Faubus warned that if the black students attempted to enter Central High, "blood would run in the streets." Dismissing charges of racism, Faubus's official justification was that he feared that the hundreds of white supremacists, who were converging on Little Rock, would harm the students.

On September 4, the first day of class, the black students attempted to enter Central High but were prevented from doing so by an angry mob of locals. As a result, President Dwight D. Eisenhower federalized the Arkansas National Guard (temporarily placing it under the U.S. Army) and ordered 1,000 paratroopers of the 101st Airborne Division to Little Rock.

With the presence of airborne soldiers, the incident was quashed. The children were permitted to enter the school and did so under Army escort. Incensed, Faubus referred to the paratroopers as an "army of occupation."

In the mid-1950s, several units were reorganized and trained at Fort Campbell, Kentucky, all subordinate to Headquarters, 101st Airborne Division (Advance). As a result, on September 21, 1956, the 101st became the first "pentomic division" in the U.S. Army.

A "pentomic division" was a short-lived U.S. Army infantry division structure developed in the 1950s to operate on a nuclear battlefield.

The term *pentomic* was a combination of the Greek word *pent* or *penta* for "five," and the contemporary English word *atomic*. The division consisted of five "battle groups," as opposed to the traditional four-regiment or three-brigade division. Each of the groups were smaller than a regiment, but larger than a battalion.

The battle groups were organized in such a manner that their tactical units were small and fast-moving, thus not presenting "lucrative nuclear targets." Additionally, the small tactical units were equipped and trained to be able to fight and survive when isolated or cut off from the main body. The division was highly mobile and able to deploy on a moment's notice. Its commanders were taught to rely on its naturally effective interior lines of communication. The division also relied heavily on nuclear artillery. By 1959, the new pentomic divisions began to feel the strain of the Army's overall reduction in force. The nuclear battlefield, with far greater dimensions than a conventional battlefield, would require more men and materiel. Additionally, battlefield technologies lagged behind strategic doctrine.

As a pentomic division, the 101st was comprised of the 2nd Airborne Battle Group 187th Infantry, the 1st Airborne Battle Group 327th Infantry, the 1st Airborne Battle Group 501st Infantry, the 1st Airborne Battle Group 502nd Infantry, and the 1st Airborne Battle Group 506th Infantry.

In 1964, after 8 years of training for an incomprehensibly terrible war, the 101st underwent its second major reorganization. The pentomic concept was scrapped, and the new Reorganization Objective Army Division, or ROAD, was created. Comprised of nine infantry battalions, a cavalry squadron, and three artillery battalions, the new airborne ROAD unit provided battlefield commanders with more firepower and great mobility, as well as command and control.

The following year, the 101st prepared to deploy an infantry brigade to Southeast Asia.

VIETNAM AND "AIRMOBILE"

On July 29, 1965, the 1st Brigade of the 101st landed at Cam Ranh Bay, South Vietnam. In so doing, it was one of the first American "combat" elements in that country. The brigade was comprised of two battalions of the 327th Infantry and one battalion of the 502nd Infantry.

Soon thereafter the brigade moved out into the Song Con Valley, near the town of An Khe. For the next three years, elements of the 101st conducted numerous long-range patrols and fought a number of costly actions in Vietnam. Those actions included bloody fights at places like Dak To, Khe Sanh, and numerous villages throughout the Quang Tri Province.

During the Vietnam War, when the Army made the decision to subdue the colors of shoulder patches for camouflage purposes, the 101st was able to retain its full colors for wear in the field; the men demanded it. Consequently, the Vietnamese people living in the backcountry were able to identify the troopers of the 101st by the stark white eagle head on the Americans' shoulders. Unfamiliar with the bald eagle, the Vietnamese began referring to the 101st troopers as "chicken men." This did not in any way hold the cowardly connotation of the term "chicken" understood by Americans. On the contrary, the "chicken men" were greatly feared by the Vietcong and the North Vietnamese Army.

During the infamous Tet Offensive of 1968, the men of the 101st, often in detached units, fought at Hue City and other points throughout the countryside. One of the division's most dramatic moments during Tet was when a single platoon was helicopter-lifted onto the rooftop of the U.S. Embassy in Saigon. From there, the soldiers swept through and cleared the building; they also engaged a few enemy holdouts on the embassy grounds after Vietcong forces had infiltrated the compound.

Also in 1968, the 101st was radically restructured. No longer were the Screaming Eagles to be a division of paratroopers. Instead, they were to descend onto the battlefield from helicopters, and the division was to be known as the 101st "Airmobile" Division.

As airmobile soldiers, The 101st's final large-scale action in Vietnam was a terrible 10-day slugfest on a steep rise in the 28-mile-wide A Shau Valley known as Hamburger Hill.

In August 1968, the division was ordered into the A Shau, under the code name Somerset Plain, in an attempt to rid the region of the enemy. Fighting was sharp, only limited objectives were achieved, and the Americans were withdrawn. It was then determined that if the valley was to be completely controlled, further operations were needed.

HAMBURGER HILL

The following spring, the 101st again moved into the A Shau Valley. The soldiers were helicopter-ferried into the heart of the area. There, as part of an operation known as Apache Snow, they fought a tough engagement, forcing the enemy to fall back on the valley's northwestern sector and a steep hill near the Laotian border, known to the Vietnamese as *Dong* (translated as "mountain") Ap Bia.

Officially designated Hill 937, the Ap Bia mountain was dubbed "Hamburger Hill" by the Americans because it seemed to chew up their buddies like a hamburger meat grinder. Local Montagnard tribesmen referred to it as "the mountain of the crouching beast." The North Vietnamese Army (NVA), who lost even more men attempting to defend the hill, referred to it as *Thit Bam* (or "meat chopper").

Ap Bia was a difficult obstacle. Its slopes were covered in a tangled morass of undergrowth, vines, and thick groves of bamboo. Positioned on the heights was the 29th NVA Regiment, nicknamed the "Pride of Ho Chi Minh." The 29th was a crack force of 1,200 regulars who were dug in behind an extensive network of log bunkers. Having been there for several years, they had taken great pains to ensure that the hill's defenses could withstand ground attacks from any direction. Subterranean tunnels honey-combed the mountain and offered surprisingly good protection from heavy artillery and aerial bombardment. Also, being only one mile from the Laotian border, the defenders were constantly resupplied by their compatriots moving along the Ho Chi Minh Trail.

> The Ho Chi Minh Trail was a vital North Vietnamese supply line that ran south from North Vietnam just inside the Laotian and Cambodian borders before turning east at various points into South Vietnam. Both Vietcong guerrillas and regular North Vietnamese forces were resupplied and reinforced from the trail throughout the war.

On May 10, 1969, a brigade-size force of the 101st and elements of the Army of the Republic of (South) Vietnam (ARVN) were ferried into a clearing near Ap Bia. The entire group was under the direction Maj. Gen. Melvin Zais, the 101st's commanding general. The American brigade, under Col. Joseph Conmy, was composed of three airborne infantry battalions: the 1st Battalion of the 506th Regiment, the 2nd Battalion of the 501st, and the 3rd Battalion of the 187th.

As the 506th and 501st began fanning out into the A Shau backcountry, Lt. Col. Weldon Honeycutt's 3rd Battalion of the 187th Infantry Regiment landed some 2,000 yards west of Ap Bia with little opposition. The 3rd Battalion was known by the Japanese term *Rakkasans*, which translates as "umbrella men" or "parachutists." The Rakkasans then launched a reconnaissance in force toward the base of the mountain.

Honeycutt, a North Carolina native who lied about his age to enlist as a private at 16, loved the Army. He was fiercely loyal, and despite the growing antiwar movement, he believed that America's place was in Vietnam. He had once physically thrown a subordinate officer, who expressed his opposition to the war, headfirst out of his headquarters building. He then accused the officer of cowardice and treason, and had him shipped to another unit. The incident was not isolated as Honeycutt was known for getting rid of those whom he deemed to be cowards, duty shirkers, conscientious objectors, or even marginal fighters. Honeycutt was a warrior. He expected every soldier under his command to be the same. Consequently, by the spring of 1969, he had honed his 3rd Battalion into one of the best combat units in South Vietnam.

Confident that his Rakkasans could defeat all comers, Honeycutt temporarily violated one of the great principles of war and divided his force over unfamiliar ground. Some elements moved around to the north and northwest of Dong Ap Bia. Others swept west toward the Laotian border, and still others moved up toward the base of Ap Bia's southern slopes.

On May 11, having made virtually no contact with the enemy, Honeycutt ordered one of his companies to assault and seize the summit. The first assault was beaten back and, even worse, supporting helicopter gunships mistook Honeycutt's command post for an NVA unit and attacked. The friendly fire incident killed two sky soldiers and another 35 were wounded, including Honeycutt.

The Americans then pulled back into hastily erected defensive positions and radioed for supporting fires. American air and artillery fire pounded the hill in an attempt to knock out the NVA positions. Enemy soldiers caught in the open were killed, but most remained underground and survived.

The bombing and shelling stripped the hill of its vegetation, enabling pilots and artillery forward observers to have a better visual idea of what they were hitting. However, it also eliminated most of the cover and concealment needed for attacking forces. Making matters worse, heavy rains turned the hill's slopes into giant mudslides. The following day Honeycutt launched the second of several attempts to take Ap Bia.

By May 13, it had become obvious to Col. Conmy that far more NVA soldiers were dug in on the hilltop than Honeycutt's force could deal with. To support Honeycutt's men, Conmy dispatched the 1st Battalion of the 506th toward Ap Bia.

The 506th, also known as the Currahee Regiment, was best known for its stellar performance at Normandy and Bastogne during World War II. More than two decades later, the Currahees were trudging forward through the A Shau, the regiment's 1st Battalion having been ordered to force-march across the backcountry toward Ap Bia's northern slopes and attack the enemy from the rear. In so doing, the battalion would also sever any NVA supply columns moving in that direction. Conmy had hoped that his Currahees would be in position to attack Ap Bia the following day. Instead, rugged terrain and enemy snipers delayed the Americans for five days.

Honeycutt launched coordinated attacks against the heights on both May 14 and 15. Both attacks were beaten back by fierce enemy resistance. In fact, the elusive crest began to seem impregnable to the men trying to take it. Each time the exhausted GIs struggled up the hill, they either tripped explosive booby traps, got shot, slipped and slid back down in the mud, or were ordered to fall back short of reaching the top. Those in the advance elements who got close enough to the top were either killed, maimed, or pinned down by the enemy who poured machine-gun fire into their ranks and rolled grenades down on them. Each time Honeycutt was hoping to be reinforced by the battalion from the 506th, but they were still battling their way across the countryside.

The precariousness of the situation quickly permeated the ranks, from rifle company private to battalion commander. At no time was this more evident than when Honeycutt appealed to Conmy for help. On the night of May 14, the two commanders held a powwow, standing in the rain as artillery fire pounded the heights above.

"Joe, this fight is getting awful rough," said Honeycutt. "I don't know how many of the bastards are up there, but I know there's a helluva lot of them. The bastards have got heavy weapons. They've got communications. They're dug in. They've got a defense in depth, and they're movin' fresh troops up those draws from Laos every night. Every night. And I don't have the manpower to stop them."

On May 16, elements of the 506th reached closing distance of Ap Bia and attacked. But the attack was diverted when they were forced to move against and seize nearby Hill 916. Conmy then ordered Honeycutt to halt his ongoing attacks against Ap Bia and wait for the 506th to catch up.

Meanwhile, the battle began to take on a new dimension. Reporters, having gotten wind of the numerous unsuccessful assaults to seize Ap Bia, began to question the fruitlessness of it all. Subsequent newspaper accounts began to ignite a firestorm of controversy, which heaped criticism on Gen. Zais, stirred the ire of the antiwar movement, and unsettled Washington policymakers. Moreover, journalists began flocking to rear-area headquarters and forward bases supporting the Ap Bia battle in an attempt to glean anything from the front. This forced commanders to divide their focused efforts between the battle and a brewing public relations nightmare.

But Zais, Conmy, and Honeycutt were determined not to fail. On May 20, the Rakkasans—now joined by the two battalions from the 506th and the 501st, as well as one of two ARVN battalions—attacked Ap Bia in force. After a bitter struggle and 11 uphill assaults, Zais's men punched through the enemy's summit defenses and became the kings of Hamburger Hill.

Rifling through the remnants of the NVA position, the Americans discovered more than 630 enemy bodies scattered along the slopes and the crest. Two NVA battalions had been virtually destroyed. More enemy soldiers may have been killed and either buried under debris after the bombings or carried across the border into Laos.

Some 70 Americans were also dead. Another 372 were wounded. (Over the years, a number of sources have erroneously claimed that 241 members of the 101st were killed at Hamburger Hill. This information has been fostered by the fact that a month after the battle, *Life* magazine published photographs of the faces of all the Americans killed in Southeast Asia during the time that the Battle for Hamburger Hill was being waged. Many readers assumed that those were the faces of the men who struggled on the slopes of the hill. It was "a misleading feature," according to the late Dr. John Pimlott, who oversaw the War Studies Department at the Royal Military Academy in Sandhurst, United Kingdom.)

In terms of losses, Hamburger Hill had not been the bloodiest fight of the war, nor had it been the longest. But no battle of the war faced more public scrutiny. Although it was a victory for the Screaming Eagles, commanders were roundly criticized for ordering their soldiers up the hill time and again under relentless enemy fire. Worse, the hill, located in a remote region of Vietnam, was later deemed to be of little strategic value. Thus, it was abandoned weeks after being captured.

Hamburger Hill was, in the words of outspoken Col. David H. Hackworth, a "totally useless piece of real estate" that had been assaulted by Gen. Zais "as if he thought he was in Korea or storming Kraut positions at Normandy."

Gen. Westmoreland was of a different opinion. In his memoir, *A Soldier Reports*, Westmoreland defended the decision to capture Hamburger Hill. "To have left the North Vietnamese undisturbed on the mountain would have been to jeopardize our control of the valley and accept a renewed threat to the coastal cities," Westmoreland wrote. "A prolonged siege would have been costly and tied up troops indefinitely." He added that Gen. Zais "quite properly ordered an attack."

When the book was closed on America's involvement in Vietnam, some 58,000 soldiers, sailors, airmen, and Marines were dead. More than 4,000 of them were members of the 101st. The division withdrew from Southeast Asia in 1972.

Two years later, Maj. Gen. Sidney B. Berry, the 101st's commanding general, authorized the wearing of the "airmobile badge." The badge, which closely resembled the basic parachutist's badge (a helicopter instead of a parachute is the centerpiece element of the badge), was later renamed the "air assault badge" and approved for wear by all soldiers completing air assault training.

Located at several U.S. Army bases across North America, "Air Assault" school is a demanding 10-day course that trains soldiers for helicopter-borne combat assault operations. The school focuses on rappelling, rope-climbing, and fast-roping techniques (fast-roping is a means by which soldiers wearing leather gloves slide down heavy, nylon ropes from helicopters to the ground), sling-loading equipment onto helicopters, tactical marches with full combat gear, and running obstacle courses.

For the next several years, the Screaming Eagles perfected the art of heliborne operations, becoming a true "air assault" division. For a brief time, the division was renamed the 101st Air Assault Division, reflecting the division's primary means of delivering troops to the battlefield. But traditions die hard, and the division became permanently and officially known as the 101st Airborne Division (Air Assault). As such, the 101st also became the only true "air assault" or helicopter assault division in the world.

THE FIRST GULF WAR

Apache helicopters from the 101st Airborne Division fired the initial shots of the allied invasion of Iraq—Operation Desert Storm—in early 1991. On the night of January 16 and 17, the helicopters blasted away at Iraqi early warning radar sites, knocking them out 22 minutes before the actual air war began.

When the ground war was launched on February 24, the 101st penetrated deep into Iraqi territory and attacked Saddam Hussein's forces on their own turf in what would become the largest air assault in military history. The division's soldiers, operating under the XVIII Airborne Corps, were fighting alongside their brothers in the 82nd Airborne, as well as other U.S. Army and allied ground force units.

A decade later, after the September 11, 2001, attacks on the United States, the 101st was again called into action. Placed on full alert, the 101st quickly prepared to deploy anywhere in the world, seek, engage, and destroy the perpetrators of the September 11 attacks as well as their supporters in the new war against terror.

In March 2002, the soldiers of the 101st participated in Operation Anaconda, a major battle against Taliban and al Qaeda forces in Afghanistan. The division participated in other offensive operations in the region throughout the spring and summer.

THE SECOND GULF WAR

During the 2003 invasion of Iraq, the 101st participated in numerous operations aimed at destroying Saddam Hussein's Iraqi army, replacing the existing Ba'ath Party leadership, and capturing the party's top henchmen.

On July 22, 2003, more than two and a half months after President George W. Bush announced the end of major combat operations in Iraq, soldiers of the 101st advanced toward a sector of the northern city of Mosul believed to be harboring Saddam Hussein's sons, Odai and Qusai. Holed up in the palatial home of one of Saddam Hussein's cousins were the Iraqi leader's sons, both of whom were considered to be two of the most dangerous members of the regime, and second in power only to their father.

Elements of the 101st Airborne as well as a special operations team known as Task Force 20 (a special army unit tasked with routing out Saddam Hussein and his chief lieutenants) were directed to search the premises and apprehend the occupants.

Once there, the Screaming Eagles quickly surrounded the residence and ordered everyone inside to surrender. The demand was met with small-arms fire. The Americans then returned fire and what has since been described as a "ferocious shootout" ensued.

For four hours, fighting raged in what a CNN reporter described as "all hell broken loose." The soldiers were supported by Apache helicopters, tank-busting A-10 Warthogs, and other fighter aircraft.

When the fighting subsided, elements of the 101st secured the area while Task Force 20 operatives and personnel from the Central Intelligence Agency gathered up documents and other potential pieces of intelligence.

"They [the Hussein brothers] died in a fierce gun battle," said Lt. Gen. Ricardo S. Sanchez, senior commander of allied ground forces in Iraq during a post-raid news conference. "They resisted the detention and the efforts of the coalition forces to go in there and apprehend them, and they were killed in the ensuing gunfight and the attacks that we conducted on the residence."

President George W. Bush, elated over the success of the Screaming Eagles, said the following day, "Saddam Hussein's sons were responsible for torture, maiming, and murder of countless Iraqis. Now more than ever, Iraqis can know that the former regime is gone and will not be coming back."

CHAPTER 6

ANGELS: 11TH AIRBORNE DIVISION

> This was an outfit which could operate amphibiously, by parachute, with gliders, and as elite ground combat teams with equal enthusiasm and skill.
>
> —U.S. Army Lt. Gen. William Pelham "Bill" Yarborough (one of the founding fathers of airborne and special operations forces), describing the 11th Airborne Division

> Giants of ordinary men.
>
> —U.S. Army Lt. Gen. Edward M. Flanagan Jr., describing members of the 11th Airborne Division

Ask most any American schoolboy to name his country's two famous airborne divisions, and he will be quick to say the 82nd and the 101st. After all, those two divisions not surprisingly became legendary during World War II. Their notoriety rose quickly in the early hours of the Allied invasion of Normandy, and they survived the postwar deactivation of so many celebrated units. They also went on to earn new laurels in America's postwar conflicts, including the war on terror and the recent invasion of Iraq. And both divisions continue to be the subject of countless newspaper and magazine articles, books, movies, and television documentaries.

But only a career soldier, a military historian, or perhaps the families of certain World War II veterans would immediately be able to recall the exploits of the 11th Airborne Division, also known as "the Angels."

Like the Army's other two short-lived airborne divisions—the 13th and 17th (both were disbanded after World War II)—the 11th was a crack outfit, organized and equipped to drop behind enemy lines, locate, close with, and destroy any and all opposition it faced. Unlike the other wartime-only divisions, the 11th existed for two decades after the war.

The 11th Airborne Division was activated at Camp Mackall, North Carolina, on February 25, 1943, and placed under the command of Maj. Gen. Joseph May Swing.

The former commander of the 82nd Airborne Division's artillery, Swing was a ruggedly handsome "soldier's general" who had earned a stellar reputation decades earlier as a halfback on the West Point football team (one of his teammates had been Dwight D. Eisenhower). As a general, however, he avoided the publicity that so often seemed to follow airborne generals like Slim Jim Gavin, Matt Ridgway, and Max Taylor. But Swing knew how to fight, and he believed that the key to success on any battlefield was rigorous training and retraining.

In terms of physical fitness, Swing was hard-as-nails tough with a powerlifter's strength and a boxer's endurance, and he expected his men to be the same. He often participated with his men on 15-mile runs through the swamps and piney woods of Georgia and North Carolina. Few could keep up with him. Officers who fell back were promptly kicked out of the division. He was the perfect leader at the perfect time with what would soon be the perfect division.

Comprised of many veteran glider soldiers and a number of qualified paratroopers, the 11th Airborne Division needed to be crash-trained for readiness. The outcome of World War II was still far from being decided and time was critical. The battle for Guadalcanal had just ended in the Pacific and lots of tough campaigning lay ahead. The Axis powers were still making gains on all fronts. In North Africa, the U.S. Army's inexperienced II Corps had just suffered a severe beating at the hands of Germany's crack Afrika Korps at Kasserine Pass.

America needed more combat-ready paratroopers and fast. As part of the crash-training program, Gen. Swing was directed to establish his own in-house jump school. Soon thereafter the 11th's newly joined soldiers and glidermen strapped on parachutes and were "sent aloft" with little formal ground training. They learned quickly, however, most in less than a week, and in less than a year the 11th was fully trained and ready for overseas deployment.

SOUTH PACIFIC BOUND

In January 1944, the division participated in maneuvers at Camp Polk, Louisiana. In May, the 11th was in San Francisco, California, boarding troop transport ships bound for the South Pacific, specifically New Guinea.

For the next five months, the paratroopers honed their jumping and ground combat skills by training in the rugged mountains and jungles of New Guinea.

On November 11, 26 years to the day after the end of World War I, the 11th Airborne Division boarded transports for the invasion of the Philippines. One week later, the 11th landed at Bito Beach on the island of Leyte in the Philippines.

For the first few days, the paratroopers busied themselves offloading supplies and setting up a base camp just behind Bito. During their idle time, they watched as American fighters shot down numerous Japanese Kamikaze planes trying to crash into offshore American ships. The sky soldiers also witnessed a successful Kamikaze attack that struck the bridge of a transport ship and sank it.

On November 22, Maj. Gen. John R. Hodges, commanding the XXIV Corps (the 11th was assigned to the XXIV Corps on Leyte), issued the following field order: "The 11th Airborne Division will relieve the 7th Infantry Division along the line Burauen-La Paz-Bugho and destroy all Japs in that sector."

BURAUEN TO ORMOC

The men of the 11th broke camp and moved inland, securing a route from Burauen to Ormoc along the mountains of southern Leyte, and destroying all Japanese forces in their path. Leading the division was the 511th Parachute Infantry Regiment. Guarding the rear around Bito Beach was the 187th Glider Infantry Regiment.

Within days of moving out, the division found itself strung along some of the most difficult terrain imaginable: deep swamps darkened by a thick jungle canopy, uncharted trails, knee-deep mud, and incessant rain. Making matters worse, the enemy was deeply entrenched and determined to fight to the death.

The only resupply the paratroopers received as they advanced were from air-drops over small openings in the jungle from small L-4 and L-5 Cub planes based at the San Pablo, Buri, and Bayug airstrips near Bito Beach. The airplanes, normally used for artillery spotters, were affectionately referred to as "biscuit bombers" by the men of the 11th.

On December 6, 1944—nearly three years to the day after the attack on Pearl Harbor—the Japanese conducted their only parachute assault of the war. The attack, preceded by a series of bomb runs and fighter strikes, was launched against the San Pablo and Buri airstrips. Swing immediately rushed the 187th Glider Infantry Regiment from Bito toward San Pablo. Fierce fighting ensued, and the Japanese airborne force was destroyed. Meanwhile, the main body of the 11th slashed its way toward Ormoc.

On Christmas Eve, Swing penned a letter to the former U.S. Army chief of staff who had been his boss during World War I, Gen. Peyton C. March (Gen. March was also Swing's father-in-law). Portions of the letter read:

> Dear General,
>
> Am just back from a few days in the mountains, as a matter of fact I've walked clean across this d____ island and it wasn't the most pleasant jaunt I ever took. Wish you could see these young men of mine fight. It would do your heart good to see the calm joyful manner in which they kill the rats. ...
>
> The last day, the 22d, when we busted out of the hills to where the 7th Division was sitting on the beach—the dawn attack caught 300 Japs sleeping outside their foxholes and we slaughtered them with bayonet, knife, and hand grenades. ...

In late January 1945, the weary paratroopers reached Ormoc. There the division rested, regrouped, and refitted. The campaign had been one of the war's toughest. It took two months "of bitter fighting, often hand-to-hand to drive the Japanese defenders from the pass and surrounding heights," reads a unit history of the 11th Airborne Division. "In the end, the 11th Airborne had killed almost 6,000 enemy soldiers."

ON TO MANILA

The division had not rested but a few days when it was ordered back into action. The airborne soldiers were to land in-force on a stretch of coastline some 70 miles from Manila and attack toward the capital, wiping out all enemy resistance along the way.

In less than a week, the bulk of the 11th destroyed all Japanese opposition along Highway 17—the primary road artery—and struck the enemy's main body at Tagaytay Ridge. The 511th Parachute Infantry Regiment and supporting elements then launched a combat airborne assault on and near the ridge.

Filipino guerrillas had cleared the predetermined drop zones, but the transport pilots had little experience in mass parachute operations. The result was that some of the paratroopers jumped too early and landed far too short of their target areas. Others leapt at dangerously low altitudes and aircraft speeds of between 125 and 135 miles per hour. Making matters worse, the wind speed on the ground was between 20 and 30 miles per hour. This resulted in several harder-than-average landings. Nevertheless, the jumps were successful and, once landed, the combined forces of the 11th Airborne Division quickly captured the high ground. The Japanese launched a few futile counterattacks but for the most part crawled into their caves or fell back on their main body at Manila.

According to the division's official reports as published in Lt. Gen. E. M. Flanagan Jr.'s *Angels: A History of the 11th Airborne Division,* "several thousand" Japanese soldiers remained. They were isolated in "scattered groups," however, and they were "so demoralized" that they never regained the offensive and failed to launch any real aggressive action. Instead, they remained "in their hideouts to be searched out and killed months later."

With close air support provided by both Army Air Forces and Navy aircraft, the airborne soldiers continued moving forward, but often the thick vegetation slowed the advance to a mere few hundred yards in a 24-hour period. By February 4, the 11th's advance elements began reporting a visual sighting of buildings burning in Manila. Soon thereafter, the division attacked and captured several Japanese strong points, wresting from the enemy Fort McKinley, Clark Field, and Nichols Field.

The Japanese put up a last-ditch effort hoping to hang on to Manila, but the Philippine capital soon fell to the Americans. There the airborne forces linked up with the U.S. 1st Cavalry Division and the 37th Infantry Division.

LOS BAÑOS

With the capture of Manila, Gen. Swing relocated his headquarters a few miles south of the city. It was there in the early morning hours of February 8 that the division's night duty officer received a top-secret wire. The message read, "Imperative you move on Los Baños ASAP."

Within hours, a meeting was held between Gen. Douglas MacArthur and Swing. "Joe, I want you to rescue the American civilian prisoners at Los Baños," MacArthur ordered.

The situation was grave and time was critical. Some 2,200 frail men, women, children—many ill—were being held by the Japanese at a camp located deep behind enemy lines. With the Americans in the Philippines, the Japanese knew their situation was at best tenuous. Some Japanese holdouts were willing to fight to the last man, whereas others were waiting on orders to withdraw and prepare to regroup closer to the Japanese home islands. Either way, they were still in the fight. Worse, fresh intelligence indicated that the enemy garrison was planning to execute the civilians at Los Baños and then evacuate the camp.

> The Japanese camp at Los Baños was located at the former University of the Philippines Agricultural School in Los Baños. The town itself was located on the main Philippine island of Luzon approximately 40 miles southeast of Manila. When the Japanese took the Philippines at the beginning of the war, they converted the agricultural school into an internment camp.

The prisoners housed in the camp included approximately 2,200 civilians from a variety of countries—though most were Americans—and all ages from infant to elderly. The only American military personnel in the camp were 12 Navy nurses, and the Japanese garrison numbered 243 armed men.

The Angels had to move quickly, but with precision. One mistake could result in a catastrophic bloodletting of both civilians and paratroopers. On top of this, the intelligence regarding enemy troop strength and available fire support, as well as the actual location and conditions of the prisoners, was sketchy.

Fortunately, one of the prisoners, Pete Miles, escaped prior to the operation and made his way to the 11th's lines with a wealth of fresh information. Miles knew Japanese numerical strength and available weapons. He knew where the Japanese were and what they were doing at any time of day. He was able to confirm the layout of the camp. Best of all, he revealed that every morning at 7, the Japanese stacked their arms, removed their tunics, and gathered for calisthenics in the camp's common area. Based on Miles's information, Swing made the decision to attack on February 23 at 7 A.M. The operation was to be a closely synchronized assault with elements attacking from land, sea, and air.

First Lt. George Skau's 31-man reconnaissance platoon would advance overland toward Los Baños some 36 hours before kickoff. Once in the area, the platoon would make contact with friendly guerrilla forces, "integrate those forces into the rescue effort," and then move into position around the camp. Skau's men were not ordinary soldiers. Trained in the skills of deep reconnaissance, they were the combat equivalent of modern Army Long-Range Reconnaissance or Marine Force Reconnaissance teams.

Fifty-nine amphibious tractors (amtracs) would also be used during the rescue. Driving up from the beach, they would arrive at the camp after the enemy force had been neutralized. Meanwhile, 1st Lt. John M. Ringler would lead a company of the 511th in an airborne assault near the compound.

On the night of February 21, Skau's team moved out toward the objective. The mission kicked off on the morning of February 23.

At 7 A.M., as most of the weaponless enemy guards were stripped to the waist and conducting their morning physical fitness training, the Angels attacked. On the ground, Skau's reconnaissance men and guerrillas were in position.

The 10-plane airborne element roared overhead in V formation at an altitude between 400 and 500 feet, as opposed to the previously considered 700 to 1,000 feet. The planes were homing in on a plume of green smoke from a signal grenade hurled by one of Skau's troopers.

Inside the camp, the attention of most of the Japanese soldiers shifted from their morning calisthenics to the sounds of droning airplanes. The few enemy soldiers not exercising were armed sentries who were busy changing the guard. The prisoners were lining up for roll call.

Suddenly, the C-47 transport planes appeared overhead, and the paratroopers began leaping from the aircraft doors. Lt. Ringler was the first man to jump, and when his chute blossomed, the ground element attacked all along the perimeter, knocking out bunkers and guard towers with rifles, machine guns, and grenades. As the bare-chested Japanese raced toward their stacked weapons, they were cut down.

Meanwhile, Ringler's men were on the ground, unharnessing themselves and racing toward the fence line with weapons blazing and wire cutters at the ready. Amazingly, all the paratroopers landed in the drop zone on target with virtually no casualties. The only injury suffered was by a paratrooper who was knocked unconscious when his head hit the railroad tracks near the edge of the drop zone.

Once inside the camp, enemy resistance was quickly defeated. The American prisoners had mixed emotions, but most were jubilant. "Thank God for the paratroops," shouted one prisoner. "These are the angels He sent to save us." Others who were physically and emotionally drained became frightened and confused. Many of them rushed back to their dank huts when the shooting started and refused to leave until the dwellings caught fire.

Aside from fighting the enemy, the paratroopers were tasked with herding the enormous number of civilians into one area and getting them ready to leave as quickly as possible. Some of the children and the infirm, elderly civilians had to be physically carried.

At one point, the rumbling of tracked vehicles was followed by a shout of "Enemy tanks!" Immediately, the Angels moved into defensive positions. Fortunately, the rumbling was the sound of the approaching American amtracs.

The one humorous anecdote associated with the raid was detailed in William B. Breuer's *Geronimo!* According to Breuer, when one of the airborne rescuers burst into one of the barracks, he found a number of frightened priests and nuns lying on the floor attempting to protect themselves from the hailstorm of bullets and grenade fragments. One of the nuns, having recently listened to radio reports of the American Marine landings on Iwo Jima, asked nervously, "Are you a Marine?" In an exasperated tone, the tall, blond teenager replied, "Hell no, I ain't a gyrene! I'm an American paratrooper!"

Sister Mary Kroeger, one of the nuns, remembered her rescuers as giants. "They were massive compared to our malnourished men in the camp."

One of the priests, overcome with joy, dropped to his knees and raised his hands to Heaven, offering thanks to God. One of the paratroopers approached the priest and helped him back to his feet. "Come on, Father," the soldier said. "Let's get the hell out of here."

By 9 A.M., just two hours after the first shots were fired, the prisoners who were fit enough began calmly walking toward the beach. Those who were sick or too feeble to walk were transported in the amtracs. Oddly, many of the Filipino guerrillas who assisted the Angels melted into the jungle without so much as a handshake or a good-bye. Amazingly, every one of the prisoners was liberated without injury. Not one single paratrooper was killed and only two were wounded (from Skau's platoon). With the exception of a handful of terrified Japanese soldiers disappearing into the jungle, the entire garrison was wiped out.

Despite the success of the Los Baños raid, the mission resulted in an unforeseen tragedy. Days after the raid, a force of Japanese soldiers moved back into the area with captive Filipino families in tow. In reprisal for the American raid, the Japanese tied the Filipino civilians to the foundation stilts of their huts and set them ablaze, burning men, women, and children alive. After the war, one of the ringleaders, Warrant Officer Sadaaki Konishi, was implicated in the murders, tried for war crimes, and executed.

The day after the raid, Gen. Douglas MacArthur, commanding general of U.S. forces in the Far East, issued the following statement to the 11th Airborne Division: "Nothing could be more satisfying to a soldier's heart than this rescue. I am deeply grateful. God was certainly with us today."

Indeed. According to Ringler in an article for the 511th Parachute Infantry Association, "One point of the operation that I have never understood is how could you have over two thousand persons in the target area and live fire coming in from four sides and yet not have a casualty within the camp. It is actions like this that makes us think of who controls our destiny."

Following Los Baños, the 11th refocused its efforts on cleaning out pockets of resistance throughout southern Luzon. In May 1945, the Angels were ordered to the rear where they were patched up, rested, resupplied, and reinforced with fresh paratroopers. Moreover, they began training for what they believed would be their next major operation: the invasion of mainland Japan. Code-named Operation Olympic, the invasion was cancelled after the atomic bombings of Hiroshima and Nagasaki in early August.

On August 10, the division was transferred to Okinawa. There they began preparations to "spearhead the occupation" of Japan. The first elements of the 11th began landing on Japanese soil a few weeks later.

> One ongoing, albeit friendly, dispute between the 11th Airborne Division and the 1st Cavalry Division centers around who was the first military force to land in Japan after the Japanese surrender in 1945. The 1st Cavalry Division claims it was the first on Japanese soil. Veterans of the 11th Airborne Division contend that they not only landed first, but their band played "The Old Gray Mare Ain't What She Used to Be" on the docks in Yokahama while the 1st Cavalry Division was landing.

"It was a small division, half the size of a standard infantry division in men and firepower, which, nonetheless, took on missions of a full-sized division and proved that heart and courage and training and camaraderie and esprit and loyalty, not only up but down, engender self-confidence and invincibility, making giants of ordinary men," wrote U.S. Army Lt. Gen. Edward M. Flanagan in his book, *The Angels*.

POSTWAR OCCUPATION, TRAINING, AND "TEST" DUTIES

After the war, the 11th assumed occupation duties in Japan. During that time, the division's 187th Glider Infantry Regiment, destined to become an Airborne Regimental Combat Team, was nicknamed by the Japanese *Rakkasan* (translated as "umbrella men" or "parachutists"). Although it would eventually drop its "glider" designation, the 187th would distinguish itself in the coming decades, most notably at Hamburger Hill in Vietnam (see Chapter 5).

The 11th Airborne Division was relieved of occupation duties in 1949 and sent to Camp (later Fort) Campbell, Kentucky, where it assumed the role of a training division.

In 1950, the Korean War erupted and the 11th continued to train soldiers for combat. By the time the shooting on the Korean peninsula ceased three years later, some 13,000 combat-ready soldiers had been trained by the 11th. In 1956, the division deployed to Germany, where it spent the next two years.

In July 1958, the 11th returned to Fort Campbell, where it was disbanded. It was reactivated in 1963 at Fort Benning, Georgia, and the division's "airborne" designation was replaced with "air assault." The unit in fact became the 11th "Air Assault" Division (Test). As such, it was not deployable. For the next two years, the division's soldiers conducted training exercises as they experimented with and developed the Army's new concept of air-assaulting (or delivering by helicopter) a large armed force into a combat zone. Commanding the division was Maj. Gen. Harry W. O. Kinnard.

Tests completed, the 11th was disbanded in 1965. Kinnard assumed command of the 1st Cavalry Division, and the 1st Cav—having long retired its horses—became the first airmobile (air assault) division in U.S. Army history.

At this time the war in Vietnam began heating up, and the 1st Cavalry Division was soon shipped to Southeast Asia. In November 1965, Kinnard's helicopters thundered toward what would become the famous battle for the Ia Drang Valley. Riding helicopters into battle was still something of a novel concept, but despite heavy losses among the ranks of the 1st Cavalry Division's 7th Cavalry Regiment, the troopers of the 1st achieved a stunning victory in the valley. Troop-ferrying helicopters would thereafter be used extensively in Vietnam and with great success, thanks to the troopers of the old 11th Airborne Division who had perfected the art.

CHAPTER 7

BLACK CATS:
13TH AIRBORNE DIVISION

Even though most people who undergo it rarely get to use
their skills in action, the training itself has proven a useful
way to prepare troops for the rigors and uncertainty of combat. You might say it has been concluded that soldiers who
will jump out of an airplane will be capable of doing just
about anything.

—James F. Dunnigan, author of *The Perfect Soldier*

Though an unbloodied and short-lived military organization, no
history of America's airborne forces would be complete without a
look at the story of the U.S. Army's crack 13th Airborne Division.

Soon to be known as the "Black Cat Division," the 13th Infantry
Division was designated "airborne" at Fort Bragg, North Carolina,
on Friday, August 13, 1943. The paratroopers and glidermen
began referring to themselves as the "Black Cats" in defiance of
the superstition associated with that date and the numerical designation of the unit. By the end of World War II, the somewhat
unstoried Black Cats believed they had indeed been cursed (veteran paratroopers who had jumped over some of the most hellish
drop zones of the war would argue the 13th had been blessed).

Upon forming, command of the 13th Airborne Division was awarded to Maj. Gen. George Griner, but the general would serve in that capacity for only four months. Griner was replaced in December by Maj. Gen. Eldridge Chapman, an old corps veteran who had seen action with Gen. John J. "Black Jack" Pershing during both the 1916 Mexican Expedition and with the American Expeditionary Force (AEF) in World War I. When America entered World War II in late 1941, Chapman was considered by his peers to be one of the Army's more progressive-thinking officers who grasped the value of airborne warfare when others did not. That fact, combined with his combat experience, helped raise Chapman's name high on the list of those officers whom the army was considering for future airborne commands.

The 13th's history stretches back to the summer of 1918, the last few months of World War I. On July 5 of that year, the 13th had been established as an infantry division at Camp Lewis, Washington. It was considered to be a "square division" because it was comprised of four fully manned infantry regiments. After a short period of training, the 13th deployed to France, where it was slated to join the frontline forces of Gen. Pershing's AEF. But the war ended on November 11, as the 13th was preparing to move up into the trenches. The following March the division was disbanded.

WORLD WAR II

Nearly a quarter-century after it was disbanded, the 13th was reactivated and designated as an airborne division. The charter units included the paratroopers of the 513th Parachute Infantry Regiment and the glidermen of the 189th and the 190th Glider Infantry Regiments. For the next several months, the 13th increased its numbers and trained for a war in which it would never fight.

Soon after Gen. Chapman arrived in December, the 13th was strengthened with the addition of three new regiments: the 515th Parachute Infantry Regiment, the 88th Glider Infantry Regiment, and the 326th Glider Infantry Regiment. The 189th and 190th were disbanded and their men were transferred to the two new glider infantry regiments. The division, with its four regiments and supporting units, was then transferred to New York, where it was stationed for overseas deployment.

In the spring of 1944, the 513th Parachute Infantry Regiment was reassigned to the 17th Airborne Division. Thus, for the next year, the 13th's only parachute infantry regiment was the 515th.

The distinctive shoulder patch of the 13th Airborne Division consists of a blue shield, bordered in black, with a golden, winged unicorn in the center. The unicorn is symbolic of both the soldier's qualities of "virtue, courage and strength" and the division's relationship to winged flight. Arcing above the blue shield is a black tab with the inscription "AIRBORNE" in gold letters.

On January 26, 1945, the men of the 13th boarded ship and set sail for Cherbourg, France, where they would arrive the following month. In Cherbourg, the division was assigned to the XVIII Airborne Corps under the command of Maj. Gen. Matthew B. Ridgway (the XVIII, which had been formed on August 25, 1944, also included the battle-proven 101st, 82nd, and 17th Airborne Divisions). The men then linked up with most of their supplies and moved into assembly and staging areas near the French towns of Sens, Joigny, and Auxerre. From those staging bases, the Black Cats continued training, honing their skills in airborne operations, land navigation, and ground combat tactics. But like the 13th *Infantry* Division's late arrival on the western front in 1918, the 13th Airborne Division arrived too late to the European theater.

On March 1, the 517th Parachute Infantry Combat Team joined the Black Cats at Joigny. Known affectionately as the "battling buzzards," the 517th was a combat-seasoned force under the command of Col. Rupert Graves that had fought in Italy, southern France, Belgium, and Germany. Meanwhile, the 88th Glider Infantry Regiment was disbanded. Its glidermen were then absorbed into the 326th Glider Infantry Regiment, thus increasing the 326th from two to three battalions.

THE "ALMOST" OPERATIONS

Slated to jump in Operation Varsity—an over-the-Rhine airborne/ground forces assault into Westphalia on March 24, 1945—the division was instead ordered to stand fast. The 17th Airborne Division and a British division conducted the operation. To the dismay of the eager paratroopers and glidermen from the 13th, a dearth of transport aircraft and the division's lack of combat experience forced them into strategic reserve status. Decision-makers at XVIII Airborne Corps headquarters instead gave the nod to the 17th Airborne based on its stellar combat performance during the Battle of the Bulge. Varsity was to be the first airborne assault into Germany and the last major airborne operation of World War II.

After losing Operation Varsity to the 17th, the 13th's untested soldiers got their hopes up and dashed three more times. The first was when the Black Cats saddled up for Operation Choker in mid-March, a planned airborne assault on the town of Worms, Germany.

"The day before the division was to take off the 13th's paratroopers and glider-troopers again moved out of their barbed wire enclosed assembly areas," wrote author James E. Mrazek in his brief *History of the 13th Airborne.* "Division paratroopers marched to the airfields, found the C-47's, climbed in the ones they were assigned to, and secured drop loads. Glider troopers loaded and lashed ammunition, pack howitzers, Jeeps and trailers into the gliders ready to take off at dawn." But the surging tank forces of Gen. George S. Patton Jr.'s Third Army attacked and captured Worms before the airborne operation could get off the ground.

On April 3, 1945, the 13th was assigned to the First Allied Airborne Army under the command of Gen. Lewis H. Brereton. But under the Airborne Army, the division's soldiers found themselves carrying out frustratingly menial supply and administrative duties. It was a tough pill to swallow for an elite unit like the 13th. However, the war's combat veterans would have loved to have taken over such cushy, rear-echelon responsibilities. By early 1945, the war was winding down and the division had yet to fire a shot.

The buildup to an attack known as Operation Effective soon followed the cancellation of the Worms invasion. Operation Effective was to be a parachute assault into a remote area of the Alps where it was believed a quarter of a million German troops led by SS diehards were regrouping for either a counterstrike against the Allies or to lure Allied forces into the mountains. Strategists believed the Germans, fighting as guerrillas, would temporarily have the upper hand in the Alps; thus, the war would continue as a partisan conflict.

As the kickoff for the operation drew closer, fresh intelligence began indicating that the enemy was collapsing on all fronts and no regrouping was occurring in the Alps. In fact, a German plan to battle the Allies in the Alps never existed. The plan, as perceived by Allied intelligence forces, was nothing more than a ruse fabricated by Dr. Joseph Goebbels, the Nazi propaganda minister. Goebbels hoped his deception would lure the Allied armies into the Bavarian backcountry and away from Berlin.

The paratroopers were again boarding C-47 transports when word came down that the mission had been scrubbed. Except for the 517th Parachute Infantry Regiment, the Black Cats were again disappointed. The veterans of the old 517th were relieved. They had seen more than enough action prior to joining the "Black Cats."

The 13th was also considered for a top-secret jump into Denmark during the last days of the war, but it too was cancelled.

Regardless of the 13th Airborne's lack of combat service as a division, many of the 13th's paratroopers and glidermen saw a great deal of action during World War II.

According to the divisional history on the XVIII Airborne Corps' official website, throughout the 13th's existence, the division was on more than one occasion "depleted of trained soldiers to provide replacements for the 82nd, the 101st, and the 17th Airborne Divisions." The history further states that in one instance, all "private" soldiers and lieutenants were sent to units that had suffered the greatest losses among those ranks.

Additionally, the 13th Airborne Division's late-joining 517th Parachute Infantry Regimental Combat Team had previously seen a great deal of combat action since the Italian campaigns of 1943.

On April 30, German leader Adolf Hitler committed suicide. When the enemy surrendered the following month, the command elements of both the 13th and 101st Airborne Divisions were notified that their divisions would be reassigned for possible combat action in the Pacific theater. But three months later, American atomic bombs were dropped on the Japanese cities of Hiroshima and Nagasaki. The war was over.

"Many of us in the 13th felt cheated to have volunteered for an elite fighting force only to have a European vacation at the expense of the United States government," said Jack W. Bauer in William B. Breuer's *Geronimo!* "We had exceptionally fine leadership in the 13th Airborne, and could have given a good account of ourselves in any mission. We could have measured up with any of our other airborne outfits.

"I was really disappointed," Bauer added. "My older brother, Joe, had always beaten me in everything from childhood on up, and he had been a combat paratrooper with the 509th Parachute Infantry Battalion [the first American Airborne unit to make a combat jump], so he was one up on me again."

On August 26, 1945, just over two years after having been activated, the 13th Airborne Division returned to Fort Bragg. There, on February 25, the only World War II airborne division with no combat history was deactivated.

"Thus ended the saga of the 13th, perhaps confirming the putative unluckiness of its designation," wrote Lt. Gen. E. M. Flanagan Jr. in *Airborne*. The unlucky 13th Airborne Division has never been reactivated.

CHAPTER 8

THUNDER FROM HEAVEN: 17TH AIRBORNE DIVISION

> Paratroopers were at times a quarrelsome lot because they
> could never believe that anybody could beat hell out of them.
>
> —U.S. Army paratrooper Ross S. Carter

One of the late bloomers in terms of "combat" airborne divisions,
the 17th Airborne "Thunder from Heaven" Division was activated
at Camp Mackall, North Carolina, on April 15, 1943. As such, it
was the last division-size parachute unit formed to see action
before World War II ended two years later.

The division fell under the command of Maj. Gen. William M.
Miley, former commander of the 501st Parachute Infantry Regiment.
The 17th was initially comprised of the 193rd Glider Infantry Regi-
ment, the 194th Glider Infantry Regiment, and the 513th Parachute
Infantry Regiment. The 513th was in fact transferred to the 17th
from the 13th Airborne Division.

Following the Normandy invasion of June 6, 1944, the 507th
Parachute Infantry Regiment was transferred from the 82nd Airborne Division to the 17th. After 33 days of continuous fighting,
the 82nd—including the 507th—had been withdrawn to Great

Britain. The untested 17th arrived there from the States in August, and the bloodied 507th then joined the ranks of the 17th.

> The distinctive shoulder patch of the 17th Airborne Division consists of a black circle bordered in gold, with a gold eagle's talon in the center.
> The patch's black background is symbolic of the enemy's surprise. It symbolizes the seizure of a "golden opportunity" through surprising the enemy.
> Arcing above the black circle is a black tab with the inscription "AIRBORNE" in gold letters.

On August 25, the U.S. XVIII Corps was redesignated the XVIII Airborne Corps. The 17th became one of the Corps' divisions, as did her sister divisions, the 101st, the 82nd, and, later in the war, the 13th. In September, Maj. Gen. Matthew B. Ridgway was named commanding general of the XVIII, and the 17th began an intense training regimen.

FILLING THE GAP

On December 16, approximately 3 months after the 17th's deployment to Great Britain, the Germans launched a massive counterattack against the Allies in Belgium.

Almost immediately, the 82nd and the 101st Airborne Divisions, both of which had been regrouping in France after the invasion of Holland, were rushed forward to stem the tide. Within days, the 82nd was slugging it out with the enemy near St. Vith and the 101st was holding the line at Bastogne. The 17th, however, was still in Great Britain, straining at the reins to get into the fight, but poor weather kept the division grounded.

As Christmas approached, however, the skies cleared. From December 23 through 25, the 17th was airlifted in a series of what was later described by the U.S. Army Almanac as "spectacular night flights" across the English Channel into staging areas near Reims, France.

Once on the ground, the advance elements, including the 513th Parachute Infantry Regiment, moved toward Mourmelon. There, attached under legendary Gen. George S. Patton Jr.'s Third Army, the paratroopers positioned themselves to defend the Meuse River sector from Givet to Verdun.

Oddly enough, they found themselves digging in for defensive action between the graves of a previous generation of Americans who had fallen during the bloody Meuse-Argonne offensive of World War I, an eerie reminder to the sky soldiers that history often repeats itself.

THE DIVISION FIGHTS

On Christmas Day, the paratroopers left their positions and struck out for Neufchateau, Belgium. Meanwhile, Gen. Patton's forces had finally smashed through the enemy lines at Bastogne and made contact with the battered paratroopers of the 101st. At that point, the 513th and the other elements of the 17th broke camp and marched through the snow to Morhet. There, on January 3, 1945, they relieved the 28th Infantry Division.

The 507th Parachute Infantry Regiment along with the 193rd and 194th Glider Infantry Regiments were held in reserve in the event the Germans counterattacked. But within days of relieving the 28th, the two glider regiments were called up to support the 513th.

The fighting was fierce, and the glider regiments were hit hard, so much so that one of the regiments, the severely battered 193rd, was cannibalized to form an additional battalion for the 194th.

From January 4 through 9, the 17th's sky soldiers fought the Germans in a series of bloody engagements known as the Battle of Dead Man's Ridge. During that period, they seized a number of Belgian villages, including the town of Flamierge. Almost always, the enemy retreated and then launched aggressive counterattacks. Finally, the Germans were beaten back across the Ourthe River.

In mid-January, the division relieved the 11th Armored Division at Houffalize. Following this, they attacked and captured Wattermal and Espeler. The 17th, under the temporary command of the U.S. III Corps, then advanced on Luxembourg, capturing Eschweiler and Clervaux after wiping out isolated pockets of enemy resistance along the way.

At the Ourthe River, reconnaissance teams were organized that crossed the river and probed the defenses along the famous Siegfried Line. Additionally, a limited bridgehead was established near Dasburg. There, on February 10, the 6th Armored Division relieved the 17th.

Although the 17th's paratroopers and glidermen had proven themselves to be tough, committed fighters, the Germans fought like fanatics throughout the entire Ardennes (Bulge) campaign. Their desperation was analogous to a rat that's been backed into a corner. The Ardennes offensive was Germany's last, desperate hope of stopping the Allies before they launched their final thrust across the border into Germany's heartland. Hitler knew it, and so did his senior commanders and the rank-and-file soldiers. If the German army was defeated in Belgium, the German people would soon be at the mercy of invading forces.

Additionally, Nazi officers told German soldiers going up against American airborne forces that U.S. paratroopers never took prisoners. Thus, surrender was not an option. The only hope of survival, in the German soldier's mind, was to fight to the last round. When that was spent, he would use the bayonet and the rifle butt.

German soldiers faced with immediate death in combat did, however, surrender and were surprised when—instead of a summary execution—they received food, rest, and medical attention.

One wounded and terrified German prisoner asked his captor, U.S. paratrooper Kurt Gabel, if he was going to shoot him now that he had been taken prisoner.

"Is that what you've been told?" replied Gabel, a German Jew who had emigrated to America prior to the war and later joined the 17th Airborne Division's 513th Parachute Infantry Regiment. "Don't be idiotic. Hell, man, I'm taking you to the aide station to get a bandage on you."

The German prisoner told Gabel he had been informed by a Nazi political officer in his unit that "American paratroop units were made up of convicted murderers who had been given a choice either to die or to go into the paratroops [not unlike the film *The Dirty Dozen*] and that they always killed prisoners." Of course, it was misguided propaganda, but it was enough to keep the individual German soldier fighting when all seemed lost.

Having achieved all its objectives, the 17th Airborne Division returned to Chalons-sur-Marne, France, in mid-February 1945. In just over a month, the division returned to Belgium in order to prepare for a massive airborne assault across the Rhine River.

LAST JUMP

In early 1945, the decision had been made to cross the Rhine from the west and punch into Germany's industrial Ruhr region. Code-named Operation Varsity, the 2nd British Army was slated to attack from the ground, whereas the American XVIII Airborne Corps were to strike from the air.

It was to be the last major airborne operation of World War II, and the vanguard of the XVIII Airborne Corps was the 17th Airborne Division, specifically the division's 507th Parachute Infantry Regiment.

On the hazy morning of March 24, 1945, some 4,000 transport aircraft and gliders loaded with airborne soldiers of the 17th and the British 6th Airborne Division began roaring above their advance staging areas in France. Soon the great air fleet crossed the Rhine and was over enemy territory. Near Wesel, in Westphalia, just north of the Ruhr, heavily armed American paratroopers and their British cousins began jumping from the transport planes.

Unlike Operation Market Garden, where the sky soldiers were dropped far from their primary targets, the paratroopers and gliderborne soldiers of the 17th landed close to their targets, achieving complete surprise and quickly overwhelming the defenders.

The invasion was characterized by individual heroism from all quarters. Moments after Pvt. First Class George G. Peters and 10 of his buddies from the 507th landed, a German machine gun opened up on them from about 70 yards away. Everyone hit the deck, except Peters, who personally charged the enemy gun nest with his rifle and a handful of grenades. A burst of fire knocked him down, but the determined PFC crawled to within a few feet of the Germans and lobbed a couple grenades at their position. Peters killed the German gunners before he himself died of his wounds. He was posthumously awarded the Congressional Medal of Honor.

Then, in one of the most dramatic scenes of the war, Gen. Miley landed under fire, separated from his staff but near three young privates. Unbuckling himself from his parachute, the general spotted a parachute-dropped container he knew contained a machine gun. Shouting to the privates to meet him at the container, the four men—a two-star general and three slick-sleeve privates—sprinted toward the gun. Quickly assembling the weapon, they were soon able to return fire.

The day following the landings, the division seized a number of bridges over the Issel River and set up a defensive position along the Issel Canal. It was during this action that elements of the 194th Glider Infantry Regiment encountered stiff resistance near Lembeck Castle, and a young glider soldier from West Virginia, Tech. Sgt. Clinton M. Hendrick, won the Congressional Medal of Honor.

Following three failed frontal assaults on German positions, Hendrick rushed an enemy machine-gun nest, hip-firing his Browning Automatic Rifle (BAR) all the way. This dramatic performance rallied other members of his company, who charged behind him. The Americans quickly overran the German positions, and several of the surviving German soldiers retreated into the castle with Hendrick hot on their heels.

Unfortunately, one of the Germans, feigning surrender, lured the American glidermen into a trap. Sensing the ruse, Hendrick tried to warn the others but was immediately hit by a burst of enemy fire and mortally wounded. Still, he managed to signal his men to fall back. The young sergeant then resumed the attack and single-handedly wiped out the remaining German defenders.

When the shooting subsided, Hendrick's men approached their young sergeant, who had collapsed and was bleeding profusely. He died shortly thereafter and was posthumously awarded the Congressional Medal of Honor.

Days later, the paratroopers and glidermen of the 17th attacked and seized the towns of Haltern (March 29) and Munster (April 2). Soon thereafter they smashed into the Ruhr pocket, where they linked up with and relieved the U.S. 79th Infantry Division. On April 6, the Rhine-Herne Canal was crossed. The division regrouped and then pressed on toward the city of Essen. Upon arrival, the division's soldiers captured the famous Nazi diplomat Franz von Papen. The city itself fell to the Americans four days later, followed by the capture of the towns of Mulheim and Duisberg.

Operation Varsity was a stunning success. The German army was collapsing and Hitler himself was days from committing suicide.

Enemy opposition ceased on April 18, and on April 24, the 17th was transferred to the U.S. XXII Corps. On June 15, the 17th was withdrawn to France. In September, the war ended and the division was shipped back to the United States, where it was disbanded.

CHAPTER 9

GLIDERBORNE FORCES

Flying caskets.

—Universal nickname for combat gliders during World War II

Gliderborne infantry forces and glider assaults were a short-lived—and today often underappreciated—means of delivering specially trained combat infantrymen behind enemy lines during World War II. As part of the early airborne triage—parachute, glider, and airfield-landed forces—gliderborne infantrymen attacked almost always in concert with large-scale parachute drops. As such, the glider units were attached to the Army's airborne divisions.

In the 1920s and early 1930s, both the Army and Navy experimented with gliders as a practical method of delivering forces to a predetermined point, but both services deemed the glider impractical and thus abandoned the idea.

That belief changed in early May 1940, when nine German Luftwaffe gliders silently landed on the rooftop that covered the subterranean fortress of Eben Emael in Belgium. The glider soldiers successfully seized the supposedly impregnable fortress, causing surprised American military leaders to take a second look at the concept of using gliders as a component of airborne warfare. At the time, the only existing gliders in North America were small sport gliders.

On February 25, 1941, U.S. Army Air Corps commander Gen. Henry Harley "Hap" Arnold issued orders for the procurement of "suitable" training gliders. Thus, the proverbial wheels were set in motion for glider forces that would complement the newly forming American parachute forces. The Marine Corps also experimented with gliderborne forces but dissolved them early in the war (see Chapter 14).

The gliders were engineless transport aircraft that were towed by large transport aircraft—usually C-47s—via cable at top speeds of about 150 miles an hour through enemy antiaircraft fire. A few miles from their intended landing area, the gliders were disconnected from the towing aircraft. At that point, the gliders would silently descend to the earth, usually under cover of darkness, and land in preselected fields in the enemy's rear areas. Once on the ground, the planes would skid to a stop. The aircraft doors would then burst open and out would rush the assault troops, who—like their parachuting brothers—would seize bridges and highway junctions or attack power plants and communications centers. In a sense, the glider craft *itself*—packed with armed men—was the airborne version of a Trojan Horse.

Constructed primarily of wood and canvas—and without armaments—the craft were extremely vulnerable to both enemy fire and the stresses of flight and landing. Many of them landed hard or crashed, often killing everyone on board. Sometimes this was due to poor landing sites or marginal-to-zero visibility during the approach to landing. Other times the pilots were killed or incapacitated by enemy fire. Flak and bullets could also damage the wings, flaps, and ailerons, resulting in a total loss of control.

British glidermen were transported in the big Horsa gliders, whereas the Americans preferred the slightly smaller Waco CG-4A troop-carrying gliders. The Wacos were capable of transporting 13 infantrymen (not including the 2 pilots) with full combat loads, or fewer men and more equipment. Often the gliders would transport one 75mm howitzer and 6 fully equipped soldiers.

"DON'T GO BY GLIDER!"

Riding a glider into battle was not nearly as glamorous as parachuting from an airplane, but the risk of death or injury to a glider soldier or pilot was often far greater.

"I'll tell you straight out: If you've got to go into combat, don't go by glider," said retired CBS News anchorman Walter Cronkite, who rode a glider into battle while a correspondent for United Press International in September 1944. "Walk, crawl, swim, float—anything. But don't go by glider!"

Cronkite, who landed with the glider elements of the 101st Airborne Division during the Allied invasion of Holland, remembered being terribly frightened before, during, and after the glider ride.

"I didn't want to go by glider," he wrote in the foreword to John L. Lowden's *Silent Wings at War*. "I had seen what happened to the gliders in Normandy. The wreckage of hundreds of them was scattered across the countryside. Many were impaled on the spiked posts [Rommel's asparagus] the Germans had planted to defeat them."

In the end, Cronkite went. "I decided that the only thing worse than going to Holland in a glider was the ignominy of not going at all on a mission for which I had volunteered, of having those guys at airborne headquarters and my fellow newsmen back in London know how chicken I really was." Cronkite echoed the concerns of the soldiers whose deeds he was reporting.

"I had heard many say that the word glider was a synonym for suicide," said Ferd Moyse, an artillery officer who rode a glider into Normandy. During World War II, both the Allies and the Germans used gliders to ferry assault troops into predetermined landing zones behind enemy lines.

GLIDERS AT NORMANDY

On June 6, 1944, gliders attached to the 82nd Airborne Division were used to land silently behind the Normandy beaches and wreak havoc in the enemy's rear.

On one of those gliders was Lt. Col. J. Strom Thurmond, a 42-year-old circuit court judge from South Carolina who left the bench to fight the Germans. Thurmond, who would ultimately become the longest-serving U.S. Senator in American history, was nearly killed upon landing and during subsequent fighting with the enemy.

Crash-landing in an apple orchard near St. Mere-Eglise, Thurmond's glider bounced from tree to tree and was literally torn to pieces before skidding to a halt. Miraculously, the future senator survived. "Thurmond suffered cuts on both hands and another jagged wound on a severely bruised knee," wrote authors Jack Bass and Marilyn W. Thompson in *Ol' Strom*. "Yet he and the four paratroopers were able to walk out of the wreckage."

Almost immediately, the men came under enemy mortar, rifle, and machine-gun fire. Moreover, Thurmond and his fellow glidermen were surrounded. They successfully fought their way out, made contact with friendly forces, and later captured four German soldiers. Of his experiences, Thurmond would later write, "There were so many narrow escapes that it is a miracle to me that any of us who landed by glider are still alive."

ROMMEL'S ASPARAGUS

At Normandy, one of the most lethal weapons employed against the gliders were "Rommel's asparagus"—long wooden poles sticking straight up from the ground across potential glider landing zones (the poles were the brainchild of German field marshall Erwin Rommel, who was responsible for the physical defenses of Fortress Europe). The poles, resembling telephone poles, varied in size from 6 to 12 inches in diameter and 8 to 12 feet long. They were sunk approximately 2 feet into the ground and spaced 75 to 100 feet apart.

Despite their size, they were nearly impossible for pilots to detect from the air. As the gliders swooped in close to the ground, the pilots would sometimes make the terrifying discovery seconds from touching down and try to maneuver between them. If they were lucky, only the wings would be sheared off. In most cases, however, gliders unfortunate enough to land in one of Rommel's "asparagus" fields did not fare very well. The poles would literally rip open the underbellies of the planes, tearing the craft to pieces, killing or maiming the occupants, and destroying any equipment being transported to the landing zone.

Adding to the destructive nature of the asparagus fields, explosive devices were often attached to the poles, and barbed wire was strung from pole to pole.

Ditches were also dug to thwart the glider landings. Most were 10 to 12 feet across and 5 to 6 feet deep. Many were filled with water.

GLIDER INFANTRYMEN

Glider infantry soldiers were a hardy breed. In terms of ground combat training, they learned to fight like paratroopers. During combat, they carried all manner of personal weapons, including submachine guns, grenades, trench knives, and commando daggers. After all, their mission, like that of their parachuting brothers, was to land in the enemy's rear and engage him in close-quarter fighting. Unlike paratroopers, however, glidermen were not always volunteers.

Glider training was almost as dangerous as combat glider assaults. In the months before the invasion of Normandy, the U.S. Army reported an alarmingly high number of glider accidents: three to six gliders daily. As dangerous as glider training was, the glider soldiers often felt as if they were the unwanted stepchildren of American airborne forces.

"One poster at Laurenberg, Maxton Army Air Base, North Carolina, summed up the glider rider's feelings," wrote Lt. Gen. E. M. Flanagan Jr. in *Airborne*. "Beneath a series of photos showing glider wrecks, one glider man had written: 'JOIN THE GLIDER TROOPS! No flight pay; no jump pay; BUT never a dull moment.' Such was the birth of the glider program and the glider soldier—'Those who were roped in.'"

Early glidermen did not receive flight pay (like conventional military pilots), nor did they receive hazardous duty pay (like paratroopers). They also had no special emblem signifying their gliderborne capabilities, and they were often looked down on by their parachuting brothers.

"Rivalry between the paratroopers and the glider troops was quite high, with the chest-thumping paratroopers claiming they were the bravest and toughest in the airborne kingdom," writes Gerard M. Devlin in *Paratrooper!* "But deep inside, the paratroopers knew it took just as much guts to ride a flimsy glider down out of the sky into a small square of partially cleared earth as it did to step out of an airplane above a huge, cleared field wearing two parachutes [the primary parachute and the reserve chute]."

Attitudes changed after both glidermen and paratroopers had tasted battle. In the summer of 1944, glidermen began receiving hazardous duty pay: $50 per month extra for enlisted soldiers and $100 for officers—just like the paratroopers. Glidermen also received a badge (see Appendix E) and a hat patch.

GLIDER PILOTS

Unlike glider infantry trainees, who were drawn from among the toughest fighters in regular infantry units, glider pilot candidates were a mixed bag of would-be aviators with varying levels of experience. And they were not members of the Army's ground force branches; they were airmen serving in the Army Air Forces. Also, unlike the troops they would be ferrying into battle, glider pilots were all volunteers. Many of them had an extensive number of flight hours under their belts, either civilian or military. Others were fighter pilot hopefuls who either failed to pass the flight physical or the written examinations.

The primary difference between a glider pilot and an engine-driven aircraft pilot is that the former was always on a "one-way" flight with no hope of a happy landing, just a successful one.

(National Archives)

Gen. Anthony C. McAuliffe, destined to refuse the German appeal to surrender at Bastogne with the word "Nuts," addresses a group of glider pilots before the Invasion of Normandy, June 1944.

"Imagine flying a motorless, fabric-covered CG-4A glider, violently bouncing and jerking on a one-inch thick nylon rope 300 feet back of the C-47 tow plane," said a veteran glider pilot during a 2002 interview for the Silent Wings Museum in Lubbock, Texas. "You see the nervous glider infantrymen behind you, some vomiting, many in prayer, as you hedge-hop along at treetop level instinctively jumping up in your seat every time you hear bullets and flak tearing through the glider. You try not to think about the explosive aboard. It's like flying a stick of dynamite through the gates of Hell."

Hell indeed. The men on board had no parachutes and no opportunities to make a second go-round if the landing zone was deemed poor. The glider pilot had to crash-land his aircraft on every mission, after which he would find himself in a ground combat environment. On the ground, the American glider pilot was not tasked with fighting like an infantry soldier (British and German glider pilots were trained to fight on the ground), but in reality he often had no choice. If he remained at the front, he could either fight or risk death or capture, unless he chose to move out of the area and hopefully link up with friendly forces in the rear. Either way, there was an enormous chance he would make contact with enemy forces on the ground. Consequently, the glider pilot prepared himself to fight.

"As glider pilots we were allowed to have whatever arms we wanted," said Fred Sampson, a former British glider pilot in a 2003 interview for the *Toronto Globe and Mail*. "I packed an American carbine and a commando knife, which was illegal … [We weren't] allowed to have a fixed blade by the Geneva Convention." American glider pilots often equipped themselves similarly, but they also carried silk-fabric maps to guide them if they chose to solitarily make their way to the rear.

Throughout the war, approximately 6,000 men earned their glider pilot wings. Not all saw combat action, but many were responsible for literally leading the charge in many major invasions—Sicily, France, Holland, the Philippines, and the China-Burma-India theater. Some felt that if they had known what they were in for, they would have never volunteered for glider pilot training. Glider pilot Pete Buckley, the youngest to earn his glider wings, was among that bunch.

"Thirty minutes before takeoff the engines of the tow ships started up," Buckley recalled in Gerald Astor's *June 6, 1944: The Voices of D-Day*. "The muffled noise and throbbing of their motors spread around the field like a distant, approaching thunderstorm, and contributed to our uneasiness. We all climbed aboard trying not to show our true feelings. My own were that in roughly three and a half hours I might be dead. It was a very sobering moment, and I wondered why I had been so foolish as to volunteer for this job. When I first went into the glider program, nobody had ever explained to me how gliders were going to be used."

However, it did not take more than one mission for a glider pilot to ascertain the tremendous risk. Some could not handle it and quit outright.

"There were glider pilots who flew one mission and packed it in," wrote former glider pilot John L. Lowden. "We didn't ask why; we knew why. But we accepted their decisions without question or criticism. You could be shit-faced with fear, but not frozen with it. You had to function under fire, and paralyzing fear does not make for good foxhole fellows."

Though rarely elaborated on in wartime histories, there was in fact a shortage of trained glider command pilots for the Normandy invasion. As a result, less-experienced "co-pilots" assumed command of many of the gliders, and airborne soldiers became copilots.

"The training for the new co-pilots took place about thirty minutes before takeoff and consisted of a few minutes' ground instruction by their respective command pilots," wrote Mike Kelly, a contributing writer for Thomas E. Simmons's *Forgotten Heroes of World War II*. According to Kelly, the instruction was little more than, "If I get wounded or killed going over, here's what you do to land ...."

Over France, some of the new command pilots were knocked out of action, and the glider soldier in the adjacent seat had to take the controls and land. Many of those landings were disastrous.

"Having to land a glider for the first time in combat is a chastening experience," said Gen. James M. Gavin, the famous commanding general of the wartime 82nd Airborne Division. "It gives a man religion."

Nearly 14,000 gliders were manufactured between 1942 and 1945, and about 30,000 American glider soldiers were ferried into action during World War II. Although gliders were not used in action after World War II, the U.S. Defense Department did not officially disband the military glider program until 1952.

CHAPTER 10

INDEPENDENT AIRBORNE AND PARACHUTE INFANTRY UNITS

Courage is doing what you are afraid to do. There can be no courage unless you are scared.

—Edward V. "Eddie" Rickenbacker to Peggy Streit on "What Is Courage," *The New York Times* magazine, November 24, 1963

Numerous Army airborne battalions, regiments, regimental combat teams, brigades, and even one task force were formed during World War II. Most were broken up or folded into airborne divisions by the close of hostilities in 1945. A few remained and went on to earn laurels in the second half of the twentieth and early twenty-first centuries.

One airborne brigade, the 173rd (quite possibly the best known of the independents—a unit that exists and operates separately from a parent unit), was formed nearly two decades after the end of World War II.

173RD AIRBORNE BRIGADE

Of all the independent U.S. Army airborne units, none is more storied than the 173rd Airborne Brigade. "One of the finest units in the history of the American fighting man," said Gen. William C. West-moreland in 1967, less than 5 years after the 173rd Infantry Brigade earned its airborne wings.

Best known for its numerous "firsts" during the Vietnam War, the 173rd was the U.S. Army's first brigade-size ground combat unit in Vietnam. It was the first Army force of its size to engage the enemy. It was one of the first brigade-size or larger units to conduct a helicopter-borne air assault against the enemy. It was also the first and only American unit to make a mass combat jump during the war, but the unit's beginnings were modest.

In August 1917, the 173rd Infantry Brigade was established at Camp Pike, Arkansas, and would later become the 173rd Airborne Brigade. Upon its establishment, the brigade was placed under the 87th Division. The following year the 173rd deployed to France as part of the American Expeditionary Force, but it did not participate in any of the campaigns of World War I.

The brigade was demobilized in early 1919. For the next two decades, the 173rd existed both as an active and reserve unit. It also still held its numerical and brigade designations, but it was rarely more than a head-quarters company for the 87th Division.

In December 1941, America entered World War II. The following February, the 173rd Infantry Brigade was redesignated as the 87th Recon-naissance Troop and was ordered into active military service. As a recon-naissance troop, the future 173rd Airborne Brigade fought in the European theater under Gen. George S. Patton Jr.'s vaunted Third Army and partici-pated in three campaigns, including the Battle of Bulge from late 1944 to early 1945.

At the close of the war in 1945, the 87th was ordered into reserve status. It was briefly reactivated as the 87th Mechanized Cavalry Reconnaissance Troop from 1947 to 1951. In December 1951, the troop (brigade) was dis-banded.

The 173rd Infantry Brigade/87th Reconnaissance Troop was reactivated on March 26, 1963, as the 173rd Airborne Brigade. Command of the brigade was awarded to Brig. Gen. Ellis W. Williamson, and the unit itself became a Pacific area quick-reaction force.

In the years following its new airborne designation, the 173rd trained extensively in friendly, Pacific countries, particularly Taiwan. There the brigade honed its skills in jungle fighting and guerrilla warfare. Additionally, the paratroopers made countless training jumps, which earned the brigade the nickname "sky soldiers."

Sky soldier is a casual term widely used to describe all U.S. Army paratroopers and has been so since the early days of American airborne forces. However, the only Army airborne unit with the semiofficial designation "sky soldiers" is the 173rd Airborne Brigade. The title was bestowed on the 173rd by Nationalist Chinese soldiers, who referred to the brigade's paratroopers as *tien bien* (translated as "sky soldier").

In May 1965, the new 173rd Airborne Brigade deployed to Vietnam, where it became the Army's first major ground combat force to serve in that country (elements of the 101st would arrive in July). Originally slated for security duties around Bien Hoa, the sky soldiers instead began routing out the enemy in the Vietnamese backcountry, destroying enemy base camps along the way. During that period, the 173rd's soldiers began perfecting the art of long-range reconnaissance patrols.

On February 22, 1967, under the command of Brig. Gen. John R. Deane Jr., the 173rd made airborne history when the brigade's paratroopers conducted the first—and only—mass parachute jump of the Vietnam War. The jump, part of Operation Junction City, was conducted by nearly 850 paratroopers of the brigade's 2nd Battalion, 503rd Infantry Regiment, and a supporting battery of airborne artillery.

Just after 9 A.M., the sky soldiers jumped from 16 C-130 transport planes over a drop zone near Katum, South Vietnam. Landing against virtually zero opposition, the paratroopers quickly assembled, deployed into defensive positions, and set up a command post and artillery firebase. Following this, they began moving toward their objectives where they were to link up with helicopter-borne infantry forces.

The jump was textbook. Only 11 minor injuries were sustained during the jump, with no killed or wounded from enemy action. Soon the paratroopers were engaging the enemy in a series of firefights. Within a week, the sky soldiers attacked and destroyed a Vietcong intelligence and propaganda complex. Junction City then evolved into a series of larger engagements with both Vietcong guerrillas and North Vietnamese Army (NVA) soldiers. By mid-May, the enemy had either been destroyed or driven across the Cambodian border.

The 173rd later participated in fighting inside the famous Iron Triangle, and in November fought in one of the bloodiest battles of the war at Dak To.

On November 13, a savage close-quarters struggle ensued between a company of the 503rd and a battalion from the crack 174th NVA Regiment at Dak To. A second American company was hurried forward to reinforce its fellow paratroopers. The fighting—literally cold steel and grenades—raged throughout the night. Casualties soared on both sides. By first light, the NVA had withdrawn.

"The fighting had been so intense that one log was found in the morning with six dead paratroopers on one side and four dead NVA sprawled out on the other side," wrote Dr. Shelby L. Stanton, historian and former U.S. Army Special Forces officer. "At the end of the log were two more NVA, one of them an officer who still clutched an M-16 rifle taken from one of the Americans."

On the November 19, the 173rd was ordered to capture one of the area's most commanding heights, Hill 875. The fighting was grim, characterized by close combat, attacks, and counterattacks. Four days later, on Thanksgiving Day, the bloodied sky soldiers seized the heights. At the top, some of the men shouted "Airborne!" and "Geronimo!" Some collapsed from exhaustion. Others openly wept. A few simply sat down and opened cans of C rations for their Thanksgiving dinner.

The following year, the brigade launched an amphibious assault against the enemy as part of an overall effort to drive NVA and Vietcong forces out of the strategic lowlands along the Bong Song River.

"There are volumes of statistics in war," wrote Brig. Gen. H. S. Cunningham, commanding general of the 173rd, in June 1970. "But the cold calculated columns of figures are void of the personality, dedication, and sacrifice made by the paratrooper of this brigade. Charts and reports fail to communicate the tension of the man who strains his eyes searching for the hidden enemy. They fail to picture the blood and sweat that soak and stain ... the heat, the rain, the rocks and mud, the jungle and mountains that wear and grate on the man with the rifle. But—a sky soldier knows."

On January 14, 1972, the 173rd Airborne Brigade was deactivated at Fort Campbell, Kentucky.

On June 12, 2000, more than 28 years after furling their colors, the 173rd was reactivated at Vicenza, Italy. Almost immediately, the brigade began participating in a variety of combat exercises throughout the world.

Soon after the terrorist attacks of September 11, 2001, the 173rd was placed on full alert. When the U.S. and coalition forces invaded Iraq in early 2003, the 173rd's paratroopers prepared for the big show.

On March 26, 2003—40 years to the day after the brigade was established as an airborne force—some 1,000 sky soldiers from the 173rd jumped over northern Iraq and quickly seized the enemy-held Harir airfield. The brigade was a key combat element in securing the city of Kirkuk. Although its current missions are classified, the brigade continues to operate with success in northern Iraq.

THE 187TH RAKKASANS

Often referred to as the only U.S. airborne regiment that has fought in every American war since the inception of airborne forces, the 187th Infantry Regiment was established at Camp Mackall, North Carolina, on November 12, 1942. The following February, the regiment was designated "glider infantry" and assigned to the 11th Airborne Division, also known as "the Angels." The 187th fought within the ranks of the Angels in the Pacific theater during World War II (see Chapter 6).

When the war ended in 1945, the 187th Glider Infantry Regiment, as well as other elements of the 11th Airborne Division, assumed occupation duties in Japan. During that time, the Japanese nicknamed the regiment's soldiers *Rakkasans* (translated as "falling-down umbrella," "umbrella men," or "parachutists").

In the spring of 1949, the 11th, including the Rakkasans, returned stateside and moved into garrison at Camp (later Fort) Campbell, Kentucky. In June, the regiment was redesignated as the 187th Airborne Infantry Regiment.

During Exercise Swarmer, "the largest peacetime airborne maneuver in history" held in April 1950, the exemplary performance of the 187th was a key factor in the regiment's being selected to form the nucleus of an airborne-trained regimental combat team.

On the night of June 24 and 25, 1950, Communist North Korean ground forces crossed the 38th parallel—dividing North and South Korea—and attacked in great strength. Two months later, the 187th was again redesignated, this time as the 187th Airborne Regimental Combat Team (ARCT).

On September 22, a week after U.S. Army Gen. Douglas MacArthur's historic amphibious landing at Inchon, elements of the 187th ARCT began landing at Kimpo airfield, near the South Korean capital of Seoul. Almost immediately, the ARCT was engaging the North Korean army as it cleared the area of enemy forces between the Han River and the Yellow Sea. Within days, the tide was turning against the Communists and the Americans were attacking north above the parallel.

MacArthur then decided on a parachute assault near the Communist capital of Pyongyang. In the first airborne operation of the Korean War, an air fleet of 71 C-119 and 40 C-47 transports ferried nearly 2,900 paratroopers of the 187th ARCT to drop zones near the capital on October 20 and 21, 1950. Jumping over the North Korean towns of Sukch'on and Sunch'on, the Americans landed as part of a surprise attack. During the jump, 1 sky soldier was killed and another 36 men were injured. On the ground, the 187th RCT linked up with other U.S. forces who were driving north toward the Yalu River.

The 187th conducted a second airborne assault on March 23, 1951, near the 38th parallel. In late June, the ARCT returned to Japan, where it was placed on strategic reserve. In early 1952, the ARCT briefly deployed to Korea, was transferred back to Japan in October, and made its final redeployment to Korea in June 1953. Two years later, the 187th returned home to Fort Campbell.

In 1956, the 187th ARCT was redesignated as the 2nd Airborne Battle Group, 187th Infantry, of the newly reactivated 101st Airborne Division.

In 1963, the unit was redesignated as the 3rd Battalion, 187th Infantry, placed under the 11th Airborne Division (recently redesignated as the 11th Air Assault Division for testing purposes), and transferred to Fort Benning, Georgia. There the Rakkasans worked under the 11th, testing and perfecting the new concept of helicopter-borne air assault operations.

(National Archives)

Rakkasans of the 187th ARCT during a training jump in Korea, January 1952.

After a year as a test unit, the 187th was reassigned to the 101st. Upon being folded into the 101st, the Rakkasans were no longer an independent regiment. They were and are permanent members of the Screaming Eagles.

The 187th would distinguish itself in the coming decades, most notably at Hamburger Hill in Vietnam (see Chapter 5), and has since fought in most of America's post-Vietnam conflicts.

503RD AIRBORNE (PARACHUTE) INFANTRY REGIMENT

Known as "the Rock," the 503rd Regiment was one of the first American airborne units formed during World War II. It eventually became an ARCT, retook the Philippine island of Corregidor, and existed as an airborne regiment throughout most of the Cold War.

The team's first element was conceived on August 21, 1941, with the establishment of the 503rd Parachute Infantry Battalion in Fort Benning, Georgia. The battalion, the third of four parachute battalions (the others being the 501st, the 502nd, and the 504th), was placed under the "Provisional Parachute Group" commanded by then-Lt. Col. William C. "Bill" Lee.

In early 1942, the 503rd Parachute Infantry Regiment was formed, with the 503rd Parachute Infantry Battalion forming the nucleus around which the regiment would be grown. A second battalion was added (the original 504th Parachute Infantry Battalion, which would later be redesignated as the 509th).

In March, the 503rd Parachute Infantry Regiment was transferred to Fort Bragg, North Carolina. However, the 2nd Battalion would not remain long with the regiment. It was separated and shipped to England, from where it would soon strike North Africa in the first-ever American combat jump. (In early November, the 2nd Battalion would be redesignated the 2nd Battalion, 509th Parachute Infantry Battalion, and later as simply the 509th Parachute Infantry Battalion.)

By the fall, the 503rd Parachute Infantry Regiment was staged for deployment in San Francisco, and on October 20, the regiment—minus its 2nd Battalion—departed for Panama. There it linked up with the 501st Parachute Infantry Battalion (the first-ever U.S. Army airborne battalion). The 501st then became the 2nd battalion of the 503rd.

In December 1942, the 503rd landed in Australia. There the unit trained for airborne warfare in the Pacific theater.

In the early fall of 1943, the regiment made history. On September 5, paratroopers from the 503rd made the first combat jump in the Pacific when they leapt over the Markham Valley in New Guinea. The airborne assault forced the Japanese defenders to abandon a major base of operations. The jump also convinced U.S. military planners that large-scale parachute operations were a viable means of taking the war to the enemy. Many cynics had begun raising a clamor against the use of parachute forces after the 509th Parachute Infantry Battalion's near disaster in North Africa in November 1942.

With the addition of a parachute field artillery battalion in March 1944 and an airborne engineer battalion in September, the 503rd Parachute Infantry Regiment became a Regimental Combat Team (RCT).

On July 3 and 4, 1944, less than one month after the historic invasion of Normandy, two parachute infantry battalions of the 503rd made a jump on strategic Noemfoor Island, off the coast of New Guinea. The two battalions were followed by a third, which landed by sea. The 503rd was tasked with knocking out Noemfoor's Japanese garrison. After accomplishing this, the Allies were able to use the island as an advance base for the upcoming invasion of the Philippines.

The fighting on Noemfoor had been tough. The terrain was rugged, and the Japanese fought to the death. Isolated and with virtually no food, the enemy resorted to cannibalism, often eating the flesh of both their own dead and any killed American soldier whose own body might be found on some remote trail.

In mid-November, the 503rd was placed on temporary reserve status and shipped to the island of Leyte.

In December, the regiment conducted an amphibious assault on the island of Mindoro, landing under heavy enemy air and naval bombardment. Upon arriving, the 503rd battled isolated pockets of Japanese soldiers. The toughest fight was waged over an enemy air raid warning station on the island's north end. There the enemy battled stubbornly, refused to surrender or abandon the station, and had to be wiped out.

In mid-February 1945, the 503rd RCT, under the command of Lt. Col. George Jones, parachuted over Corregidor to liberate those held within the Philippine fortress since the Japanese occupation in 1942. The 503rd landed on the western heights, known as "Topside," while the U.S. 24th Infantry Division came ashore on the island's eastern shoreline.

The jump over Corregidor was one of most difficult of the war. The Japanese defenders had been thoroughly pounded by a massive pre-assault air and naval bombardment, but few of the enemy were killed as they were deeply burrowed in the island's labyrinth of caves and tunnels. Those enemy defenders had been ordered by their commander, Japanese navy Cpt. Akira Itagaki, to fight to the death. Additionally, the winds over the drop zone were between 15 and 25 miles per hour—difficult for any parachutist to jump in.

Nevertheless, at 8:33 on the morning of February 16, the first paratroopers leapt onto the island, scattering widely over the drop zone. The Japanese were waiting, however, and a quarter of Jones's entire force was injured, wounded, or killed in the earliest moments of the assault (a full 50 percent loss had been estimated by U.S. military planners prior to the assault).

Fortunately for the Americans, Itagaki himself was killed during one of the initial clashes with the paratroopers.

Jones was soon making headway, beating back all counterattacks. A second reinforcing jump was made in the early afternoon, but many of the paratroopers were shot to death in midair. On the ground, resistance was stiff. For the next several nights, the enemy launched a series of banzai suicide attacks against the 503rd. The Japanese used every conceivable weapon at their disposal. A few even rushed, screaming at the Americans with bayonets fixed to the ends of long sticks. In many instances the fighting was hand to hand. Nevertheless, Jones's regiment held, and by February 27 all resistance had been eliminated. Between 4,000 and 5,000 men of the 6,500 Japanese garrison had been killed.

Upon returning to Mindoro, the 503rd was again ordered into action, this time to reinforce the U.S. infantry forces fighting on the island of Negros in the central Philippines. Landing by boat, the regiment encountered enemy resistance almost immediately. For the next five months, the men of the 503rd RCT battled the Japanese in the Negros mountains.

When the war ended in the fall of 1945, many of the 503rd's paratroopers were quickly withdrawn from the Pacific and shipped back to the States. Newly joined sky soldiers were transferred to other airborne units, most of them going to the 11th Airborne Division. On Christmas Eve, the storied 503rd was deactivated.

In February 1951, the unit was reactivated and designated as Company B, 503rd Airborne Infantry. It was then folded into the 11th Airborne Division at Fort Campbell, Kentucky.

Five years later, the 11th deployed to Germany. In July 1958, the division returned to Fort Campbell and was disbanded, and the orphaned 503rd was soon reassigned to the 82nd Airborne Division at Fort Bragg, North Carolina. With the 82nd, the 503rd was organized into two airborne battle groups.

In March 1963, the battle groups were redesignated as battalions, and the regiment was transferred to the newly established 173rd Airborne Brigade.

The 173rd shipped to Southeast Asia in 1965. As a consequence, the 503rd became the first Army regiment to deploy to Vietnam. There the 503rd was the vanguard force of the 173rd, fighting throughout the Vietnamese backcountry, making the first and only mass parachute jump of the war, and fighting in the terrible battle of Dak To.

In 1971, the 503rd shipped back to the States and was reassigned to 101st Airborne Division. The fabled 503rd was disbanded in 1984.

FIRST AIRBORNE TASK FORCE

The short-lived First Airborne Task Force was a division-size airborne unit comprised of American and British paratroopers and glidermen. Commanded by U.S. Maj. Gen. Robert T. Frederick, the task force was established on July 11, 1944, as a special combat element. Their responsibilities consisted of both reinforcing the Allied forces driving north from the Normandy beaches and blocking any enemy forces attempting to overrun the Allies.

Frederick was the ultimate airborne leader. He had commanded the First Special Service Force, a joint U.S.–Canadian unit, later made famous by the movie *The Devil's Brigade*. In Italy, Frederick's force had earned the sobriquet "the Black Devils of Anzio." Frederick himself was known by his men as "the Head Devil," a title he relished.

The "independent units" that comprised the First Airborne Task Force included the American 509th Parachute Infantry Battalion, the 463rd Parachute Field Artillery Battalion, the 517th Parachute RCT, the 550th Glider Infantry Battalion, the 551st Parachute Infantry Battalion, and the British 2nd Independent Parachute Brigade.

Code-named Operation Dragoon, the August 1944 invasion of southern France was initially known as Operation Anvil. The name was changed by British prime minister Winston S. Churchill, who purportedly claimed to have been "dragooned" into accepting the plan. Churchill in fact proposed an invasion of the Balkans.

In the predawn hours of August 15, 1944, the First Airborne Task Force launched an airborne assault on Le Muy, France, between Toulon and Cannes. Though fraught with danger, the mission was simple: Strike from the sky at dawn, capture the high ground, and destroy any enemy forces attempting to outflank the Normandy invaders.

Although the drops were less than accurate, the majority of the paratroopers landed in their predetermined drop zones. French resistance forces in the area were heartened by the landings and began attacking numerically superior German forces at every opportunity. German reinforcements hurrying to the front were often hit hard by surprise attacks from both the French partisans and the Allied paratroopers and glidermen. German garrisons in the immediate area either stood fast and surrendered or fled north in a near state of panic. Dragoon was a complete success, and the performance of the First Airborne Task Force was considered "exemplary."

In late November, the task force was disbanded, and each of its units were withdrawn to Soissones.

During World War II, a number of "phantom" combat divisions existed as a ruse intended to deceive the enemy into believing that the U.S. Army could field more divisions than it actually had. The ruse worked. German intelligence operatives in England spotted soldiers wearing the "phantom" division patches on their sleeves and reported these findings to Berlin. As a result, many combat-ready German units were either held in reserve or placed in defensive positions throughout Europe in anticipation of attacks by the divisions which only existed on paper.

Five of those "phantom" divisions were designated "Airborne": They included the 6th, 9th, 18th, 21st, and 135th Airborne Divisions.

509TH PARACHUTE INFANTRY BATTALION

The first American airborne unit to *jump* into combat was the U.S. Army's 509th Parachute Infantry Battalion (see Chapter 3). The battalion did so over North Africa on November 8, 1942. (Three months earlier, the U.S. Marine Corps' 1st Parachute Battalion became the first American airborne unit to engage an enemy in combat, but they did not jump into action; see Chapter 14.)

Although it is one of the most colorful units in American airborne history, the fact that it has gone through several confusing unit-numerical designations throughout its existence has created a number of published historical inaccuracies. On October 5, 1941, the battalion was formed and officially designated the 504th Parachute Battalion. In late February of the following year, the 504th (the future 509th) was redesignated the 2nd Battalion of the 503rd Parachute Infantry Regiment. On November 2, the battalion was renamed the 2nd Battalion of the 509th Parachute Infantry Regiment. Then on December 10, 1942, it became known as simply the 509th Parachute Infantry Battalion. The battalion held this designation for the remainder of the war.

After making headlines with the first three dramatic combat jumps in American airborne history—two over Algeria on November 8 and 15, and one over Tunisia on Christmas Eve, 1942—the battalion spent the next six months training in Algeria, Tunisia, and Morocco for the upcoming invasion of Sicily and Italy.

The third combat jump for the 509th was over Avellino, Italy, on September 14, 1943 (the same night elements of the 82nd Airborne Division were jumping over Salerno). The 509th's mission was to land behind enemy lines and sever German supply routes. Unfortunately, intelligence failed to report that the battalion would be jumping on top of a newly arrived German Panzer division.

"There was a full moon," wrote Lt. Col. Doyle R. Yardley in his diary. Yardley had replaced Col. Edson Duncan Raff, the first commanding officer of the 509th. "The fighting commenced immediately. Some of my men were killed while hanging in their parachutes in pine trees. As each parachutist dropped with either a rifle, a pistol or a carbine attached to his body, they were able to protect themselves to a certain extent."

Yardley was captured and many of his men were killed. For the survivors who had not been taken prisoner, the situation seemed grave. For the next couple weeks, the paratroopers of the 509th found themselves slugging it out with the enemy alone and with dwindling supplies of food and water. Though battered, the battalion survived and was able to reassemble at Salerno in late September.

On January 21, 1944, the 509th participated in the amphibious assault at Anzio. On the beach, the battalion stopped a savage German counterattack.

"Many dead paratroopers were strewn about," wrote William B. Breuer in *Geronimo!* "Some had heads blown off. Others had been bayoneted in their holes. A shell fragment had sliced off the face of a trooper. One five-o-niner lay dead with stumps for legs. Two trails of blood, one from each stump, indicated that he had tried to carry on the fight. A few badly wounded survivors, their faces ashen, were gasping for breath; they had been shot through the lungs."

Battalion surgeon Carlos C. "Doc" Alden, who described the battle as the "saddest day" of his life, wrote in his diary, "We brought out bits and pieces of bodies all afternoon and evening. Our men were greatly outnumbered, pinned down by artillery, assaulted by infantry, then tanks. But our guys stopped the German attack! They didn't budge an inch."

Over the next few months, the 509th became the first airborne unit to be awarded a Distinguished (later Presidential) Unit Citation, and one of its members became the first paratrooper to win the nation's highest honor.

On February 8, Cpl. Paul B. Huff, a Tennessee native and a future sergeant major, was leading a reconnaissance patrol when his team made contact with the enemy. During the ensuing action, Huff distinguished himself as a true airborne leader against a numerically superior enemy force. He ultimately won the Congressional Medal of Honor. A portion of his citation reads:

> Cpl. Huff volunteered to lead a six-man patrol with the mission of determining the location and strength of an enemy unit which was delivering fire on the exposed right flank of his company. The terrain over which he had to travel consisted of exposed, rolling ground, affording the enemy excellent visibility. As the patrol advanced, its members were subjected to small arms and machinegun fire and a concentration of mortar fire, shells bursting within five to 10 yards of them and bullets striking the ground at their feet. Moving ahead of his patrol, Cpl. Huff drew fire from three enemy machineguns and a 20 mm weapon. Realizing the danger confronting his patrol, he advanced alone under deadly fire through a minefield and arrived at a point within 75 yards of the nearest machinegun position. Under direct fire from the rear machinegun, he crawled the remaining 75 yards to the closest emplacement, killed the crew with his submachine gun and destroyed the gun. During this act he fired from a kneeling position which drew fire from other positions, enabling him to estimate correctly the strength and location of the enemy. Still under concentrated fire, he returned to his patrol and led his men to safety. As a result of the information he gained, a patrol in strength sent out

that afternoon, one group under the leadership of Cpl. Huff, succeeded in routing an enemy company of 125 men, killing 27 Germans and capturing 21 others, with a loss of only three patrol members. Cpl. Huff's intrepid leadership and daring combat skill reflect the finest traditions of the American infantryman.

In late March, the 509th was pulled off the line at Anzio and shipped to Great Britain. After 73 days of continuous combat action in Italy, the paratroopers needed some rest, but it was not to be. Enormous plans were in the works. While Allied seaborne and airborne forces were preparing for the largest amphibious operation in history (at Normandy, which was slated for June), the 509th had to immediately begin preparing for its role as the spearhead element of Operation Dragoon, the Allied invasion of southern France. Dragoon was slated for late summer. On the night of August 14 and 15, 1944, the 509th became the vanguard parachute force of the First Airborne Task Force's assault on Le Muy, France.

The following December, the paratroopers of the 509th were attached to the 101st Airborne Division during the Battle of the Bulge. Following the battle, the Army deemed the existence of independent airborne units to be inefficient in terms of command and control. Thus, the 509th was slated for deactivation. When the battalion was dissolved on March 1, 1945, only a handful of its original complement remained. Many had been killed or wounded so severely they were out of the war. Additionally, Army leadership felt that separate parachute infantry battalions were no longer necessary.

The remaining paratroopers were absorbed into the 82nd and 13th Airborne Divisions. Two years later, the 509th was reconstituted as Company A, 509th Parachute Infantry Battalion. In the spring of 1963, the battalion was redesignated the 1st Battalion of the 509th Infantry and assigned to the 8th Infantry Division.

Over the next decade (during the Vietnam War), the unit swelled to two battalions and was then reduced to one battalion in the summer of 1973. In the fall, the 8th Army released the 509th, and the battalion shipped to Vicenza, Italy.

In 1975, one company of the 509th returned to the States, where it was reconstituted as an airborne pathfinder company supporting the Army's

Aviation Training Center at Fort Rucker, Alabama. During the 1980s and 1990s, the battalion went through several redesignations and transfers.

Today the 509th is based at Fort Polk, Louisiana. There it serves as "the world's premier opposing force for light infantry and Special Operations Forces."

550TH AIRBORNE INFANTRY BATTALION

Being neither parachute- nor glider-trained, the 550th Infantry Airborne Battalion is one of the often-overlooked units in airborne history. The 550th was formed on July 1, 1941, at Fort Kobbe, an American post over-looking the Bay of Panama on the west bank of the Pacific side of the Panama Canal (Kobbe was established as a small defensive position in 1918). Command of the 550th was awarded to Lt. Col. Harris M. Melasky.

Although they were considered to be "airborne," the 550th's soldiers were not trained in either parachute or glider operations. Instead they were conventional infantrymen who were to aircraft-land on airfields seized by paratroopers. Air-landing infantry was not a new concept. The Germans had successfully employed such forces at the beginning of the war, and the 550th was based on the German model.

No initial plans had been made to deploy the battalion to either the European or Pacific theaters of operation. Instead, the soldiers were to remain in Panama as a regional quick reaction force. Increasing German influence in Central America caused alarm among Army planners, who felt a need to position combat forces below North America's southern flank. By 1943, however, concerns diminished, and the 550th was ordered to the States for glider warfare training.

In the summer of 1944, the 550th joined the First Airborne Task Force in Operation Dragoon, the Allied invasion of southern France. By that time, the battalion had been redesignated as the 550th Glider Infantry Battalion. But after landing in France in mid-August, the battalion's soldiers found themselves fighting as mountain troops in the French Alps. In November, the 550th was withdrawn and shipped to England.

When the Battle of the Bulge erupted in December, the battalion was attached to the 194th Glider Infantry Regiment of the 17th Airborne Division (see Chapter 8). For the next two months, the glidermen were heavily engaged and suffered terrible losses.

In February 1945, the remaining elements of the 550th—along with the 193rd Glider Infantry Regiment—were permanently folded into the 3rd Battalion of the 194th Glider Infantry Regiment.

551ST PARACHUTE INFANTRY BATTALION

A short-lived independent airborne unit, the 551st Parachute Infantry Battalion was so badly mauled during the Battle of the Bulge in 1944 and 1945 that its surviving elements were absorbed into the 82nd Airborne Division.

Established in Panama on November 1, 1942, the independent 551st Parachute Infantry Battalion replaced the first-ever U.S. airborne battalion, the 501st, which had become a part of the 503rd Parachute Infantry Regiment.

The initial plan for the 551st was that the battalion would launch a parachute assault on the Caribbean island of Martinique, a French territory. With France having been overrun and occupied by the Germans early in the war, U.S. military planners feared that Martinique might become an advance base for Nazi U-boats prowling the East Coast of North America. The operation was scrubbed when the island's French military commander surrendered.

The following August, the battalion left Panama for Camp Mackall, North Carolina. There the battalion's paratroopers honed their fighting skills until March 1944. The battalion then deployed to the Mediterranean where the unit's airborne skills were further sharpened at an airborne warfare training center in Sicily.

In August, the 551st joined other independent units of the First Airborne Task Force for the invasion of southern France—Operation Dragoon. Like their brothers in the 550th Airborne Infantry Battalion, the paratroopers of the 551st fought as mountain soldiers in the French Alps.

Soon thereafter, the 551st was attached to the 82nd Airborne Division. The battalion suffered heavy losses during the Battle of the Bulge in December 1944 and January 1945. Among the losses was Lt. Col. Wood Joerg, the battalion commander. Joerg was killed on January 7, when an enemy shell struck and detonated at the top of a tree under which he was standing.

Ultimately, the battalion's losses were so great that the unit was cannibalized. Its survivors were transferred to the 82nd Airborne.

THE TRIPLE NICKELS

In December 1943, an all-black paratrooper company—the 555th Parachute Infantry Company (Colored)—was formed. Soon thereafter the company was redesignated Company A of the 555th Parachute Infantry Battalion. Affectionately known as the "triple nickels," the unit was comprised of men who had been drawn from the ranks of the all-black 92nd Infantry Division, which was based at Fort Huachuca, Arizona.

Like their white brothers, the black soon-to-be-airborne soldiers attended jump school at Fort Benning, Georgia. There they performed well; 17 of the first group of 20 won their silver wings, despite alleged betting among the white parachute instructors that none of the black students would jump. But their successful completion of jump school was not enough. Institutional racism in the early 1940s also called into question their ability to perform well in armed combat.

As a consequence, the 555th was never deployed overseas. Instead, the paratroopers were sent to the western United States, where they participated in a series of forest fire-fighting operations code-named Firefly. During the operation, they served as smoke jumpers, dropping into—and fighting—forest fires set by Japanese incendiary balloons in the Pacific Northwest.

In 1948, the U.S. armed forces were completely integrated, and most of the men of the 555th were absorbed into the 82nd Airborne Division.

On July 26, 1948, President Harry S. Truman signed Executive Order 9981, which officially ordered the desegregation of the U.S. armed forces. A portion of the order reads: "It is hereby declared to be the policy of the President that there shall be equality of treatment and opportunity for all persons in the armed services without regard to race, color, religion, or national origin." The order also established "the President's Committee on Equality of Treatment and opportunity in the Armed Services."

CHAPTER 11

ARMY SPECIAL OPERATIONS FORCES

> These [Special Operations Forces] are the guys who can do a zillion push-ups, wear dirty underwear for six months, and kill a man with a ball-point pen.
>
> —*Charleston City Paper*, South Carolina, December 18, 2002

The U.S. Army has clearly been the pioneering branch of service in the realm of airborne-qualified special operations forces. This is due to five primary reasons:

- Infantry and cavalry units—two of the three primary branches of any army (artillery being the third)—have for centuries been the most logical repositories of candidates for special operations forces. This is because the basic function of any rifleman or horse-mounted soldier has always been to locate, close with, and destroy the enemy. At times, that function has required the infantryman and the cavalryman to engage the enemy in hand-to-hand combat, and close-quarters battle has always been a primary specialty of any special operations combatant.

- Over time, specific conventional infantry and cavalry units have evolved into unconventional units in order to effectively combat guerrilla forces.
- Most special operations throughout history have been conducted on land—the primary combat domain of any army.
- The U.S. Army was the first American service to begin training airborne forces for combat.
- Airborne forces are by nature "special," and one of the most effective means of clandestinely delivering special operations soldiers into an enemy-controlled area is by parachute.

SNAKE EATERS

Affectionately known as "snake eaters" because of their ability to live off the land, the U.S. Army's special operations forces have existed as a part of the American armed forces since the Colonial era. But the operational importance of such forces was ratcheted up during World War II (when only a handful of special operations forces were required to be parachute qualified). That importance increased dramatically during the early days of the Vietnam War (when many special operations forces were required to be parachute qualified) and to an almost exponentially greater degree since the terrorist attacks of September 11, 2001 (when nearly all special operations forces were and are required to be parachute qualified).

Special operations forces have been, and will continue to be, critical frontline elements in the war against terror. In the recent war in Iraq, the overwhelming success of conventional American forces in that country's urban environs was in large measure a result of U.S. Army—and to a lesser degree Navy, Marine Corps, Air Force, and even Central Intelligence Agency (CIA)—special operations elements. Not that all branches of service did not field extraordinarily capable special warfare units, but the U.S. Army simply fielded the largest number.

WHAT IT TAKES

Army special operations combatants—including Rangers, Special Forces (Green Berets), and Delta Force—are soldiers who are specially trained and equipped to conduct special military operations that the average soldier is not normally trained or equipped to carry out. In most cases, these special operations combatants are extremely fit young men (women are not permitted to join special operations forces in any branch of the military). With the exception of Rangers, whose average age is 21, the men are usually in their late twenties and early thirties. The consensus among most military experts is that men operating in a special warfare environment need to be at least that old to have the military experience as well as the emotional and intellectual maturity required for unconventional missions. That said, with the war on terror increasing the demand for special operatives in the field, younger men are indeed appearing in the ranks. But no matter the age, all special operations soldiers must be in far better physical condition than the average soldier in his early twenties.

Many special operations warriors are college educated. They are trained to handle a variety of weapons and sophisticated navigational aids. They are capable of operating at night, in poor weather conditions, independently of large regular units, and deep behind enemy lines. They must also be first and foremost paratroopers—the parachute being their basic means of noiseless delivery beyond moving on foot.

To accomplish the latter, all Army special operations soldiers must successfully complete the basic three-week course in static-line parachute instruction—or jump school—at Fort Benning, Georgia. But jump school for snake eaters is not enough.

At some point during the early part of their careers, special operations soldiers attend the U.S. Army's Military Free-Fall Parachutist School at either Fort Bragg, North Carolina, or the Yuma Proving Grounds in Arizona. The course is five weeks long and includes instruction and hands-on training in a variety of free-fall parachuting techniques. To accomplish this, soldiers jump from high altitudes with supplemental oxygen. They learn to stabilize their bodies in both airborne-simulating wind tunnels and in actual free fall. They learn to pack parachutes, free fall at night using only altimeters to determine their altitude, jump as individuals, jump as groups, recognize oxygen deprivation in themselves, properly deploy their parachute canopies at varying altitudes, and leap from a variety of different airplanes.

The free-fall school is demanding. No less than 30 free-fall parachute jumps—including day and night jumps with oxygen equipment and combat gear—must be made before the students become fully qualified military free-fall parachutists. Although most attendees are from the Army, students include members of the Navy, mostly SEa, Air, Land (SEAL) teams; the Marine Corps, mostly Force Recon; and the Air Force, mostly Combat Controllers and Pararescuemen.

During parachute training missions for special operations soldiers, static-line jumps without an official waiver are not permitted in an environment where cloud ceilings are less than 800 feet above-ground-level and/or winds are in excess of 13 knots. Additionally, static-line jumps—both training and operational—cannot be conducted at altitudes greater than 10,000 feet above ground level.

Free-falling high altitude/low opening (HALO) and high altitude/high opening (HAHO) training jumps cannot be conducted in an environment where cloud ceilings are lower than 500 feet above-ground-level. Training safety requirements dictate good ground visibility and winds less than 18 knots for HALO/HAHO jumps.

During combat operations, HALO/HAHO jumps cannot be conducted at altitudes greater than 36,000 feet above-ground-level without a waiver.
—*Special Operations Forces Reference Manual,* Army Command and General Staff College, 2000

In addition to jumping from a variety of fixed-wing airplanes, special operations soldiers often leap from rotary-winged helicopters.

"The biggest difference [between jumping out of airplanes and helicopters] is the longer delay on the static line," says Bob Mayer, a former Army Special Forces officer-turned-novelist and nonfiction author. "You count to six rather than four because the forward velocity of a chopper is slower than a plane." Additionally, the downward rotor wash is also a factor when jumping from helicopters.

Mayer says when he was in Special Forces over a decade ago helicopters were used as jump platforms for two primary reasons. "[The] big reason was it was such a pain in the ass to request an Air Force plane, and you had to do it so far in advance," says Mayer. "And it [the helicopter jump] was really only a training thing because it would make more sense to land in the chopper, or worst case, if [the] chopper could not land, you would fast-rope in." Fast-roping is a technique where special operations soldiers wearing heavy leather gloves slide down thick, nylon ropes from a hovering helicopter to the ground.

Whether jumping from an airplane or helicopter, Army special operations forces in the twenty-first century will continue to depend on their basic airborne skills as a primary means of delivery to the battlefield.

RANGERS

The Ranger Battalion is to be an elite, light, and the most proficient infantry battalion in the world, a battalion that can do things with its hands and weap-ons better than anyone. The Battalion will contain no "hoodlums" or "brigands," and if the battalion is formed of such persons, it will be disbanded.

—Gen. Creighton W. Abrams, U.S. Army Chief of Staff, 1974

Of the U.S. Army's three primary special operating forces, Rangers are considered the special operations spearhead of the Army's conventional forces. Rangers are all airborne qualified. They specialize in light infantry operations, night fighting, and airfield seizures. They can fight as regular army units and have done so in the past.

Independent forces of partisan or irregular soldiers have been loosely attached to regular American army forces (including British colonial forces) since the French and Indian War. But Rangers may well be the oldest American special operations force still in existence.

The first recorded Ranger operations in North America took place in the late seventeenth century. Then Capt. Benjamin Church led American Rangers against American Indian forces in a bloody conflict known as King Philip's War. The war, which lasted from 1675 to 1676, was a victory for the colonists in large measure because the colonial soldiers—including the Rangers— adopted unconventional, Indian-style methods of fighting, as opposed to the linear, pitched-battle tactics of European armies.

Eighty years later, in 1756, New Hampshire native Maj. Robert Rogers recruited and trained nine companies of colonial soldiers to fight as an independent Ranger Regiment for the British army during the French and Indian

War. Rogers taught his men the tactics of backcountry warfare he had personally gleaned from years of fighting Indians on the frontier. His methods were not new, but he was the first to incorporate them into a cohesive doctrine aimed at developing a professional force of elite fighting men. As part of that doctrine, he created his now-famous "standing orders"—a set of rules that stressed "operational readiness, security, and tactics."

Rules for Rangers

Young Airborne Ranger hopefuls in the U.S. Army of the twenty-first century are introduced to Rogers's colorful "standing orders" during the earliest part of their training. In so doing, Ranger instructors are not only able to connect their charges to a past steeped in military tradition, but, despite the grammatical gaffes, the orders can be applied to modern Airborne Ranger warfare:

1. Don't forget nothing.
2. Have your musket clean as a whistle, hatchet scoured, sixty rounds powder and ball, and be ready to march at a minute's warning.
3. When you're on the march, act the way you would if you was sneaking up on a deer. See the enemy first.
4. Tell the truth about what you see and what you do. There is an army depending on us for correct information. You can lie all you please when you tell other folks about the Rangers, but don't never lie to a Ranger or officer.
5. Don't never take a chance you don't have to.
6. When we're on the march we march single file, far enough apart so one shot can't go through two men.
7. If we strike swamps, or soft ground, we spread out abreast, so it's hard to track us.
8. When we march, we keep moving till dark, so as to give the enemy the least possible chance at us.
9. When we camp, half the party stays awake while the other half sleeps.
10. If we take prisoners, we keep 'em separate till we have had time to examine them, so they can't cook up a story between 'em.

11. Don't ever march home the same way. Take a different route so you won't be ambushed.

12. No matter whether we travel in big parties or little ones, each party has to keep a scout 20 yards ahead, 20 yards on each flank, and 20 yards in the rear so the main body can't be surprised and wiped out.

13. Every night you'll be told where to meet if surrounded by a superior force.

14. Don't sit down to eat without posting sentries.

15. Don't sleep beyond dawn. Dawn is when the French and Indians attack.

16. Don't cross a river by a regular ford.

17. If somebody is trailing you, make a circle, come back onto your own tracks, and ambush the folks that aim to ambush you.

18. Don't stand up when the enemy's coming against you. Kneel down, lie down, hide behind a tree.

19. Let the enemy come till he's almost close enough to touch, then let him have it and jump out and finish him up with your hatchet.

RANGERS AFTER THE REVOLUTION

A few years later, during the American Revolution (1775–1783), the Continental Congress called for the establishment of "six companies of expert riflemen" recruited from Pennsylvania, Maryland, and Virginia. This force, under the leadership of Continental Army Gen. Dan Morgan, was referred to by Gen. George Washington as a "Corps of Rangers." British Gen. John "Gentleman Johnny" Burgoyne would ultimately call them "the most famous corps of the Continental Army, all of them crack shots."

During the American Civil War (1860–1865), both the armies of the Confederate States and United States employed Rangers in combat, the most famous being Confederate Col. John Singleton Mosby's Rangers. When the war ended, Rangers and Ranger warfare slipped into a period of dormancy that lasted nearly 80 years.

When World War II erupted in the twentieth century, U.S. Army Maj. Gen. Lucian K. Truscott proposed to Gen. George C. Marshall that an American force modeled after the famed British commandos be created.

The result was the establishment of the 1st Ranger Battalion. The title "Ranger" was given to the battalion and its men because, according to Truscott, "the name *commandos* rightfully belonged to the British, and we sought a name more typically American." Command of the battalion was awarded to Capt. William Orlando Darby, soon to be Lt. Col. Thus, the unit would be affectionately referred to as Darby's Rangers.

Though not parachute trained at the time, the Rangers were wholly effective as spearhead units for advancing conventional forces and as special soldiers tasked with independent missions deemed too difficult for regular soldiers. They performed well in North Africa, Sicily, Italy, and on the heights above Normandy on D-day, June 6, 1944. There they proved to be experts in scaling cliffs, knocking out fixed positions, and defeating numerically superior enemy forces. It was at Normandy where the famous battlefield command—"Rangers, lead the way"—was first uttered.

Rangers also fought in Norway and in the Pacific theater of operations. When the war ended, the Ranger units were disbanded.

When the Korean War erupted in 1950, Rangers were again called into action. This time Ranger companies were established for "extremely hazardous" duty in the Far East. The Rangers themselves were recruited from among the ranks of airborne soldiers.

"The training was extremely rigorous," according to Fort Benning's official *Ranger History*. Much of the training focused on "amphibious and airborne—including low-level night jumps—operations, demolitions, sabotage, close combat, and the use of foreign maps. All American small arms, as well as those used by the enemy, were mastered. Communications, as well as the control of artillery, naval, and aerial fires, were stressed. Much of the training was at night."

On the Korean peninsula, the companies were attached to regular infantry divisions. In that capacity, they performed magnificently in combat against both Communist North Korean and Chinese forces. The Rangers were considered "nomadic warriors," moving from one line regiment to the next. They operated "out-front ... scouting, patrolling, raiding, ambushing, spearheading assaults, and as counterattack forces to regain lost positions." So ferocious were the Rangers in action that the Chinese referred to them as "Devils."

CHAPTER 11: ARMY SPECIAL OPERATIONS FORCES

In June of 1954, the Army's 475th Infantry (the World War II–era Merrill's Marauders, a unit trained similarly to Darby's Rangers) was redesignated the 75th Infantry (the future 75th Ranger Regiment).

During the Vietnam War, many U.S. soldiers, as well as a handful of sailors, airmen, and Marines, were trained as Rangers. Nearly all Rangers or Ranger candidates were airborne qualified, and Airborne Rangers served in a variety of combat infantry roles, but no Ranger *units* actually existed until 1969. Then the famous Long Range Reconnaissance Patrols (LRRPs) were redesignated "Ranger" units. The LRRPs—pronounced *lurp*—were already performing Ranger types of missions, though not all LRRP team members had attended Ranger school. Non-Ranger-qualified LRRPs were permitted to remain with the units, but new LRRPs had to first become Rangers.

In 1973, as America was preparing to disengage itself from Southeast Asia, Gen. Creighton W. Abrams, who replaced Gen. William C. Westmoreland as commanding general of U.S. forces in Vietnam, ordered the formation of Ranger battalions. They were the first such battalions since World War II, and new members had to be airborne qualified.

Despite the unpopularity of the Vietnam War, Airborne Rangers and other airborne-qualified special operations forces flourished during that period. In fact, both the Ranger and Special Forces communities within the Army served to boost the flagging esprit de corps of what could have been a completely demoralized draftee force.

"In the sixties, Harvard wouldn't fight. Vietnam failed to stack up to the stuffy standards of an acceptable conflict, whatever that was," says John Temple Ligon, a former Airborne Ranger-qualified artillery officer. "For me, though, Ranger School was indeed home to the elite."

Ligon's Ranger "buddy" in Ranger school was a U.S. Navy SEAL and a graduate of Colgate, where he played varsity Lacrosse. "He was one bad son of a bitch, but a gentleman," recalls Ligon. "And that gentleman made me look good in the hand-to-gland pit. Ranger School was a confidence course that taught us to lead and to throw down hard, all kinds, and we left knowing we could do whatever we had to do."

In January 1974, the 1st Ranger Battalion of the 75th Infantry (the descendents of Merrill's Marauders) was established. In July, the battalion made its first parachute jump over Fort Stewart, Georgia. Three months later, the 2nd Battalion was formed.

(Defense Visual Information Center)

U.S. Army Rangers patrol during a field training exercise in the 1980s.

In October 1983, the airborne descendents of Robert Rogers's Rangers made a dangerous low-level combat jump over the Point Salinas airport on the Caribbean island of Grenada. The jump, part of Operation Urgent Fury, the invasion of Grenada, was conducted at 500 feet above the surface of the earth. The Rangers were under fire the entire time, but once on the ground, they quickly seized the airport and later rescued American citizens at a nearby medical school. The Rangers then conducted additional combat operations—in conjunction with U.S. Marines, elements of the 82nd Airborne Division, and a variety of special operations forces—successfully eliminating all resistance on the island.

The following year, a third battalion and a headquarters company rounded out the 75th Infantry, which then became known as the 75th Ranger Regiment. Since then, the 75th Rangers have served in combat operations throughout the world, most notably in Panama (1989), Iraq (1991), and Somalia (1993).

In Somalia, a joint U.S. Army force of Rangers, Delta Force commandos, supporting helicopter crews, and a handful of Navy and Air Force personnel were tasked with apprehending several senior members of

Somali warlord Gen. Mohamed Farah Aidid's inner circle from their city-center stronghold in the seaport capital of Mogadishu. The air-ground team achieved its initial search-and-snatch objective. Unfortunately, two Black Hawk helicopters were shot down, and the situation quickly degraded into the most violent firefight for American forces since the Vietnam War. In the end, 18 American soldiers and aircrewmen were killed, 73 were wounded, and the remaining members of what was operationally known as Task Force Ranger were barely able to escape with their lives. The operation spawned Mark Bowden's best-selling book, *Black Hawk Down*.

Eight years later, in the earliest days of the current war against terrorism, Rangers launched the first airborne assault against Taliban and al Qaeda positions in Afghanistan. Because of their unique skills and airborne capability, Rangers have since participated in numerous operations throughout the world.

Today numerous soldiers throughout the ranks of the modern U.S. Army are Airborne Ranger qualified. The largest single unit of Rangers, however, is the 75th Ranger Regiment and its 1st, 2nd, and 3rd Battalions. Generally speaking, each of the battalions' Rangers operate in company-strength units of roughly 150 to 200 men. They are also capable of operating in smaller teams, and as individuals if need be, in order to complete—as Rangers are fond of saying—the "Ranger mission."

Ranger School

Becoming an Airborne Ranger is not an easy task. U.S. Army Rangers must be either airborne qualified or willing to attend jump school before being assigned to one of the 75th's three battalions. Ranger school itself lasts two months and is divided into three phases: Benning, Mountain, and Florida.

The Benning Phase consists of two subphases. The first subphase is held in an area of Fort Benning known as Camp Rogers (named for Robert Rogers). There Ranger hopefuls are tested for physical strength, quickness, endurance, and agility. Extended marches, land navigation, water survival, and confidence tests are conducted. Bayonet and hand-to-hand fighting skills are honed, basic demolitions are taught, and patrolling skills are enhanced.

The second subphase of the Benning Phase is held at nearby Camp William O. Darby. There much of the training focuses on patrolling, including ambushes, reconnaissance, and direct action. Boxing and other close-combat skills are taught, as is the conduct of airborne and air assault operations.

The Mountain Phase at Camp Frank D. Merrill, near Dahlonega, Georgia, follows the Benning Phase. At "Mountain," Ranger candidates develop the mountaineering skills—climbing, rappelling, and navigating—needed to operate in extremely rugged terrain. They are also forced to function with little food or sleep.

Following the Mountain Phase, Ranger candidates are transported to Camp James E. Rudder, near Eglin Air Force Base, Florida, for the final phase, known as Florida. There the candidates build on what they've learned in the previous two phases and develop skills in small boat handling, ship-to-shore operations, and a variety of skills needed to fight and survive in a tropical/swamp environment. Florida culminates in an exhausting 10-day field training exercise.

Upon successful completion of the Ranger school, soldiers are authorized to wear the coveted Ranger shoulder tab.

Building on the traditions of both *Robert Rogers' Standing Orders* of 1759 and the *American Airborne Creed* (see Appendix C) is the current Ranger Creed:

Recognizing that I volunteered as a Ranger, fully knowing the hazards of my chosen profession, I will always endeavor to uphold the prestige, honor, and high esprit de corps of the Rangers.

Acknowledging the fact that a Ranger is a more elite soldier who arrives at the cutting edge of battle by land, sea, or air, I accept the fact that, as a Ranger, my country expects me to move further, faster, and fight harder than any other soldier.

Never shall I fail my comrades. I will always keep myself mentally alert, physically strong, and morally straight and I will shoulder more than my share of the task whatever it may be, one hundred percent and then some.

Gallantly will I show the world that I am a specially selected and well-trained soldier. My courtesy to superior officers, neatness of dress, and care of equipment shall set the example for others to follow.

Energetically will I meet the enemies of my country. I shall defeat them on the field of battle for I am better trained and will fight with all my might. Surrender is not a Ranger word. I will never leave a fallen comrade to fall into the hands of the enemy and under no circumstances will I ever embarrass my country.

Readily will I display the intestinal fortitude required to fight on to the Ranger objective and complete the mission, though I be the lone survivor.

Like conventional airborne units, each of America's 3 Ranger battalions can deploy anywhere on the planet within 18 hours, arriving on target from land, sea, or air, the latter being the reason why all Rangers must be parachute qualified. (In an extreme time-critical situation, one Ranger company with battalion command-and-control elements can deploy in nine hours or less.)

The primary Ranger missions include direct action operations, raids, the rescue and recovery of personnel and equipment, and conventional or special light-infantry operations, the latter being a reflection of the wishes of Gen. Abrams. He wanted his Rangers to be "the best light infantry unit in the world" and "a standard bearer for the rest of the Army." That they are.

SPECIAL FORCES (GREEN BERETS)

Fighting soldiers from the sky
Fearless men who jump and die

—The first lines of the famous "Ballad of the Green Berets" (1966) by Staff Sgt. Barry Sadler and Robin Moore

de oppresso libre (translated as "to free the oppressed")
—Motto of U.S. Army Special Forces

The second component of Army special operations is the Army's Special Forces, made famous by John Wayne in the Vietnam-era movie *The Green Berets* and during the post-Vietnam years by Sylvester Stallone, who played former Special Forces soldier John Rambo in the movie *First Blood.*

Special Forces combatants—best known as Green Berets—operate as both independent fighters and military advisors, each specializing in a particular area of expertise (that is, medicine, communications, or weapons). As advisers, Green Berets are tasked with training resistance or guerrilla troops in foreign countries. In nearly all cases, they must be able to speak at least one language other than English, and they are trained for a variety of missions such as direct action, guerrilla operations, special reconnaissance, and counterterrorism. Like nearly all modern special operations forces, volunteers for Army Special Forces must be either parachute trained or they must volunteer for airborne training.

Though American army special operations have been conducted since the Colonial Wars, the origins of modern Army Special Forces began with the 1st Special Service Force in World War II. In early 1942, Royal Navy Vice Admiral Lord Louis Mountbatten, the British chief of Combined Operations, presented to U.S. Army Chief of Staff Gen. George Catlett Marshall a prototypical mountaineering vehicle developed by Geoffrey N. Pike, a British civilian contractor. Pike's vehicle—code named Plough—was designed to move men across snow-covered, mountainous terrain and was considered for use against enemy hydroelectric plants based in Norway. Soon thereafter American manufacturing facilities began developing similar vehicles for similar missions. But Gen. Marshall also realized that a special force of men would have to be developed to carry out the raids with the vehicles. To accomplish this, he chose U.S. Army Lt. Col. Robert Tryon Frederick to organize, train, and lead a special force recruited from the ranks of the American and Canadian armies. The result was the hybrid U.S.–Canadian force known as the 1st Special Service Force.

Comprised of three regiments, the 1st became a separate branch of service, specializing in mountain warfare (including rock-climbing and snow-skiing), amphibious landing operations, demolitions, and parachuting. The force became known as "the Devil's Brigade," and their insignia were a pair of crossed arrows, a symbol of the Indian scouts who rode out and reconnoitered in advance of U.S. and Canadian army forces during the nineteenth-century Indian wars. Today the crossed arrows comprise the centerpiece of the U.S. Army Special Forces insignia.

Frederick's force, led by both American and Canadian officers, conducted a number of special operations in the Aleutian islands, North

Africa, and Europe. But the 1st was disbanded in early 1945, and many of its American members were transferred to conventional Army Airborne divisions such as the 82nd and the 101st. The war ended soon thereafter.

A second series of organizations that have since been referred to as the lineal ancestors of modern Army Special Forces were the "Operational Groups" of the wartime Office of Strategic Services (OSS). (The OSS was the wartime predecessor organization to the modern CIA.)

On December 23, 1942, a directive issued by the U.S. Joint Chiefs of Staff ordered OSS director William J. "Wild Bill" Donovan to "organize 'operational nuclei' to be used in enemy occupied territory." These "nuclei," to be known as Operational Groups (OGs), closely paralleled modern Special Forces teams in both organization and function. Trained as commandos who could link with, develop, and provide leadership for friendly underground forces, OGs required each of their members to be airborne qualified. Like other OSS elements, OGs were disbanded by the war's end.

In June 1952, the first Cold War–era special operations unit was established at Fort Bragg, North Carolina. The unit, the 10th Special Forces Group, was formed under the leadership of Col. Aaron Bank, a former operative in the OSS. Bank recruited from the ranks of those who had previously served in "the Devil's Brigade," Army Rangers, conventional airborne units, and various covert action teams within the OSS. All of Bank's men were parachute trained.

The 10th Group's official mission was "to infiltrate by land, sea, and air [thus the necessity for airborne training] deep into enemy-occupied territory and organize the resistance/guerilla potential to conduct special forces operations, with emphasis on guerilla warfare."

Though the early Special Forces claimed much of the same lineage as the Rangers, Bank differentiated between the two forces. Focusing his group's training on what he referred to as "more complex subjects" geared toward "more comprehensive missions and complex operations," Bank created a force capable of operating far outside the unconventional box. His men would be able to do things outside the realm of the "Ranger mission," if that was possible. Rangers, in fact, believed then, as they do today, that nothing falls outside of the scope of the "Ranger mission."

According to the Department of the Army's Vietnam Studies manual, the 10th "became the nucleus of the Special Warfare Center," now known as the John F. Kennedy Special Warfare Center and School.

The following November 1952, the 10th was divided into two groups. Half the force was sent to Bad Tolz, Germany, carrying with it the original numerical designation. The other half remained at Fort Bragg and was renamed the 77th Special Forces Group. Over time additional Special Forces Groups were established, and the 77th ultimately became known as the 7th.

Throughout the 1950s, a number of Special Forces "basic unit" sizes were considered. Initially, a 15-man team similar to what was employed by OSS Operational Groups during World War II was tested. Eventually, the current 12-man Operational Detachment—Alpha (ODA) or "A-Team" was adopted as the basic-level Special Forces organization.

> U.S. Army Special Forces Groups are organized into independent teams of 12 men each, known as Operational Detachments Alpha or ODAs. Though they occasionally vary in size, rank structure, and particular mission focus, a typical ODA is commanded by a captain, assisted by a warrant officer, and manned by two weapons sergeants, two engineering sergeants, two communication sergeants, and two medical sergeants. An operations sergeant and an intelligence specialist round out the team. Each is cross-trained in the others' area of expertise and can cover for another if necessary.

Bank's new organization was soon put to the test. In June 1956, the first ODA was dispatched to South Vietnam as advisors to both the South Vietnamese army and other indigenous forces who were fighting the Communist Vietcong guerrillas and regular forces of the North Vietnamese army. Other Special Forces detachments soon followed.

While the Army was experimenting with both the organizational structure of its new Special Forces Groups and their new advisory role in Vietnam, a handful of Special Forces soldiers began wearing berets without official authorization (see Appendix F).

Early in his administration, President John F. Kennedy—a former naval officer who appreciated the value of airborne and special operations warfare—got wind of the unauthorized beret-wearing phenomenon but wanted to see it for himself. On October 12, 1961, Kennedy visited the Special Warfare Center at Fort Bragg, North Carolina. There he was greeted by Brig. Gen. William Pelham "Bill" Yarborough and the Center's cadre, all of whom at Yarborough's direction were wearing green berets. The president was wholly impressed and later that day approved the wearing of the green beret for all Special Forces soldiers.

As the numbers of ODAs increased in Vietnam, the Army decided to organize them all under one roof. Thus was created the legendary 5th Special Forces Group.

By 1969, the height of America's involvement in the war, some 3,800 Special Forces soldiers were stationed in Southeast Asia. Special Forces performed a variety of roles in the country: from training the South Vietnamese to fight, to teaching conventional American forces how to "out-guerrilla the guerrilla," to building schools and providing medical care to indigenous people living in the backcountry.

In 1971, the 5th returned to Fort Bragg. Other groups were deactivated, and the stigma attached to the war in Vietnam caused Special Forces to fall out of favor in the public eye. No longer was "snake eater" an affectionate term. In fact, it carried with it the same negative connotation as "baby killer," one of the many harsh monikers leveled at all American servicemen during the last few years of—and the period immediately following—the Vietnam War.

The pendulum began to swing in the other direction in November 1979. That month, 53 Americans at the U.S. Embassy in Tehran, Iran, were taken hostage by a group of Iranian revolutionaries. After months of unsuccessful negotiations aimed at securing the hostages' release, Army special operations forces, including members of the Green Berets, attempted to free them by force in April 1980. The mission failed before it got off the ground (see "Delta Force" later in this chapter), but the anger over the hostage-taking and the bold rescue attempt by U.S. forces generated a resurgence of American national pride.

During the early years of Ronald Reagan's presidency, national pride was further fueled by an administration intent on "bringing America back" after Vietnam and the Iranian hostage crisis. The president focused much of his efforts on rebuilding the prestige and fighting capability of the

American military. Military recruiting numbers increased dramatically. The popularity of elite airborne units such as Special Forces began to rebound, and once again, it was "cool" to be a soldier.

> Building on the traditions of both Robert Rogers's Standing Orders of 1759 for Rangers, the current Ranger Creed, and the American Airborne Creed (see Appendix C) is the U.S. Army Special Forces Creed:
>
> I am an American Special Forces soldier. A professional! I will do all that my nation requires of me.
>
> I am a volunteer, knowing well the hazards of my profession. I serve with the memory of those who have gone before me: Roger's Rangers, Francis Marion, Mosby's Rangers, the first Special Service Forces and Ranger Battalions of World War II, the Airborne Ranger Companies of Korea. I pledge to uphold the honor and integrity of all I am—in all I do.
>
> I am a professional soldier. I will teach and fight wherever my nation requires. I will strive always to excel in every art and artifice of war. I know that I will be called upon to perform tasks in isolation, far from familiar faces and voices, with the help and guidance of my God.
>
> I will keep my mind and body clean, alert and strong, for this is my debt to those who depend upon me. I will not fail those with whom I serve. I will not bring shame upon myself or the forces. I will maintain myself, my arms, and my equipment in an immaculate state as befits a Special Forces soldier.
>
> I will never surrender though I be the last. If I am taken, I pray that I may have the strength to spit upon my enemy. My goal is to succeed in any mission—and live to succeed again.
>
> I am a member of my nation's chosen soldiery. God grant that I may not be found wanting, that I will not fail this sacred trust.
>
> *De Oppresso Libre!*

Since Vietnam, Special Forces have played key roles in all of America's wars and military expeditions throughout the world, from the invasion of Grenada in 1983 to the beginning of the twenty-first century. In many cases, Special Forces soldiers were on the ground and working closely with indigenous forces and local militia units long before any other U.S. forces were deployed into the region.

Winning the Green Beret

Since the terrorist attacks of September 11, 2001, the Army has begun recruiting candidates for Special Forces from "the street." Faced with a new kind of enemy—ruthless and elusive terrorists—the demand for special operations combatants has increased. Consequently, the Special Forces community is actively seeking candidates to join their ranks. It's a new phenomenon within Special Forces. For years, candidates for Green Beret training were recruited from the ranks of experienced, proven soldiers.

Today a 17-year-old civilian may enlist in Special Forces, and in just 23 weeks he may be a fully trained paratrooper entering the Special Forces Qualification Course, also known as the "Q" course. Those 23 weeks include Army basic training, infantry school, basic airborne jump school, a primary leadership development course, a special operations preparatory course, and the rigorous 23-day Special Forces Assessment and Selection (SFAS) course.

Begun in 1989, the SFAS tests the physical and mental abilities, as well as the emotional stability, of potential Special Forces men to see if they have what it takes to earn the coveted Green Beret. Officers and enlisted soldiers who pass the SFAS must then successfully complete jump school if they have not already done so.

Then comes the real test. Whether a new recruit or an experienced soldier, all candidates for Special Forces must attend the Q course. Encompassing five phases—individual skills, military occupational specialty skills, collective training, language training, and the infamous SERE (Survival, Evasion, Resistance, and Escape) school—the Q course varies in length depending upon the soldier's particular area of expertise. During individual skills training, for example, potential Green Berets further hone their land navigation, small unit tactics, and weapons skills.

Military occupational specialty (MOS) training follows, focusing on the particular skills the Green Beret candidate is best suited for. This is based on one's personal background, experience, desires, and mental and physical aptitude.

Following MOS training is collective training. During this phase, candidates work closely together developing skills in unconventional warfare, direct action, and airborne and air assault operations. This phase includes an unconventional warfare exercise in the deep pinewoods of North Carolina.

Language training is an important phase of the Special Forces Qualification Course. A number of languages are offered, but these days the Army is looking for a few good Arabic and Korean linguists.

The last phase, and what some graduates contend is one of the toughest training courses in the military, is the SERE course. SERE teaches students how to endure hardship and torture during captivity and to avoid becoming or escape from being a prisoner of war (POW). SERE training is purposefully harsh but is critical to the Special Forces soldier who—because of the nature of special operations missions—is highly susceptible to becoming a POW in the real world.

Upon winning the Green Beret, the new Special Forces soldier reports to an ODA, but training does not end there. Special Forces men are in a constant state of training to enhance their skills, not the least of which is airborne experience. Special Forces soldiers are often making jumps from varying altitudes in a variety of day and night conditions.

The "mothership" of many special operations parachutists, Combat Talons are C-130 transport aircraft that have been fitted with special instruments for special and covert operations. The aircraft's onboard electronic countermeasures systems and terrain-following radar enable it to fly extremely low, avoid enemy detection, and penetrate deep behind enemy lines. As such, the aircraft can deliver and retrieve special operations personnel and equipment in hostile territory. The Combat Talons are also able to refuel special operations helicopters at night while its crews use night-vision goggles.

Former Special Forces officer Bob Mayer made the majority of his army jumps at low altitude from the ramps of MC-130 Combat Talon aircraft with small teams of special operations parachutists. On occasion, Mayer jumped with larger, more conventional airborne units, such as the 82nd Airborne Division. "The biggest difference I remember between jumping with Special Forces and jumping with the 82nd is that we [in Special Forces] treated the jump as just part of the entire process, whereas the 82nd got really pumped for the jump itself," says Mayer.

Despite their myriad special combat skills, at the heart of every Special Forces soldier is that he is first and foremost a U.S. paratrooper. This fact is further evidenced in the chorus of the famous "Ballad of the Green Berets" by Staff Sgt. Barry Sadler and Robin Moore:

> Silver wings upon their chest
> These are men, America's best
> One hundred men will test today
> But only three win the Green Beret

DELTA FORCE

The third component in Army special operations is the super-secret Delta Force. Although the U.S. military promotes their special operators as being the best of the best, little is known about the men of Delta Force other than the fact they are considered experts in the realm of counterterrorism, hostage rescue, prisoner snatches, and surgical direct-action strikes against similarly trained enemy forces. Known officially as the 1st Special Forces Operational Detachment Delta (unofficially as the "D-boys"), Delta operatives are all airborne qualified.

Delta Force was the brainchild of U.S. Army Col. Charles "Chargin' Charlie" Beckwith. In the early 1960s, Beckwith proposed the idea of a special operations force within the U.S. Army modeled on the famed British Special Air Service (SAS). Beckwith tirelessly pushed Army leadership for his SAS-style force, but his overzealous lobbying efforts—including ignoring his chain of command and appealing to a U.S. senator—soon earned him a second nickname, "Crazy Charlie."

Col. Charles Beckwith was one of the most aggressive special operations officers in the post–World War II American Army. During the Vietnam War, then-Maj. Beckwith commanded Project Delta, a special reconnaissance force within the 5th Special Forces Group. Seeking men for his unit, he published a flyer that read, "Wanted: Volunteers for Project Delta. Will guarantee you a medal, a body bag, or both." Although it was a U.S. Army special operations unit commanded by Beckwith, Project Delta was unrelated to the future Delta Force.

After the Army bandied about Beckwith's idea and temporarily activated an interim counterterrorist force known as *Project Blue Light*, the colonel got his wish. In October 1977, Delta Force became a reality.

The creation of Delta was a result of American military forces needing some means of effectively countering the growing threat of global terrorism. Like the terrorists, the men of Delta Force would combat their opponents using whatever means available—no matter how unorthodox or dark those means might be.

Just over two years after its establishment, America's first combat mission involving Delta Force was launched. As previously mentioned, in November 1979, a group of Iranian revolutionaries stormed the U.S. Embassy in Tehran and took 53 Americans hostage. Over the next six months, the administration of U.S. President Jimmy Carter tried to secure their release diplomatically, but to no avail. It became apparent that military force would be required.

On the night of April 24, 1980, Beckwith and 132 newly trained Delta soldiers—calling themselves "Charlie's Angels"—landed via C-130 transport planes in a remote stretch of the Iranian desert some 200 miles from Tehran. The location, known as "Desert One," was a staging area and rendezvous point for the Delta commandos and eight RH-53D Sea Stallion helicopters from the aircraft carrier USS *Nimitz* stationed in the nearby Gulf of Oman. The plan called for the Sea Stallions to refuel at Desert One. Once the helicopters were gassed up, the Delta soldiers would climb aboard and the force would fly to an advance location in the mountains closer to Tehran. The following night, "Charlie's Angels" were slated to enter the Iranian capital in four trucks, drive to the embassy, and free the hostages. Navy helicopters would swoop in, pick them up, and fly to a nearby airfield that would have been previously seized by Army Rangers. But it was not to be.

Following a number of operational glitches, from missed deadlines to malfunctioning helicopters, the mission was aborted. Making matters worse, as the rescue force began to withdraw from the staging area, one of the helicopters operating in nighttime black-out conditions accidentally hovered into a C-130. A terrific explosion followed that killed or badly burned several soldiers, Marines, and Air Force personnel.

Nothing could have been worse. The American armed forces were still licking their wounds from the Vietnam War and the subsequent poor public perception of the military that followed. But military planners and decision makers on Capitol Hill realized that running away from one disaster to the next without addressing the problems head-on was not the responsible thing to do.

Instead, the decision was made to ramp up U.S. special operations forces, specifically counterterrorist-capable units such as Delta Force and the Navy's SEAL teams.

Soon thereafter, the Joint Special Operations Command (JSOC) was created. The JSOC was a joint-command group comprised of the special operations elements of the Army, Navy, and Air Force, with the Marine Corps deliberately avoiding membership. Marines believe the entire Corps is singularly "special," and Corps leaders have often been opposed to the idea that their Marines might fall under small unit combat command of leaders from other branches of service (see Chapter 14).

When President Ronald Reagan moved into the White House in 1981, Delta Force began a rapid expansion, ultimately tripling in size from 100 men in 1979 to approximately 300 by the mid-1980s. In the ensuing years, Delta commandos purportedly participated in every major American war and overt military expedition, as well as some unknown operations, from the invasion of Grenada in 1983 to the war against terror and the Iraqi war in the twenty-first century.

During the tragic 1993 Task Force Ranger operation in Somalia (refer to the previous "Rangers" section), Delta Force soldiers quickly assumed battlefield leadership positions even though higher-ranking officers were present. Had they not, the number of American dead might well have been higher than it was.

Tragically, 18 young American soldiers were killed, some of whom were members of Delta. In fact, two Delta commandos, Gary I. Gordon and Randall D. Shugart, were posthumously awarded the Congressional Medal of Honor for their actions in attempting to rescue the crew of one of the two downed Black Hawk helicopters.

D-Boys in the New World

Though exact figures are not known, Delta Force members in the twenty-first century number at least 800. Aside from the force's counterterrorism focus, Delta is unique in that it draws its numbers not only from the ranks of Army Rangers and Special Forces, but Navy SEALs and Marine Corps Force Reconnaissance men, although most Delta members *are* from the Army.

Much of Delta's organization, training, methods, and operations are classified. What is known is that Delta Force is organized into three squadrons of between 75 to 150 men each. Prior to joining a squadron, a D-Boy must first undergo a rigorous mental, physical, and emotional assessment process. This is followed by a punishing six-month Operator's Training Course. Once assigned to a squadron, individual D-Boys are capable of performing myriad special tasks, including throat-slitting, safe-cracking and lock-picking, hot-wiring automobiles, and rescuing hostages. Additionally, they are trained in self-contained underwater breathing apparatus (SCUBA), helicopter fast-roping, and parachute insertion.

All members of Delta Force must attend the Army's jump school at Fort Benning either before joining Delta or once selected. Most have, in fact, attended jump school long before being considered for Delta, but jumping out of airplanes as a basic static-line parachutist is not enough. Delta Force soldiers must be free-fall qualified and be able to perform HALO jumps, HAHO jumps, and dangerous jumps over water.

Like their Ranger and Special Forces brethren, the most important symbol of Delta's demanding and dangerous work is the "silver wings" badge of the airborne soldier.

PART 3

NAVAL PARACHUTISTS

CHAPTER 12

NAVAL SPECIAL WARFARE FORCES

The only easy day was yesterday.
—Unofficial motto of U.S. Navy SEALs

[SEAL] training is extremely demanding, both mentally and physically, and produces the best-trained combat swimmers in the world.
—Official United States Special Operations Forces Posture Statement 2000

In the fifth century A.D., Athenian general Thucydides said, "We must remember that one man is much the same as another, and that he is best who is trained in the severest school." Had Thucydides lived in the twenty-first century, he almost certainly would have agreed that one of the world's "severest schools" is the half-year of absolute hell endured by young American sailors who dream of wearing the coveted trident badge and gold parachute wings of the U.S. Navy SEALs.

Arguably, no commando in the world is better trained than a Navy SEAL. Some military experts contend that Delta Force operatives and certain foreign military special operators such as those of Great Britain's Special Air Service (SAS) and Royal Marine Commandos are equally skilled, or in some cases better. Perhaps, but certainly no underwater combatant could be superior to a SEAL.

Officially, SEALs (an acronym for SEa, Air, Land) trace their origins to the Navy frogmen, the hybrid Army-Navy Amphibious Scout/Raider teams, and even the Marine Raiders of World War II.

U.S. Navy Capt. Phil H. Bucklew, who oversaw the Amphibious Scout/Raider training program during World War II, is considered to be the "father of naval special warfare." The primary mission of Bucklew's Scout/Raiders was to conduct preinvasion reconnaissance of the beaches and guide the amphibious assault waves ashore at Normandy on D-day, June 6, 1944. Though little has been published about their role in the Normandy invasion, the efforts of Bucklew's Scout/Raiders were key to the overall success of the landings.

In fact, the roots of modern SEAL teams date back to the misty fleets of the ancient world, when the first barefoot and bare-chested swimmer slipped undetected into a harbor and made a mental note of the size and number of the enemy's ships. Such has always been one of the most basic means of gathering Naval intelligence. During the sixteenth century when masted warships came of age and great fleets were sent on expeditions far from their home shores, ships' crews were comprised of a mixed bag of impressed and often undependable seamen, dependable professional sailors, officers, and loyal-to-the-death Marines. Whenever crewmembers were needed for special landing or boarding parties, Marines and the toughest professional sailors were the combatants of choice. In this sense, the ancestors of modern Navy SEALs are in many ways also the ancestors of modern U.S. Marines. But the direct predecessors to the SEALs are Bucklew's men and the Navy's famous underwater demolition teams (UDTs).

SEALs themselves did not become a reality until January 1, 1962. After President John F. Kennedy ordered the expansion of America's unconventional warfare capabilities, SEAL Teams One and Two were formed. Soon thereafter, SEALs were conducting reconnaissance missions in Vietnam, and by 1966 they were involved in direct-action operations against North Vietnamese soldiers and Vietcong guerrillas.

SEALs performed magnificently as intelligence gatherers and covert-action combatants during the Vietnam War. They faced detractors, however, particularly from within the ranks of the Navy's celebrated ground force—the U.S. Marine Corps.

"Some of the problems were in the recon Marines' perception that the SEAL training level was inadequate," wrote acclaimed author Michael Lee Lanning, a retired U.S. Army infantry officer, in his book, *Inside Force Recon*. "Deeper prejudices existed as well. Maj. James McAlister and Capt. Patrick J. Ryan, both commanders of the First Force Reconnaissance Company in the early 1960s, were not supporters of the SEALs in general." In 1963, both officers expressed concern that operational SEALs were lacking not only in the number and variety of parachute jumps, but none had jumped at night, and only one had attended the Army's Ranger training program.

Additionally, Ryan argued SEALs were encroaching on Marine responsibilities. "I personally feel SEAL is infringing on USMC missions by moving inland from the high-water mark," Ryan was quoted as saying in Lanning's *Inside Force Recon*. "Representative type USMC corporals and sergeants could, allowing three to six months for scuba/para training, while polishing patrolling and demolition techniques along the way, arrive at the same degree of proficiency that SEAL Team members currently will take a minimum of 18 months to obtain."

According to Lanning, the Marines' complaints "were valid at the time," but SEALs under aggressive leadership ultimately proved themselves to be indispensable as special operators. Only a handful were airborne qualified during the Vietnam War, but that would change in a few short years.

MODERN SEALS

Though SEALs had proven their value in Southeast Asia, conventional-minded Navy planners believed reconnaissance-gathering frogmen to be a hyper-expensive luxury in the post-Vietnam world. Helicopters, they believed, had rendered traditional amphibious landings obsolete. Landings by Marines and other amphibious forces could skirt the dangerous beaches and land inland behind the enemy's shore defenses. Consequently, SEALs would not be needed. But in the aftermath of the ill-fated hostage rescue attempt in the Iranian desert (see Chapter 11), the demand increased for special operations forces with terrorist-thwarting skills.

The SEALs had already been developing a counterterrorist capability—similar to what the U.S. Army was doing with Delta Force—but after the Iranian hostage debacle, SEAL planners ratcheted up their training and methods several notches.

In October 1980, SEAL Team Six was established. Like Delta, Team Six was a mysterious organization. All that was known about its members was that they were experts in combating terrorists and were all airborne qualified. Moreover, the positive public perception of the Navy's new supermen was just what the American military had been seeking after Vietnam and Iran. Eventually, SEAL Teams Three, Four, Five, Seven, Eight, and Ten joined One, Two, and super-secret Six.

Commanded by a Navy commander (the equivalent of an Army lieutenant colonel), a SEAL Team is comprised of eight operational SEAL platoons and one headquarters element. The SEAL platoon, commanded by a Navy lieutenant (the equivalent of an Army captain), is comprised of 16 SEALs. The platoon is capable of dividing into two squads or four two-man elements.

The SEALs' first big show after Vietnam was during Operation Urgent Fury, the 1983 American invasion of the Caribbean island of Grenada. The overall invasion was a success, but a number of costly operational glitches and near disasters occurred among several of the units involved, not the least of which was the SEALs.

On the night of October 23 and 24, a group of SEALs and a handful of Combat Controllers (an elite Air Force Airborne element trained to set up drop zones and coordinate airborne assaults, among other special operations responsibilities) made an open-water parachute drop off Point Salinas on the southern tip of Grenada.

The SEALs were responsible for reconnoitering the airfield and determining the condition of the runway as well as the location and strength of nearby enemy forces. The combat control airmen were tasked with clandestinely positioning radar beacons on the airfield so that incoming airborne forces would be able to locate the drop zone. Sadly, four SEALs drowned in the heavy seas, and the others were ordered to withdraw before completing their mission.

During a later phase of Urgent Fury, a group of SEALs was dispatched to rescue British Governor-General Sir Paul Scoon, his wife, and staff, all of whom were being held hostage by Grenadian forces at the Scoons "Government House" residence. As two helicopters loaded with SEALs roared over the capital toward the mansion, the enemy holding Scoon prepared to fight back. Once on site, the helicopters came under heavy fire. The first of the two choppers was hit and forced to withdraw. The second, also hit, managed to hover over the mansion long enough for the SEALs to fast-rope to the ground. The SEALs quickly overwhelmed the Grenadian guards and stormed the residence, but they soon found themselves under heavy fire from the enemy's armored personnel carriers. Hours later, the SEALs, the Governor-General, and his wife were rescued by a small force of U.S. Marines. Scoon and his wife were then helicopter-ferried to an offshore American warship.

Meanwhile, another force of SEALs was dropped by helicopter at a radio transmitter site near the Grenadian capital of St. George. There the SEALs were to launch an assault to capture the transmitter without damaging it. They were successful in reaching the site and overpowering the guards in a brief hand-to-hand struggle, but an enemy counterattack forced the SEALs to withdraw.

Correcting their initial operational problems, SEALs have conducted special missions in every American military operation and expedition since Grenada. Many such missions have been carried out independently of other U.S. military forces and many are still classified and unknown to the public. In 1988, SEAL Team Six, the counterpart to the Army's Delta Force, became a subordinate entity under the Naval Special Warfare Command. Team Six was then renamed the Naval Special Warfare Development Group, or "Dev Group."

(Defense Visual Information Center)

A U.S. Navy SEAL on a combat-shooting course in Kuwait, 1998.

In the aftermath of the terrorist attacks of September 11, 2001, SEALs were among the first men on the ground fighting Taliban and al Qaeda forces in Afghanistan. SEALs have also been among the first Americans killed in combat in the current war against terrorism, a tragic reality of their extremely dangerous missions. Consequently, SEAL training is rigorous. Some SEALs have even admitted that their training was more intense than the experience of a real operation. SEAL training instructors are extremely safety conscious, but injuries among SEAL candidates are common and in a few cases some candidates have drowned or died as a result of hypothermia.

"THE SEVEREST SCHOOL"

All SEAL hopefuls must first attend Basic Underwater Demolition/SEAL (BUD/S) training: six months of the unequivocally toughest schooling on Earth.

The program begins with an eight-week "basic conditioning" course known as "First Phase." This includes swimming, running, obstacle courses, small boat seamanship, and myriad other exercises for physical and mental toughening. During First Phase, the SEAL candidate must also endure an seemingly impossible five and a half days known as "Hell Week." To the outsider, this may sound like nothing more than a mildly intense fraternity initiation. It is far more than that. During Hell Week, SEAL candidates are allowed only four hours of sleep ... not per day, but for the entire week.

"Second Phase," or the "diving course," follows. This, too, lasts eight weeks and includes self-contained underwater breathing apparatus (SCUBA) training as well as other exercises carried over from First-Phase training. The difference is that the intensity increases in Second Phase.

"Third Phase" is an intense indoctrination in the art of ground combat, known in the SEAL lexicon as "land warfare." During this five-week training cycle, SEAL hopefuls must master land navigation, small-unit tactics, combat patrolling, rappelling, marksmanship, and military explosives. The physical conditioning requirements during this phase are even more intense than Second Phase.

The completion of these phases does not yet make a SEAL. Like all other special operations forces, the parachute is a primary means of insertion into a hostile or combat environment. Consequently, all SEAL candidates must attend the U.S. Army's three-week basic parachute course at Fort Benning, Georgia. But the decades-old tradition of sailors attending army jump school may soon be coming to an end.

As of this writing, according to Naval Reserve Lt. Comdr. Mark Divine of NavySEALs.com, SEALs are scheduled to begin parachute training in-house. The reasoning is simple: "Fort Benning takes these young men out of the SEAL training loop for too long," says Divine. "We [the Navy] can achieve in roughly four days what they do in the first two weeks of jump school."

Beyond that, there is some friction that exists between many of the basically trained soldiers and the tough-as-nails SEALs.

During a conversation about Army jump school, Divine says he and former SEAL Jeff Smith humorously recalled their own experiences.

"Well, five guys got kicked out," said Smith. "They went back to the teams to get yelled at."

"That happens every class," Divine responded. "Jump school is funny because there are 3,000 Army pukes and 16 SEALs. All the 'black hat' instructors will focus on the SEALs, because SEALs will go there *en masse* as a class and literally run circles around the rest of the formations. The Army will do their formation trots and the SEALs will get bored. To get their workouts they will try to get dropped down for extra pushups."

SEALs have often been some of the most colorful characters to attend the Army's jump school at Fort Benning. During brief periods of down time, while their counterparts from other services were sound asleep in their bunks, SEALs have been known to muster the strength for nocturnal runs and calisthenics. A few have purportedly climbed the famous 250-foot towers for fun.

Nevertheless, jumping from an airplane is a gut-check experience, even for a SEAL.

"The standing joke is that your first jump will be a night water jump, because your eyes will be closed and you will pee your pants," says Divine. "However, most SEAL airborne students learn to enjoy jumping and are eager to get to free-fall school when in the teams." It is not uncommon for individual SEALs to log more than 1,000 free-fall parachute jumps and between 50 and 100 static-line jumps during their Navy careers (see Appendix G).

After graduating from jump school, SEAL candidates are authorized to wear the silver wings of the basic parachutist. Once they have completed additional jumps from a variety of different aircraft, they are awarded the gold wings of the Navy/Marine Corps parachutist.

After BUD/S and jump school, SEAL candidates are assigned to at least six months of on-the-job training/probationary service with one of the teams. The candidate becomes a SEAL only after veteran SEALs deem him worthy of serving with the teams.

Twenty-first-century Navy SEALs have several real-world areas of responsibility. They are tasked with conducting unconventional warfare, direct action, special reconnaissance (usually amphibious), foreign internal defense, and counterterrorism operations.

> Unconventional warfare [a SEAL Team specialty] includes guerrilla warfare, subversion, sabotage, intelligence activities, evasion and escape, and other activities of a low visibility, covert, or clandestine nature. When unconventional warfare is conducted independently during conflict or war, its primary focus is on political and psychological objectives. When unconventional warfare operations support conventional military operations, the focus shifts to primarily military objectives.
> —*Special Operations Forces Reference Manual,* Army Command and General Staff College, 2000

Additionally, several "collateral activities" are also conducted by the Navy's special operations sailors, such as security assistance, antiterrorism, counter-drug operations, the rescue and recovery of personnel and equipment, and what the U.S. Defense Department officially refers to as "maritime-specific special operations to meet U.S. Navy fleet-specific requirements."

Although SEALs today are all airborne qualified, they are not the only American sailors who wear parachute wings. A few non-SEAL naval officers and enlisted personnel win slots to attend jump school each year. Those sailors jump out of perfectly good airplanes either for the career-broadening airborne experience or because they are assigned to parachute-qualified units from other branches of service. Many of those sailors are Navy medical corpsmen who serve in Marine Corps parachute units, such as Force Recon or the Air Naval Gunfire Liaison Companies (ANGLICO).

PART 4

MARINE CORPS PARACHUTISTS

CHAPTER 13

LEATHERNECKS AND BLOOD WINGS

If the Army or the Navy ever look on Heaven's scenes, they will find the streets are guarded by United States Marines.

—From the third verse of the "Marines Hymn," often attributed to Henry C. Davis, 1911

Marines have it (pride) and benefit from it. They are tough, cocky, sure of themselves and their buddies. They can fight, and they know it.

—Gen. Mark W. Clark, U.S. Army

Since their inception on November 10, 1775, U.S. Marines have been developing a reputation as some of the world's most committed fighters. During the first half of the twentieth century, that reputation, combined with the leathernecks' exploits at places like Haiti, Vera Cruz, and Belleau Wood, added fuel to an already burgeoning mystique that would grow to near mythic proportion. Consequently, when the Marines began training parachutists in the early 1940s, the potential enemies of the United States took a keen interest. An armed American parachutist dropping from the sky was unsettling enough to an enemy soldier, but the possibility that the man at the end of the parachute might be a U.S. Marine was enough to strike the enemy with paralyzing fear. This fear of Marines has always been a very real force multiplier for America.

> *Leatherneck* is a synonym for "Marines." The word is derived from the fact that early U.S. Marines wore a heavy leather collar (or stock) around their necks. The collar was designed to deflect knife and saber cuts in combat. American sailors, amused that Marines had to wear the uncomfortable devices, began referring to Marines as "leathernecks," and the nickname stuck.

"Marines are mystical," writes best-selling author Tom Clancy in *Marine: A Guided Tour of a Marine Expeditionary Unit*. "They have magic." It is this same magic, Clancy adds, that "may well frighten potential opponents more than the actual violence Marines can generate in combat." But it works. During the first Persian Gulf War, more than 100,000 Iraqi soldiers were deployed along the Iraqi and Kuwaiti coastlines in anticipation of a landing by some 17,000 U.S. Marines. Terrified by what they had been taught about the combat prowess of Marines, the Iraqi soldiers had nicknamed them "angels of death."

The legendary repute of American Marines stems from a number of factors. The Marine Corps is the smallest branch of the U.S. armed forces, and it is undeniably the most unique. Although it is organized as a separate armed service, it is officially a Naval infantry/combined-arms force overseen by the Secretary of the Navy.

For much of its 228-year history, the Corps has functioned as the Navy's security force and amphibious infantry arm. It was signed into existence in an eighteenth-century Philadelphia alehouse. Its first captain was the barkeep and its first commandant, the owner of a neighboring pub. Its first recruits, a motley band of Rhode Island toughs and a few cutthroats who frequented the two drinking establishments. Soon thereafter, Marines joined ships' crews, where they were tasked with a variety of functions. In combat, they manned Naval guns, served as sharpshooters in the mast riggings, and led boarding and landing parties. Their very presence aboard ship also prevented impressed sailors, living in harsh conditions, from jumping ship or mutinying.

Over time, Marines evolved into amphibious warfare experts whose divisions today serve as forward-deployed rapid reaction forces. The performance of individual Marines and Marine units on the battlefield has always been exemplary. In combat, Marines are capable of bringing all elements— airplanes, helicopters, artillery, armor, and infantry—against an enemy. Marines guard the White House and a variety of other sensitive posts around the nation, as well as U.S. Embassies around the world. The Corps' infamous "boot camp"—more of a rite of passage than a training program—is the longest and toughest recruit indoctrination program of any of the military services. Consequently, Marines who graduate from boot camp believe themselves to be superior to other soldiers—a fact that has spawned resentment among the ranks of elite soldiers from other branches, particularly within the airborne community.

Although it fields airborne-trained special operations forces, the Corps has previously refused—sometimes almost arrogantly—to be a part of the U.S. Joint Special Operations Command (JSOC). The Marine Corps' justification is simple. Marines believe the entire Corps to be singularly "special," and Corps leaders have often been opposed to the idea that their Marines might fall under the command of small-unit combat leaders from other branches of service.

The Marine Corps' tight approach to being an independent special operations force has loosened somewhat in the days since the September 11, 2001, terrorist attacks on the United States.

On June 20, 2003, Marine Corps Special Operations Command Detachment One, under the command of Lt. Col. Robert J. Coates, was activated at Camp Pendleton, California. Within days, some 86 leathernecks—most of whom were airborne-qualified—began training for special missions in the war against terror. Training included working closely with Navy SEALs at the nearby Naval Amphibious Base in Coronado.

The Marine Corps' new Detachment One is a 12-month experiment. After one year, the Corps will decide whether or not it will remain an independent special operating force or become a permanent member of the U.S. JSOC.

Beyond the issues of extra-service command, Marines have historically been masters of the art of public relations, a fact that prompted U.S. President Harry S. Truman to once state that Marines "have a propaganda machine that is almost equal to [Soviet premier Joseph] Stalin's." Indeed, although other branches of service have lured recruits to their ranks with promises of "a great way of life," being "all you can be," and money for college, the Marines have simply asked "for a few good men" who might "pack the gear" to join their exclusive organization.

Not surprisingly, numerous unsuccessful efforts have been made—primarily on the part of some Army and Navy officers—to have the Corps disbanded or absorbed into either the Army or Navy. Most of these efforts took place in the first half of the twentieth century. But even after the Marines' stellar performance in World War II, U.S. Army Brig. Gen. Frank A. Armstrong condescendingly referred to the Corps as "a small bitched-up army talking Navy lingo."

As late as 1997, Assistant Secretary of the Army Sara Lister took aim at the Marines. "I think the Army is much more connected to society than the Marines are," Lister said before a public gathering at Harvard University's John M. Olin Institute for Strategic Studies on October 26. "The Marines are extremists. Wherever you have extremists, you've got some risks of total disconnection with society. And that's a little dangerous."

Of course, the Commandant of the Marine Corps demanded an apology. Lister was fired, and Marines secretly said among themselves, "Yes, we are extremists. We are dangerous. That's why we win wars and are feared throughout the world."

Nevertheless, the Corps has become a wholly American institution in the eyes of most Americans. The public simply loves its Marines, extremism and all. But this same "extremism" continues to lend itself to harsh criticism from many opponents like Lister with a blanket distaste for the masculo-military culture of Marines. This extremism has not escaped the Corps' elite parachute forces.

BLOOD WINGS

The same year Lister lambasted the Corps, a videotape of a parachute "blood-winging" ritual at Camp Lejeune, North Carolina, was obtained by the media and subsequently aired on CNN. The video, which showed a closed-door ritual where Marines were bloodied by their fellow leathernecks, shocked the general public and resulted in punitive actions taken against those involved.

During the ceremony, Marines having just completed their final qualifying jump before winning their gold wings had their new wings pounded into their chests. The Marines being initiated into the "brotherhood" of the gold wings were ordered to stand at attention while the wings, with quarter-inch metal spikes protruding from the back, were pinned to their T-shirts. The clasps had been removed from the wings' spikes, the points resting against the initiates' bare chests. Then one by one, senior Marine parachutists approached the men and pounded the wings with heads, fists, and open palms into their chests. Though crying out in pain, the Marines on the receiving end continued to stand fast as blood streamed down their white T-shirts. Other units have in fact also blood-winged their Marines upon their return from jump school with silver wings.

Like all other forms of hazing and physical abuse, blood winging is officially forbidden, but the Corps, more than any other branch of service, has been plagued with problems related to hazing and extreme forms of punishment stretching back to the eighteenth century.

The worst recorded incident took place in 1956 at the Marine Corps Recruit Depot, Parris Island, South Carolina. There several recruits were force-marched by one of their drill instructors into a tidal estuary known as Ribbon Creek and drowned. The Ribbon Creek deaths and other incidents of unchecked maltreatment of recruits and junior Marines have added to both the mystique and condemnation of the Corps. But for the most part, except for blood-winging initiations, parachute-qualified units have been able to skirt the problems of hazing and maltreatment found in some Marine units. The reasoning: Because they have jumped out of airplanes, the most junior Marine parachutists have earned the respect of their more senior comrades.

EARLY MARINE PARACHUTISTS

Like the Army, the Marines first began developing plans for combat parachute units in May 1940, just days after German airborne forces successfully attacked defenses in Belgium and Holland.

The commandant of the Marine Corps, Maj. Gen. Thomas Holcomb, sent a note to the Chief of Naval Operations, Adm. Harold Raynsford Stark, requesting the help of naval attaches stationed in Europe. The attaches, he believed, would be able to observe the fledgling parachute programs of friendly nations. They would also have closer access to news related to the ongoing airborne operations of potential enemies. Holcomb was, in his own words, "intensely interested" in acquiring intelligence on foreign parachute forces, particularly those of the Germans.

The following month, the Army's famous parachute test platoon was formed at Fort Benning, Georgia. It would be another five months before the Marine Corps would begin forming a similar training platoon, and only then after senior Marine officers noted the success of both U.S. Army Airborne training and Great Britain's parachute training program, which also had been launched in June. Additionally, Adm. Stark's attaches were feeding Holcomb excellent information regarding German parachute forces in combat, as well as the development of French and Soviet airborne forces. Holcomb ordered the Corps' Division of Plans and Policy to draw up plans for a battalion of "Marine parachute troops."

Maj. Gen. Thomas Holcomb's Marine parachute battalion was given three official functions. The battalion was to serve as ...

1. A reconnoitering and raiding force with a limited ability to return to its parent organization. This assumed that the objective was sufficiently important to warrant the sacrifice of the force.
2. A spearhead or advance guard to seize and hold strategic installations or terrain features until the arrival of larger forces.
3. An independent force operating for extended periods, presumably in a guerrilla role in hostile territory.

If one were to read between the lines of the first function, one would realize that the Marines in special circumstances might be justifiably tasked with conducting suicide missions. But Marines being Marines, young leathernecks were still eager to join the "chutes."

The Marine Corps' parachute program got off to a somewhat inglorious start when three Marine officers—Capt. Marion L. Dawson and 2nd Lts. Walter S. Osipoff and Robert C. McDonough—were ordered to

Hightstown, New Jersey. They were there to inspect the famous 250-foot World's Fair towers the Army was using for training. During a test jump from one of the towers, Dawson broke his leg.

On October 26, 1940, the Marine Corps launched its first parachute training class at Marine Barracks, Lakehurst Naval Air Station, New Jersey. As the Army had experienced in June, there was no shortage of volunteers flocking to the silk. In the end, Osipoff, McDonough, and 38 enlisted Marines were chosen and began a training regimen based on the model of the Army's "parachute test platoon." The only notable difference was that the Army required its airborne students to be at least 21 years old, whereas the minimum age for a Marine parachutist was only 18.

The Marine *approach* to combat training has always been regarded as the world's most demanding. Not surprisingly, the Marine "parachute school detachment" was nothing less than unforgiving. Future "Paramarines," as they were known, began the first phase of their training—ground school—at Lakehurst.

During World War II, Marine parachutists were often referred to as "Paramarines." However, the term was eventually dropped, as it sometimes connoted part-Marine or sometimes-Marine, and the Marine parachutists were certainly "all-Marine."

The Marines then moved to the tower training phase where they practiced jumping from the 250-foot towers in Hightstown. (The same towers were eventually purchased by the Army and moved to Fort Benning, Georgia.) By early November, the leathernecks had completed tower training and were transferred to Quantico, Virginia, for further physical conditioning.

By December, those who continued to meet and exceed the Corps' rigorous standards for parachute troops were leaping from airplanes and Navy dirigibles. Those who hesitated at the moment of truth were quickly eliminated from the program. After six jumps, as opposed to the Army's required five, the Marines earned their parachute wings.

The Marine Corps briefly experimented with gliderborne forces. During the conception stages, the Corps leadership planned for two-battalion glider force. This would have required 150 pilots and 75 gliders. In June 1942, two months before the 1st Parachute Regiment was to make airborne history on the Pacific islet of Gavutu, the Corps was making planes to field a division-size force of glider troops. This would have required some 3,400-plus pilots and nearly 1,400 gliders. But it was not to be. Like the Marine parachute battalions, the glider forces were short-lived. At its peak, Marine glider force strength was 36 pilots, 246 riflemen, and 21 gliders—all of which formed two squadrons of Marine Glider Group 71.

The Marines' parachute training program expanded to include parachute training schools at both New River, North Carolina, and the U.S. Marine Base at San Diego, California.

By the summer of 1941, several small units of combat-ready Marine parachutists had been formed. In late July, newspapers reported that some "40 heavily armed young gentlemen of the Marine Corps" had nearly disrupted a 17,000-man Army combat training exercise near Fredericksburg, Virginia. Four Douglas R3D-2 transport planes—each marked with the Corps' distinctive eagle, globe, and anchor, the emblem of Marines—roared over Nottingham airport at 750 feet. The airport was in the center of the Army's maneuver area, and the soldiers on the ground looked up to see men leaping from the aircraft with their parachutes blossoming above them.

Observing officers and military umpires, who were grading the Army's exercise, drove straight to the airport to find out what was going on. Upon arrival, they found that the Marine parachutists under the command of Capt. Robert H. Williams had landed and seized the airport. The Army was furious. The Marines were simply cavalier about the whole thing. A reporter for *Time* magazine made the observation that Marine parachutists were "a notably tough-looking outfit among Marines, who all look tough."

Within a year, Williams would lead many of the same men against a real enemy—the Japanese.

THE FIRST COMBAT ASSAULT BY AMERICAN AIRBORNE FORCES

Although the U.S. Army has always trained and maintained the largest number of paratroopers and is the only branch of service to field division-size airborne forces, the honor of being the first American airborne force in combat goes to the Marines, but with a qualifier. The Marine parachutists did not actually jump into battle. They made an amphibious landing in classic Corps fashion. (The Army's 509th Parachute Infantry Battalion was the first American airborne force to make a "combat jump.")

The landing took place in August 1942 on the Western Pacific islets of Gavutu and Tanambogo. Seizing the islets was part of the campaign to strike and hold the nearby island of Guadalcanal (the first American ground offensive of World War II).

The overall invasion was comprised of five landings. The main force, comprised of men from the 1st and 5th Marine Regiments of the 1st Marine Division, went ashore on Guadalcanal. The second force, a Marine Raider battalion, stormed nearby Tulagi. Elements of the 2nd Marine Regiment were responsible for Florida Island, and responsible for landing on and seizing Gavutu and Tanambogo was the 1st Marine Parachute Battalion under the command of Maj. Robert H. Williams, the former captain who led the seizure of the airport from the U.S. Army the previous summer.

Williams's parachutists fought magnificently during the first two years of America's involvement in World War II (see Chapter 16). By late 1943, the Paramarines had grown from a single battalion into four battalions, which together comprised the crack 1st Parachute Regiment. Greater require-ments elsewhere in the Corps, however, demanded that the regiment be disbanded and Marine parachute training schools closed. The parachutists were transferred to regular Marine infantry units.

POSTWAR MARINE PARACHUTISTS

In the 10 years that followed World War II, few Marines became airborne qualified. Those who did attended Army jump school at Fort Benning. But in the wake of the Korean War (1950–1953), accurate predictions on the part of Corps leaders regarding unconventional warfare and new demands for flexibility in the area of battlefield delivery began to put a premium on airborne training.

In 1956, an entire Marine platoon attended jump school at Fort Benning. As Marines would soon discover in Vietnam, one of the most effective means of delivering small teams of leathernecks into their areas of responsibility was by parachute. Although no Marine parachute regiment would again be formed, smaller units and special teams would indeed require their men to be parachute-qualified.

Today Marines still use parachutists for a variety of missions. Most of them are in the realm of special operations, such as Force Recon (deep reconnaissance) teams and Reconnaissance Battalions (scouting elements for Marine divisions). Other Marine parachute units and billets include Air Naval Gunfire Liaison Companies (ANGLICO), radio battalions, parachute riggers, and air delivery personnel.

Some Marines have served on detached duty with Army, Navy, and Air Force parachute units. Others, such as Col. Jeff Bearor, have served with the Central Intelligence Agency (CIA). Working as a counterterrorism officer, Bearor has conducted operations with the CIA throughout the world.

With 178 military jumps and about 30 civilian jumps under his belt, Bearor has also had his share of parachute emergencies. The most exciting one, he contends, was during a High Altitude/Low Opening (HALO) jump at night. "I was free falling, and when I tried to open my main chute at 2,500 feet I had a major malfunction," Bearor recalls. "I couldn't see the ground because it was dark, but I knew I was losing altitude as I momentarily struggled to deploy my reserve because I could see my altimeter."

Bearor's reserve did not initially deploy. Just under 1,000 feet from the surface of the earth, it worked. Another eight seconds and Bearor would have been killed. "It definitely increased the pucker factor," he says with a smile.

Bearor earned his jump wings because his job has often required parachuting skills, but a limited number of Marines not assigned to parachute duties also attend jump school each year. In many cases, those Marines will never jump again, but they have the career-enhancing airborne experience. The distinguishing feature of those Marines is that they wear the silver wings of a basic parachutist throughout their entire careers. Unlike Army and Air Force personnel who upgrade to a starred parachute badge after 30 jumps, Marines and sailors conceivably need only 5 additional jumps beyond airborne training to earn their coveted gold wings.

"Technically, that's correct, but within those jumps there have to be a number of *qualifying* jumps," says Marine Col. Gary S. Supnick, former ANGLICO commander and current commanding officer of the Headquarters and Service Battalion at Parris Island, South Carolina. "Different types of jumps must be made from different types of aircraft at varying altitudes, with and without equipment, at night, et cetera." Additionally, Marine parachutists receiving their gold wings can do so only after serving in a jump billet or with a jump unit for 90 days.

Consequently, the vast majority of senior Marine officers and noncommissioned officers adorned with silver wings have only made five military jumps. An Army or Air Force parachutist, however, could have conceivably made 29 jumps yet still rate the basic parachutist badge.

Although Marines are quick to say that the most important piece of their uniform is the "eagle, globe, and anchor," the individual leathernecks who wear the wings of a parachutist do feel themselves a cut above their peers.

CHAPTER 14

1ST PARACHUTE REGIMENT

The Marine parachute units of World War II never jumped into combat, but they did make an indelible impression on the history of the Corps.

—Lt. Col. Jon T. Hoffman in *Silk Chutes and Hard Fighting*

U.S. Marines have always prided themselves on being the "first to fight." And the Corps' early parachute forces put teeth into that boast.

On August 7, 1942, exactly eight months to the day after the Japanese attack on Pearl Harbor, the Marines launched America's first ground offensive of World War II. The offensive began in the southern Solomon Islands with the amphibious assault on—and subsequent battle for—Guadalcanal. The campaign included simultaneous landings on the nearby islets of Tulagi, Gavutu-Tanambogo, and Florida Island.

The primary landing force, which consisted of elements from the 1st and 5th Marine Regiments led by Maj. Gen. Alexander A. "Sunny Jim" Vandegrift, struck the island of Guadalcanal. A second force made up of elements from the 2nd Marine Regiment under Vandegrift's second in command, Brig. Gen. William H. Rupertus, stormed the south coast of Florida Island (separated from Guadalcanal by a

20-mile-wide channel). Just south of Florida Island was the 2-mile-long atoll of Tulagi and 2 tiny islets, Gavutu and Tanambogo, which were connected by a narrow 500-yard causeway.

Tasked with capturing Tulagi was a newly formed 1st Marine Raider Battalion and the 2nd Battalion, 5th Marines, both under the command of Lt. Col. Merritt Austen Edson. Known affectionately by his peers and subordinates as "Red Mike" for his red hair, Edson also had his detractors who felt he harbored something of a blood lust. To those Marines, he was referred to as "Mad Merritt the Morgue Master."

The task of seizing Gavutu and Tanambogo fell to the 1st Marine Parachute Battalion under the command of Maj. Robert H. Williams. The "chutes" battalion, as it was known, was the seedling unit that would ultimately become the 1st Parachute Regiment. The battalion was also the first airborne unit from any branch of service to see combat in World War II. They didn't jump into action, however; they hit the beach from landing craft in traditional Marine fashion.

The Marines struck Guadalcanal on the morning of August 7, catching most of the Japanese defenders asleep and wholly unprepared. Soon thereafter Rupertus's leathernecks began attacking Florida Island and Tulagi.

The first of Williams's three-company waves of parachutists rushed ashore just after noon, but they did not fair well. "The first boatloads were decimated on the beach," said J. Robert Moskin in *The U.S. Marine Corps Story*. "In two hours, one in ten Marines was a casualty and most of the rest were pinned down."

A basic tenet in military doctrine is that amphibious assault forces should always outnumber defenders at least three to one. Not so for the Paramarines at Gavutu, who knew they were up against a larger force but were banking on their superior training and esprit de corps to carry them through the day. In the end, it did, but not without them suffering significant losses. Many of the Marines were killed before disembarking from the landing craft. Others were cut down in the surf or on the beach.

On the beach, the Marines attempted to regroup and attack the Japanese positions point by point. The Japanese, however, were deeply entrenched in a labyrinth of connecting tunnels and reinforced caves, and they were prepared to fight to the death. From various fortified positions, the defenders blasted away at the invading forces and waited for the Americans to come to them.

Several minutes into the fight, Maj. Williams himself organized an assault to capture a strong enemy position on Hill 148, Gavutu's commanding heights. Leading the charge, Williams took a bullet through the chest. Coughing and gasping for breath, he ordered his men to continue forward. His executive officer, Maj. Charles A. Miller, immediately assumed command of the parachute battalion.

One of the more enterprising Marines, Capt. Harold L. Torgerson, decided that the best way to knock out the strong Japanese positions was to literally blast them out. With 30 sticks of dynamite tied together, Torgerson rushed one cave as fellow parachutists provided covering fire. Near the mouth of the cave, Torgerson "lit the fuse, shoved the TNT in amongst the Japanese—and ran like hell," wrote William B. Breuer in *Geronimo!*

Time and again, Torgerson repeated his assault against the enemy strongholds. In one instance, his wristwatch was shot away. Another time, a bullet creased his buttocks. In his final attack, he attached a five-gallon gasoline can to his dynamite sticks. The force of the ensuing blast was so terrific that the entire island seemed to quake. Scrambling to his feet, the cocksure Torgerson, his trousers blown off, faced his Marines and said, "Boy, that was a pisser, wasn't it?" From that day forward, Torgerson was known as the "Mad Bomber of Gavutu." He would go on to command the 3rd Marine Parachute Battalion.

While Torgerson was on his one-man bombing campaign, other Marine parachutists were slugging it out in close quarters with the enemy. Cpl. George F. Grady charged eight enemy soldiers with a Thompson submachine gun. He shot two. His weapon jammed, so he clubbed to death a third. He then dropped the Thompson and whipped out a trench knife, killing two more. In the end, Grady was overpowered and killed by three other Japanese soldiers.

The fighting on nearby Tanambogo was equally savage. One assault by the parachutists was repulsed, another nearly destroyed. By the end of the second day, however, both Gavutu and Tanambogo were in Marine hands.

Out of 377 Marine parachutists who participated in the Gavutu and Tanambogo landings, 28 were killed, half that number being commissioned officers sergeants, and corporals. Another 50 Marines were wounded, most of them seriously, including Williams.

BLOODY RIDGE

In late August, Vandegrift ordered the Raiders and the parachutists on Tulagi and Gavutu-Tanambogo to ship across the channel and reinforce him on Guadalcanal, known in Marine jargon as "the Canal." En route, the Marines cleaned weapons while the sailors fed them as much bread and jelly as they could eat. It was a treat the sweets-starved leathernecks relished.

On the Canal, they quickly regrouped for battle. Maj. Williams, seriously wounded but stable, was out of the game. Overall command of both the Raiders and parachutists fell to "Red Mike" Edson.

On September 7 and 8, the Marines attacked the enemy at Guadalcanal's Taivu Point and subsequently gleaned new intelligence about the enemy. They learned that a large enemy force under the command of Maj. Gen. Kiyotake Kawaguchi had landed and was preparing to attack and seize the ever-vital Henderson (Air) Field. The Japanese chose to attack the airfield from the south, believing it was not as well defended as the coastal perimeter. They were wrong. Dug in on a ridge overlooking Kawaguchi's approach were Red Mike's newly arrived Raiders and the Marine parachutists backed by artillery. The Raiders were positioned on the right flank, with the parachutists on the left. The Japanese were everywhere in the jungle below the ridge. Unseen, but heard moving in large numbers, the enemy began raising a rhythmic war whoop. Stomping their feet and slapping their rifle butts, the Japanese began chanting, "U.S. Marines, you die tonight! U.S. Marines, you die tonight!"

On the night of September 12 and 13, the enemy attacked. The fighting was a bitter slugfest with both sides suffering heavy losses. At one point, the Marine line was bowed and Edson's left was about to collapse. Committed to holding the line at all costs, Edson ordered the paramarines to fix bayonets and counterattack.

Capt. Harry Torgerson then led two companies in a desperate charge against the advancing Japanese. The Marines regained and bolstered their positions, but not before the fighting degraded into a bloody hand-to-hand struggle.

Marine parachutist Tom Lyons took several rounds in the belly, which sent him tumbling down the ridge. According to Lyons, he then felt as if he was floating out of his body, but despite his ebbing consciousness he clearly remembers the hellish minutes that followed.

"I saw a Jap come out, and he stepped on my stomach and he stabbed me in the throat with his bayonet," recalls Lyons in Patrick K. O'Donnell's *Into the Rising Sun*. "It went through the side of my neck and into the ground behind me but it didn't hurt. Jesse Youngdeer (a fellow Marine) was coming up the trail with a box of hand grenades, and this Jap stepped off me and instead of finishing me off, he made a thrust at Youngdeer."

Youngdeer smacked aside the Japanese bayonet with his box of grenades and then grabbed the enemy's rifle in an attempt to wrest it from him. "The Jap had stabbed him just above the knee," Lyons added. "Another Marine ran up with his bayonet, and he tried to stab the Jap, and he got confused and stabbed Youngdeer right in the leg."

By the morning of the 14th, the Marines were kings of the hill. The numbers vary according to who's counting, but the Americans lost between 104 and 111 killed with 278 to 283 wounded. Of those losses, the 1st Parachute Battalion suffered about 21 dead and 101 wounded. An estimated 1,200 Japanese soldiers were killed. For his leadership and for repulsing the enemy, Edson would receive the Congressional Medal of Honor, and the ridge itself would forever be known as "Edson's Ridge" or simply "Bloody Ridge."

THE REGIMENT

On September 18, the 1st Parachute Battalion was ordered off the Canal. The battalion set sail for New Caledonia. There the Paramarines began a rigorous training cycle. The first phase consisted of a reintroduction to parachute jump techniques and chute packing. Subsequent phases included advanced patrolling and scouting, as well as combat exercises from platoon to battalion level.

The 2nd Parachute Battalion, having been organized in the summer of 1941, arrived in Wellington, New Zealand, on Halloween night 1942. The following January, the 2nd joined the 1st at New Caledonia. In March 1943, the 3rd Parachute Battalion, which had been formed the previous September, joined the 1st and the 2nd.

On April 1, 1943, the 1st Marine Parachute Regiment, comprised of the three parachute battalions, was officially established (a fourth battalion had been established but remained stateside until disbanded along with the regiment in 1944). Williams, having recovered from his wounds and promoted to lieutenant colonel, was named regimental commander.

For the next nine months, the 1st Parachute Regiment fought as a unit throughout the Solomons, earning laurels on the islands of Vella Lavella, Choiseul, and Bougainville. But a dearth of landing zones large enough to handle large-scale airborne operations, a lack of transport aircraft, and insufficient land-based staging areas prevented the Marines from ever jumping over their target areas.

On December 30, 1943, Lt. Gen. Thomas Holcomb, commandant of the Marine Corps, ordered "the disbandment of all parachute forces." The parachutists themselves were transferred to regular Marine infantry units, most of them filling the ranks of the new 5th Marine Division in early 1944. The 5th was destined to slug it out with the enemy at Iwo Jima in February and March 1945 (see Appendix B).

Although they never made a unit-level combat jump during World War II, Marine Corps parachutists fought and died in many of the bloodiest campaigns in the Pacific theater. Several individual Marine Corps parachutists also made a number of clandestine jumps over German-occupied territory in the European theater. Most of them were on detached service with the Office of Strategic Services (OSS), the wartime predecessor of the modern Central Intelligence Agency. Additionally, at least two Marine officers serving as military observers were known to have jumped with Army airborne forces.

CHAPTER 15

RECONNAISSANCE AND OTHER SPECIAL OPERATIONS FORCES

The Lord said to Gideon, "There are still too many men. Lead them down to the water and I will test them for you there."
—Judges 7:4

Every [Marine] Recon type, past, present, and future can stand tall in the shadow of the daring exploit of [Capt. Jerome] Paull and twelve 1st Force Recon Marines, who made the first successful jump 37 miles deep into Vietcong territory. I am honored they served with us.
—Maj. Gen. Lewis J. Fields, commanding general of the 1st Marine Division, in a statement recognizing the first combat jump by a Marine unit in history, June 1966

The U.S. Marines, long considered an elite military force, has often bowed its back at the prospect suggested by outsiders that certain units within the Corps are more elite than others. Clearly, the entire Marine Corps is elite. Every Marine—from the lowliest private dishing out mashed potatoes in a mess kitchen to a four-star general serving on the Joint Chiefs of Staff—is first and foremost a combat rifleman. It is this philosophy that has set the Corps apart from its sister services for more than two centuries.

Some units within the Corps are, in fact, more highly skilled in terms of special combat operations than others. The units' members know this, but they are quick to say they are just doing their jobs as Marines.

FORCE RECON

One such unit is a Marine Force Reconnaissance Company, known simply as Force Recon. Unlike other parachute-trained special operations forces— Navy SEALs, Army Rangers, and others—little is known about the responsibilities and mission scope of Force Recon. The reasoning, again, hearkens back to the idea that the entire Corps is special. In fact, if one were to line up uniformed Marines from a variety of units and try to determine which leathernecks served in Recon companies or any other special operations-capable Marine units, it would be nearly impossible. Of course, Recon Marines wear airborne wings and SCUBA badges, but so do many other Marines, some of whom serve in noncombatant billets.

Unlike the SEALs who wear the distinguishing "trident" badge, Rangers who wear their famous shoulder "tab," and Special Forces who wear the identifying green beret and "flash," the men of Force Recon wear nothing that separates them from their fellow Marines.

A lesson plan issued to members of Force Recon in the 1960s further illustrates this approach by the Corps to its best-trained units:

> The Recon Marine is no more and no less than an infantryman with special skills. He is not a superman, nor is he really a particularly special kind of Marine. He is simply and proudly a Marine doing a job which has to be done.

Nearly four decades later, that same sentiment is echoed by the men of Force Recon.

"We're not supermen, we're Marines," says Gunnery Sgt. Kevin R. Helms of the 2nd Recon Battalion at Camp Lejeune, North Carolina. "Sure, we do amazing things and people respect the jewelry [parachute wings]. But no matter how high speed we are, or how high speed we are perceived, we always focus on the fundamentals required of Marines."

"No room exists for inflated egos among Recon Marines," says Helms. "Egos will only cause someone to write a check that he can't cash," he says. "If someone comes here wanting the wings, we send them back."

Force Recon Marines fast-roping from a helicopter to the deck of the USS Boxer *in 1999.*

Admittance into the ranks of Force Recon is not easy. Candidates most go through a rigorous selection process that includes a swim test, a physical fitness test, a forced march with packs and rifles over rugged terrain, and a psychological evaluation. Some of the candidates are already airborne qualified, but many are not. Those without wings must be willing to attend the Army's basic parachute training at Fort Benning.

Once they pass the Force Recon selection process, the Marines must undergo a five-phase training cycle. During Phase I, Marines attend "basic recon" training taught by Marines and sailors at the Navy's amphibious training center in Coronado, California. Then they must attend dive school and jump school.

Following Phase I, candidates begin Phase II, or "unit training," where they develop skills in deep reconnaissance, land navigation, and amphibious operations. In this phase, they hone their skills in all types of environments from snow-covered mountains to sweltering swamps. They also learn to handle all manner of weapons, both foreign and domestic. By the end of Phase II, the Force Recon hopefuls have been training for one solid year.

They then move into Phase III, where they find themselves training for a real-world deployment with a Marine Expeditionary Unit (MEU). While with the MEU, some Marines attend the U.S. Army's Military Free-Fall Parachutist School at Fort Bragg or the Yuma Proving Grounds in Arizona. Some train as pathfinders. Some attend Army Ranger school, while some go to Marine sniper school. All receive hands-on training in explosives.

In Phase IV, candidates actually deploy with an MEU for six months where they may participate in combat operations with Force Recon.

In Phase V, the Marines return from their deployment and are permanently posted to Force Recon.

BIRTH OF MARINE RECON

Amphibious reconnaissance is as old as naval warfare, but no official form of such reconnaissance existed within the U.S. Department of the Navy until the 1920s. It was then that U.S. Marine Lt. Col. Earl H. "Pete" Ellis developed a doctrine for the conduct of amphibious warfare with a focus on amphibious—and deep—reconnaissance that would become standard for the Marine Corps, the Navy, and the Army for the next several decades.

Considered a prophet in terms of amphibious warfare, Ellis left on a fact-finding mission of South America and the Pacific in early 1921. He died mysteriously two years later in Japan's South Sea Islands, but not before publishing his *Advanced Base Operations in Micronesia*.

Ellis accurately predicted how the future war with Japan (1941–1945) would be fought. This included his outlines for amphibious assault and the need for excellent pre-assault reconnaissance. Ellis's work served as the foundation of the Corps' 1934 *Tentative Landings Operations Manual*. The manual became known as the bible of amphibious doctrine, including amphibious reconnaissance.

Marine as well as Army and Navy reconnaissance units were developed during World War II, and their work was critical to the success of amphibious operations in both the European and Pacific theaters. But few if any of the men who served in those units were airborne qualified. Parachutes were simply not a practical means of delivery for men who would only be reconnoitering beaches from the surf line to a few hundred yards inland. That would change within a decade.

When the war ended in 1945, most reconnaissance units were disbanded. In the late 1940s, Marines paired up with U.S. Navy underwater demolition teams (UDTs) to further hone their skills.

In 1950, war erupted on the Korean peninsula, and Marine reconnaissance units were quickly organized for service. During the period following the 1953 cease-fire in Korea, Marine Corps planners accurately predicted that future Marine battlefields would extend much farther inland than those of previous wars. Insertion by boat and submarine would not be sufficient, nor would insertion by helicopter, which was still in its infancy and incapable of all-weather/night flight, too noisy, vulnerable to enemy fire, and with limited range. Thus, it was determined that Marine Recon personnel would have to be able to be dropped by parachute from high-performance airplanes. They would also have to undergo pathfinder training, because a recon team's only means of extraction from their given reconnaissance zone would be to hump it out on foot.

In April 1956, an entire Marine reconnaissance platoon attended jump school at Fort Benning, Georgia, and Marine Recon teams have been trained to jump out of airplanes ever since.

During the Vietnam War, airborne-qualified Marine Recon teams were key special operators. They were, in fact, the only deep reconnaissance-trained combatants from any of the services until 1965. Their work included not only scouting, but enemy-prisoner snatches and direct-action combat.

Although a World War II–era Marine parachute battalion was the first American airborne unit to engage an enemy in combat (see Chapter 15), the Corps' 1st Force Reconnaissance Company was the first Marine unit in history to actually make a combat jump. In fact, 1st Force Recon made the first *three* Marine Corps combat jumps, and they were all in Vietnam. The first was on June 14, 1966, when a squad from the 4th Platoon, 1st Force Reconnaissance Company jumped west of the American base at Chu Lai in order to seize an observation post. It was a night jump, 37 miles deep into enemy territory, and all 12 men and 1 officer, Capt. Jerome Paull, lived to tell about it.

The second jump was conducted by nine men of the 5th Platoon southwest of Da Nang on September 5, 1967. Led by Gunnery Sgt. Walter Webb, the team was separated by extremely high winds, and the mission was scrubbed. The third jump was made by six Recon Marines commanded by 1st Lt. Wayne Rollings on November 17, 1969. The parachutists landed on a stretch of beach near the village of Nui Tran, then regrouped and moved out on a scouting mission.

By the end of the Vietnam War, four Force Recon companies had been established. Three of those companies slipped into dormancy during the postwar downsizing of the Corps, but in recent years, one such company has been reactivated, providing the modern Marine Corps with two active Force Recon companies.

FORCE AND BATTALION RECON

Modern parachute-qualified Reconnaissance Marines come in two speeds—high and super-high.

Most Recon Marines are members of Reconnaissance Battalions (known unofficially as Battalion Recon Marines). Unlike Force Recon, the Battalion Recon Marines are not required to be parachute qualified, though many of them are. They are required to provide highly sophisticated advance-force scouting for each of the Corps' divisions. Thus, the term *Battalion Recon* confuses outsiders who might assume that such a unit is a scouting/reconnaissance team supporting an individual battalion. Because the entire Marine Corps only has three active divisions with one reserve division, only four Marine Reconnaissance Battalions exist.

High-speed Battalion Recon Marines operate within 18 miles from the edge of friendly lines. The operational area several hundred miles beyond the 18-mile line is the responsibility of the super-high-speed Force Recon Marines. Force Recon Marines, though experienced in a variety of modern special operations, train for two primary missions: deep reconnaissance and direct action against an enemy, always in support of regular Marine units.

In a January 2000 article for *The Accurate Rifle*, Patrick A. Rogers may have described the men of Force Recon best when he wrote, "They are tough, rugged men, whose job is to support the guy who does the real fighting—the Marine Infantryman."

ANGLICO

Although most parachute-trained Marines serve in reconnaissance units, other leathernecks' job descriptions call for them to "put their knees to the breeze." The second largest group can be found among the elite ANGLICO Marines.

ANGLICO, an acronym for Air Naval Gunfire Liaison Company, has historically been responsible for jumping into or near a combat zone and then coordinating air strikes against enemy targets. ANGLICO Marines have also been responsible for coordinating naval gunfire against enemy targets from offshore warships. The coordination efforts have been conducted between the Marines and their sister U.S. services, as well as with foreign allies.

Currently, no ANGLICO units are active, only small liaison teams, but definitive plans are being made to resurrect these companies in the near future.

RADIO RECON TEAMS

In addition to Recon and air/naval gunfire elements, the Marine Corps maintains parachute-qualified radio reconnaissance teams. Whereas little is known about Recon and ANGLICO, even less is known about the Radio Reconnaissance Teams. The reasoning is simple. Radio Recon Teams are responsible for jumping into or near a battle zone with ultra-sophisticated radio equipment and then providing the Marines on the ground with classified signals intelligence and electronic warfare (SIGINT/EW) capabilities.

Other Marine parachutists include "chute-packing" riggers and Marines working as air-delivery (cargo) personnel.

PART 5

AIR FORCE PARACHUTISTS

CHAPTER 16

AIR FORCE SPECIAL TACTICS FORCES

These airmen have endured a great deal during their 36 weeks of arduous training. I'm told they started with a group of almost 130. Seven out of 130—that should tell you how difficult this training is and how exceptional these men are.

—Dr. James G. Roche, Secretary of the Air Force, addressing graduates of U.S. Air Force Combat Control school and their families, December 17, 2002

Although airmen make up only 2 percent of jump school graduates, the U.S. Air Force and its predecessor organizations have been at the forefront of airborne force development and operations since the conception years. Today, any major American airborne operation anywhere in the world is preceded by Air Force parachutists, who are almost always the first armed men on the ground.

PIONEERS AND PATHFINDERS

Airplanes have been around for only 100 years. Consequently, the Air Force is the newest branch of the U.S. armed forces. A product of the post–World War II National Security Act of 1947, the Air

Force traces its lineage back through the old Army Air Forces, Army Air Corps, Army Air Service, and eventually the Lafayette Escadrille and *Escadrille Americaine* (translated as "American air flotilla" or "American squadron"). The latter two organizations were groups of American mercenary flyers piloting French airplanes during the early days of World War I. Prior to that, the only real American airmen were the balloonists of the U.S. Army's Signal Corps.

During the closing days of World War I, U.S. Army Air Corps Brig. Gen. William P. "Billy" Mitchell proposed a plan to launch the first large-scale airborne operation in American military history. Mitchell, the senior air officer in the American Expeditionary Force (AEF) in France, wanted to attack the French city of Metz deep behind German lines with armed parachutists, but it was not to be. The war ended in November 1918, months before his massed jump was to take place (see Chapter 1).

In the interim period between world wars, Mitchell and the Air Corps were instrumental in the development of both the parachute assault tactics and the equipment to be used in such an operation. Air Corps officers, in fact, lobbied hard to bring all airborne assets under their respective umbrella. In the end, airborne forces would become an arm of the infantry, which never would have occurred without the direct involvement of the Air Corps.

During World War II, the Army Air Forces—the predecessor of the modern U.S. Air Force—was tasked with a number of air warfare missions, not the least of which was transporting paratroopers and towing gliders to their respective drop zones. Additionally, Air Force elements were responsible for resupplying isolated units of airborne soldiers if and when friendly, conventional ground forces were unable to reach them.

Today Air Force pilots and crewmembers are still responsible for both delivering paratroopers to their targeted drop zones and delivering air-dropped supplies to those airborne soldiers on the ground. A handful of specially trained airmen known as Combat Controllers also have the responsibility of jumping ahead of major airborne forces, then prepping the drop zone with navigational aids, clearing the area of unforeseen obstacles, and sometimes eliminating the defenders.

COMBAT CONTROLLERS

When most Americans hear or read the term Air Force, the first images to come to mind are supersonic jet fighters like the F-15 Eagle or the new F-22 Raptor. Perhaps they think of B-2 stealth bombers, the big lumbering B-52 Stratofortresses, or C-130 and C-141 cargo planes. Some Americans may think of nuclear-tipped intercontinental ballistic missiles or super-secret subterranean command posts like the great fortress that lies beneath Colorado's Cheyenne Mountain. But few think of parachuting airmen trained and equipped to fight in a ground combat environment, when in fact they are often first on the scene during airborne or special operations.

(National Archives)

An Air Force Combat Control team coordinating a parachute assault by South Vietnamese paratroopers near Saigon, South Vietnam, April 1966.

True to their motto, "First There," Air Force Combat Controllers are specially trained paratroopers who often jump in advance of large-scale airborne forces in order to set up, secure, and provide on-ground navigational assistance on landing or drop zones for pilots and paratroopers. As his title suggests, the Combat Controller's specialty is establishing and maintaining air traffic control in a combat zone, but as parachuting commandos who are almost always vastly outnumbered by defending enemy forces on the ground, they are often tasked with conducting special operations "outside the box."

Often isolated behind enemy lines or far out in front of advancing friendly armies, a Combat Controller might be tasked with coordinating an airstrike on a enemy air defense position. Equipped with special range-finding binoculars, a palm-top computer, a global position system (GPS) receiver, and a rifle, the Combat Controller can clandestinely spot the target and direct the pilot toward it. He'll then leap on a motorcycle and race to another target where he will repeat the process.

On another mission, Combat Controllers might be tasked with making a high-altitude/low-opening (HALO) parachute jump onto a field slated to be assaulted by a large airborne force. There they will silently land, overwhelm and kill any defenders who discover them, and prepare the way for inbound planes and paratroopers.

For instance, just prior to the 1983 invasion of Grenada (see Chapter 4), a handful of Combat Controllers and U.S. Navy SEALs (the Navy's elite SEa, Air, Land commandos) conducted an open-water parachute drop off at Point Salinas on the southern tip of Grenada. The SEALs were responsible for reconnoitering the Point Salinas airfield, determining the condition of the runway, and ascertaining the location and strength of nearby enemy forces. The airmen were tasked with clandestinely positioning radar beacons on the airfield so that parachuting U.S. Army Rangers and other airborne forces would be able to find the drop zone.

Sadly, four SEALs drowned in the heavy seas, and the others were ordered to withdraw before completing the mission.

Nevertheless, Operation Urgent Fury was a "go," and just over 24 hours later, a team of Combat Controllers made the first parachute jump over the island's heavily defended Point Salinas airport. Weighted down with nearly 100 pounds of vital equipment, the airmen jumped from an altitude of only 500 feet. A malfunctioning main parachute would have killed a paratrooper.

On the ground and under constant fire from Cuban forces, the airmen then directed transport aircraft ferrying two parachuting battalions of the Army's 75th Ranger Regiment over the airport. At Point Salinas, the Combat Controllers and the Rangers encountered the toughest overall resistance of the operation. "Salinas hung in the balance for a few very nervous minutes," writes Dr. Daniel P. Bolger, a military history professor at the U.S. Military Academy, West Point. In the end, the airmen and soldiers carried the day.

The airmen who make up the Combat Control teams trace their lineage to the U.S. Army's pathfinders of World War II. During some of the earliest American airborne operations, paratroopers were inadvertently dropped several miles short of their drop zones by pilots utilizing crude methods of navigation (by today's standards). As a result, the Army began training company-size units of pathfinders—scouts who parachuted over the target drop zone before the main airborne assault, secured the field, and then guided the aircraft in over the target. As a means of signaling the pilots, the pathfinders used all manner of visuals, from smoke pots to flares to flashlights and small fires. They also used crude radio homing devices that the pilots could follow.

In 1943, the first trained pathfinders were used during airborne operations in Italy. The following year, during the invasion of Normandy, pathfinders were inserted in advance of the behind-the-lines drops of the 82nd and 101st Airborne Divisions. The pathfinders were critical in the overall success of the airborne landings.

Even so, some of the sky soldiers found themselves off target by as much as 35 miles and were separated from their units. The scattered drops were primarily the result of the transport pilots who broke ranks, strayed off course, and lowered their altitudes to evade the heavy antiaircraft fire. Nevertheless, without the pathfinders the landings could have been disastrous. Pathfinders honed their skills after Normandy, as did the transport pilots, and as a result, future drops were far better coordinated.

When the war ended in 1945, pathfinder units were some of the first to be disbanded as a direct result of the Army's massive downsizing. Two years later, the National Security Act of 1947 was passed, which, among other things, established the U.S. Air Force as a separate and equal arm of military service. Soon thereafter the Army dissolved its few remaining pathfinder units, albeit temporarily. The responsibilities previously assumed by those units were then passed to the Air Force's new Air Resupply and Communications Service, the direct predecessor organization to the modern Air Force Combat Control teams. After all, Air Force leaders argued, Air Force personnel should be the only ones guiding Air Force planes.

In 1951, the Army closed its pathfinder training program at Fort Benning, Georgia. But with the emergence of the helicopter and the development of Army helicopter-borne "air assault" forces and tactics, the program was reestablished in 1955.

Unlike Air Force Combat Controllers, not all Army pathfinders today are airborne qualified. Most are, but it is not a requirement. Pathfinder school, though challenging, is not quite as long or demanding as Combat Controller training, the latter being more akin to the Air Force's version of Ranger school. Beyond that, Combat Control hopefuls must complete air traffic control school, jump school, and a series of survival training courses.

Combat Controllers are one of three primary Air Force airborne forces under the umbrella of Air Force Special Tactics. The Special Tactics Squadrons include Combat Controllers, Pararescue units, and Combat Weather Teams. A unique force indeed, a Combat Weather Team is comprised of parachute-qualified meteorologists armed with pistols and assault rifles for personal protection on the ground. Their mission is to gather real-time weather data for Army Special Forces, Ranger, and airborne missions. Combat Controllers and Pararescuemen also carry weapons for personal protection, but they have often had to use them in larger combat actions.

"Good men" are not enough to apply for Combat Controller slots. The Air Force wants "men between the ages of 18 and 27 who are athletic enough to enter the ranks" and tough enough to remain there.

All applicants for Combat Controller slots must pass a rigorous "Physical Abilities and Stamina Test." The test includes a demanding swim-performance evaluation, a three-mile run, pull-ups, sit-ups, push-ups, and flutter kicks, all accomplished within a three-hour time frame. The test is followed by a grueling 10-week indoctrination course, affectionately referred to as

"Ironman 101." The course is characterized by constant running and calisthenics. But the most difficult portion is the "pool work." During pool work, students must demonstrate a natural ability to swim with a weightbelt, tread water, drown-proof, and work closely with a "buddy" swimmer. The course is meant to both eliminate those who don't have the physical prowess to be Combat Controllers and to enhance the water confidence of those who do.

(Defense Visual Information Center)

Air Force special tactics paratroopers leap from a C-130 transport aircraft during a training exercise near Ben Guerir airfield, Morocco, in 2001.

Following the indoctrination course, combat control team students must attend a variety of special operations-related schools, including the following:

- Four weeks at the U.S. Army's combat diver (scuba) school at Key West, Florida

- One day of Navy "underwater egress" training at Pensacola Naval Air Station, Florida

- Three weeks at Fort Benning's basic static-line parachute jump school in Georgia

- Five weeks at the Army's Military Free-Fall Parachutist School, held at both Fort Bragg, North Carolina, and Yuma Proving Grounds in Arizona
- Two and a half weeks of Air Force survival training at Fairchild Air Force Base in Washington State
- Twelve weeks of Combat Controller field tactics at Pope Air Force Base, North Carolina

Additionally, students receive advanced combat training and are trained in the use of ropes, skis, and motorcycles.

Upon successful completion of the combat training programs, the students must earn the second part of their title, "Controller." To do so, they attend the Air Force's 15½ week Air Traffic Control School at Keesler Air Force Base, Mississippi (the training cycle is occasionally reversed, particularly in the case of those students who have previously attended the air traffic control school). The Keesler phase of training is the same course that all other Air Force air traffic controllers attend. There the Combat Control hopefuls master the most critical portion of their trade and are eventually certified by the Federal Aviation Administration (FAA) in air traffic control procedures.

To suggest that their training is tough is an understatement. In fact, only 7 men out of a total of 130 candidates in Combat Control class 02-04 stayed the course and graduated in December 2002.

Like other airborne special operations forces, Combat Controllers are inserted into hostile areas by a variety of methods, almost always involving the use of parachutes. For instance, if a night jump is to be made over open sea, Combat Controllers might shove deflated rubber boats out of an aircraft and then free-fall parachute jump behind them. Once in the water, the airmen would locate the boats, inflate them, climb aboard, and row ashore.

Like all combat parachutists, Combat Controllers are usually deployed with the bare minimum supplies and equipment needed to complete their mission: just the minimum to sustain them for up to 72 hours without resupply. Beyond the 72-hour time frame, the airmen will find themselves in dire need of what the Air Force refers to as "consumables"—food, water, batteries, vehicle fuel, and additional equipment that may not have been factored in to the needs of the original mission.

Scarlet berets are worn by Combat Controllers. Their Pararescue brothers wear maroon.

PARARESCUEMEN

U.S. Air Force Pararescuemen are considered some of the world's most skilled parachuting combatants. But more than killing enemy soldiers or coordinating airborne operations aimed at killing enemy soldiers on the ground, Pararescuemen are tasked with saving lives. It is this primary responsibility that is best articulated in the pararescueman's motto (taken from the creed), "that others may live."

One of three primary Air Force Airborne units, Pararescuemen are highly skilled rescue and recovery personnel who are trained to jump—as just one means of being delivered—into hostile territory in order to rescue wounded soldiers or downed pilots.

> It is my duty as a Pararescueman to save a life and to aid the injured.
> I will perform my assigned duties quickly and efficiently, placing these duties before personal desires and comforts.
> These things I do, that others may live.
> —Pararescue Creed

Like Combat Controllers, Pararescuemen trace their lineage to World War II. In August 1943, 21 occupants of a crippled C-46 transport were forced to bail out over an isolated stretch of uncharted territory near the border between China and Burma. The terrain surrounding the crash site was mostly thick, twisting jungle, and the location was so remote that the only means of rendering assistance to the survivors was by parachute. Sent to rescue the survivors were an Army Air Forces flight surgeon, Lt. Col. Don Davis Flickinger, and two medical corpsmen (all three volunteered). Jumping near the site, the three men worked their way through the jungle, reached the survivors, and, with the help of a few natives, were able to provide immediate medical assistance. The party then made its way toward friendly lines, which it reached a month later.

One of the survivors was legendary print and broadcast journalist Eric Sevareid, who later wrote of his rescuers: "Gallant is a precious word; they deserve it."

This successful parachute drop of military medical personnel into a potentially dangerous area was the genesis of the modern Air Force Pararescue team.

Admission into the ranks of modern Pararescuemen is not easy. Today all Pararescue hopefuls must meet the same Physical Abilities and Stamina Test requirements as Combat Controllers. The attrition rate is high among those taking the test, but if the applicant for Pararescue duty can endure it, he has a far greater chance of completing the grueling 10-week Ironman 101 course.

Following the indoctrination course, Pararescue students must attend a variety of special operations-related schools, similar to the Combat Controller training cycle. This includes four weeks at the U.S. Army's combat diver (scuba) school, one day of Navy "underwater egress" training, three weeks at Fort Benning's basic static-line parachute jump school, and five weeks at the Army's Military Free-Fall Parachutist School. They also receive 2½ weeks of Air Force survival training and 22 weeks of special operations combat medical training, followed by the grueling 20-week Pararescue Recovery Specialist Course.

The job of airborne-qualified Pararescuemen is rewarding, but it is also fraught with danger. Pararescuemen have served in nearly every single American combat action since the Air Force was established as a separate service in 1947.

One of the most dramatic tales in Pararescue history is that of the actions of Airman 1st Class William H. "Pits" Pitsenbarger, a 21-year-old Pararescueman during Operation Abilene, which took place near Vung Tau, South Vietnam, on April 11, 1966. Close to making his 300th combat mission, Pitsenbarger and fellow members of the Air Force's 38th Aerospace Rescue and Recovery Squadron were attempting to rescue wounded members of the Army's famed 1st Infantry Division. The 1st, known as the "Big Red One," had been ambushed by the enemy. The infantrymen were surrounded and being shot to pieces when two Air Force helicopters arrived. From one of the hovering helicopters, Pitsenbarger rode one of the cable-attached litter baskets down through the trees until he was on the ground. There he appeared to be an angel of mercy.

"Pitsenbarger was a great source of comfort," recalls Charles F. Epperson, a soldier with the 1st Infantry Division. "I was very scared. The bullets [were] flying around constantly from every direction. I was young and had been wounded. I didn't even know where my weapon was. He had a great calming effect on myself and the other wounded. He calmed me down. Once he treated me, I began to help him treat and evacuate the other wounded. He gave me clear orders in a calm manner as to how to aid the injured men. He was unarmed and was going from casualty to casualty while seemingly ignoring the bullets that were flying everywhere."

Pits continued to treat the wounded and stayed on the ground when the helicopters began transporting the wounded back to the aid station. Soon the surviving soldiers were running low on ammunition, so Pitsenbarger raced around the battlefield gathering ammo from the dead and distributing it to those still able to fight. He then joined the infantrymen and returned fire with his own rifle.

Before the day was over, Pitsenbarger was killed. For his actions, he would be posthumously awarded the Air Force Cross and later the Congressional Medal of Honor.

Aside from its direct involvement in airborne and rescue operations, the U.S. Air Force has also always played a key role in the development of the parachute. In so doing, test airmen have set some of the world's most impressive jump records.

The most notable record was set by Air Force Cpt. Joseph W. Kittinger Jr. on August 16, 1960. This date was 20 years to the day after the first jump was made by the Army's parachute test platoon, and 18 years to the day after the 101st Infantry Division was redesignated the 101st Airborne Division. On that day, Capt. Kittinger leapt from a large balloon gondola some 19 miles (102,800 feet) above the surface of the earth. For 4 minutes and 37 seconds, Kittinger's free-falling body plummeted to the earth, reaching speeds of up to 714 miles per hour (mph) in the stratosphere (supersonic speed or Mach 1 is 760 mph). Despite a high-altitude pressure suit and supplemental oxygen, the 32-year-old captain experienced breathing difficulties between 90,000 and 70,000 feet. At approximately 50,000 feet, where the atmosphere became much denser, his rate of descent dropped to around 250 mph, but he was suffering tremendous pain in his right hand due to a partial loss of pressure in his right-hand glove.

When he reached 18,000 feet, Kittinger's main parachute deployed, and 8 minutes later he landed safely at the White Sands Missile Range in New Mexico.

In less than 15 minutes, the young Air Force officer had set three world records. He had made the highest parachute jump in history, his jump had been the longest free fall in history, and, at 714 mph, he had also become the fastest man alive without an aircraft. Aside from the danger of jumping, his environment was without life-sustaining oxygen (he was equipped with a supplemental breathing device) and the temperatures at the higher elevations dropped to –94 degrees Fahrenheit.

PART 6

PARACHUTISTS IN THE OFFICE OF STRATEGIC SERVICES (OSS) AND THE CENTRAL INTELLIGENCE AGENCY (CIA)

CHAPTER 17

LONE SPIES AND SPECIAL TEAMS

All the business of war, and indeed all the business of life, is to endeavor to find out what you don't know by what you do; that's what I called "guessing what was at the other side of the hill."

—The Duke of Wellington, quoted in *The [John Wilson] Croker Papers*, 1884

When the Japanese attacked Pearl Harbor on December 7, 1941, the only American foreign intelligence service that existed was the sparsely manned Office of the Coordinator of Information, or the COI (the first official predecessor of the modern Central Intelligence Agency [CIA]). The COI had been established the previous July, but it consisted only of former U.S. Army officer William J. "Wild Bill" Donovan and a handful of men. By September, some 40 employees were working for the Office. After Pearl Harbor, the COI's ranks quickly swelled to more than 600.

In June 1942, President Franklin D. Roosevelt redesignated the COI as the Office of Strategic Services (OSS). Established as an intelligence/counterintelligence/covert action entity during World

War II, the OSS was the largest and most storied of the CIA's predecessor organizations.

The OSS was responsible for espionage and sabotage in countries that were overrun and occupied by the Germans, Italians, and Japanese. Thus, Donovan made the decision to recruit his OSS officers from among the nation's toughest, most experienced soldiers as well as from resourceful civilian leaders in the private and public sectors. A high percentage of those recruited were well-heeled members of the "eastern establishment" elite: Wall Street lawyers and Ivy Leaguers. Donovan's reasoning for hiring such men was simple: He wanted operatives who could think outside the box.

"You can hire a second story man and make him a better second story man," Donovan was quoted in Evan Thomas's *The Very Best Men*. "But if you hire a lawyer or an investment banker or a professor, you'll have something else besides."

As a result, the OSS earned the nicknames "Oh So Social" and "Oh Such Snobs" (the organization's covert nature resulted in a third nickname— "Oh So Secret"). Still, many of those recruited were seconded from American armed forces. The U.S. Army, including Army Air Corps personnel, comprised approximately two-thirds of OSS strength. Civilians comprised another quarter. The remainder was drawn from the ranks of the U.S. Navy, Marine Corps, and Coast Guard.

OSS candidates had to undergo grueling combat training that tested mental, physical, and emotional limits. Trainees were encouraged to be creative and inventive in their thinking, and trained operatives were allowed a great deal of freedom in accomplishing their missions.

At peak strength in 1944, more than 13,000 Americans (8,500 men and 4,500 women) worked for the OSS, performing myriad tasks and working in concert with resistance forces and the intelligence/special operations units of other Allied nations. Roughly 7,500 OSS employees (including 900 women) served in overseas posts, and many of them—men and women— had to be inserted by parachute.

"Intelligence agencies didn't have much need for airborne-qualified agents in peacetime," said NBC news analyst James F. Dunnigan in his book *The Perfect Soldier*. "It was easier and safer to travel by ship and train. Moreover, parachutes were a new technology, and it was feared that most landings would result in some kind of injury. So [being that there were practically no parachute-trained spies at the time] the intelligence people had to learn about parachutes in a hurry once World War II broke out."

Indeed, and as their handlers quickly discovered, physically fit operatives could be trained to handle parachutes in a short period of time. And as dangerous as the new parachute method of delivery seemed to the operatives making the jump, it was in fact far safer than the previous method: landing a light airplane in a remote field behind enemy lines and dropping off the operative.

Additionally, many intelligence-gathering specialists and related technicians worked closely with both airborne forces and parachute-trained commandos. In that capacity, the intel types had to be able to go in with the troops. That usually meant jumping out of airplanes.

The OSS operatives were parachute trained at a variety of jump schools. Many were trained as Army and Marine Corps parachutists prior to joining or being detached from their respective services to the OSS. Others trained in jump schools located in remote regions of the world like the OSS's jump school in Algiers.

OSS operatives who had trained at military jump schools found OSS parachute training a bit different. Instead of using standard American equipment and jumping from the door of a transport aircraft, OSS parachutists literally "fell out of the bottom." Utilizing both U.S. and British parachute equipment, OSS trainees practiced jumping from bombers through an opening in the floor of the aircraft where the ball turret gunner's position would normally be.

OPERATIONAL GROUPS

In late December 1942, the U.S. Joint Chiefs of Staff issued a directive that stated that Donovan's OSS should "organize 'operational nuclei' to be used in enemy occupied territory." These Operational Groups (OGs) were in many ways America's first Special Forces teams. Organized into 15-man units, the OGs were responsible for mastering commando fighting techniques. Then they were to be parachute-dropped behind enemy lines, where they were to harass the enemy at every conceivable opportunity and work closely with local resistance forces. As such, all members of an OG were required to be airborne qualified.

One of the most colorful airborne spies in the European theater—and the leader of an OSS OG—was Peter Julien Ortiz. A multilinguist and a former French Foreign Legionnaire who later became an officer in the U.S. Marine Corps, Ortiz had attended both Legionnaire parachute training and U.S. Marine jump school at one of the Corps' wartime parachute training centers. In 1943, while working with the OSS, he was dropped by parachute into German-occupied France to aid units of the French underground and to assist in the rescue of downed Allied pilots.

Although his peers wore civilian clothes in order to blend with the populace, Ortiz often wore his Marine uniform when mixing with the locals. This thrilled the French, who cheered his defiance, but the Nazis were alerted by rumors of an American commando in Marine green.

One of Ortiz's most fascinating, albeit little known, exploits occurred one night while patronizing an ale house in the town of Lyon. Uncharacteristically dressed in civilian attire, Ortiz entered the pub where he spotted several German army officers seated around a table. He approached the table and was offered a seat. Drinks were flowing freely, jokes were told, and the Germans, unaware that Ortiz was an American spy, began cursing all things American. One of the officers cursed President Franklin D. Roosevelt. Another followed it with a curse of the U.S. Marine Corps. Why or if the Corps was actually cursed is unknown since the Germans had probably never met a U.S. Marine on the battlefield. (Although a handful of leathernecks were serving on detached duty with the OSS and other specially tasked combat organizations in Europe, the vast majority of American Marines were in the Pacific fighting the Japanese.) Nevertheless, it was a blanket condemnation of everything Ortiz held dear.

Ortiz, politely excused himself from the table and returned to a nearby safe house where he changed into the dress green uniform of an American Marine captain, complete with parachute wings and combat decorations. He then draped a cape over his shoulders, concealing his uniform, and returned to the pub. There his drinking partners raucously greeted him.

Ortiz took a seat and ordered a round of drinks. When the beverages were served, he stood up and tossed back the cape, revealing his uniform and a .45 automatic pistol. The Germans were speechless.

"A toast," Ortiz shouted. "To the President of the United States."

He leveled his pistol at each officer as they emptied their glasses. Another round of drinks was ordered, and Ortiz proposed a toast to the U.S. Marine Corps. Again the Germans drained their glasses. A smiling Ortiz then eased backward out of the bar and vanished into the night. (An unconfirmed version of the story had Ortiz shooting it out with the Germans, even killing a few, before disappearing into the back alleys of Lyon.)

Ortiz later returned to Great Britain and was reassigned to an OSS OG. In that capacity, the flamboyant parachutist led a special team tasked with sabotage and direct action against German forces days before the famous invasion of Normandy on June 6, 1944. As effective as they were, the OGs were not the only parachute-trained special teams in the OSS.

THE JEDBURGHS

The "Jedburgh teams" operation was a joint effort between the OSS, the British Special Operations Executive (SOE), and free French units during World War II.

The operation consisted of recruiting, training, equipping, and inserting three-man teams of specially trained covert operatives into Nazi-occupied France, almost always by parachute. There they would coordinate resistance activities supporting the Allied effort. Each team was comprised of two officers and one enlisted radio operator, ideally one man from each of the three participating Allied nations. The Jedburgh teams would link up with French Resistance units of usually 30 to 50 fighters. They would then lead the resistance forces in commando raids against the Germans, creating diversions, disrupting communications, destroying key installations, and gathering intelligence for the Allied forces.

Legend has it that the code-name Jedburgh was taken from the Scottish village of Jedburgh. There, along the Jed River, much of the training was conducted by British commandos and intelligence operatives from the SOE and OSS. However, the truth is somewhat less romantic. The code-name Jedburgh was randomly picked from an English schoolbook. In addition to the Jedburgh training in Scotland, training was held in England at Milton Hall in Peterborough and Tatton Park in Manchester.

Milton Hall was a stone-walled seventeenth-century manor house with 50 rooms. The officers were quartered six to a room. Each morning the trainees were awakened by a houseboy with a mug of tea and a cheery "Good morning, sir." Meanwhile, a lone Scottish Highland bagpiper marched throughout the corridors of the house skirling his pipes.

"It was truly a warrior's domain," writes Col. Aaron Bank, a retired U.S. Army officer who served in the OSS. "The atmosphere was Elizabethan with paneled walls and oak-beamed ceilings. In the corridors, Cromwellian armor, swords, and shields competed for space and the clank of armor from bygone days was echoed by the pounding of our boots."

Much of the training was held on the grounds of Milton Hall. In his book, *From OSS to Green Berets*, Bank recalls the grounds shaking from explosives training. Crackling small arms fire echoed across the estate. From the open windows of the manor home, the tapping sound of Morse code signals could also be heard. Trainees learned knife fighting and instinctive shooting techniques from legendary British officers Maj. William Ewart "Delicate Dan" Fairbairn and Capt. Eric Anthony Sykes (the famous Fairbairn-Sykes commando dagger was designed by the two men).

Instruction in the art of silent killing was conducted in the estate's sunken gardens. "However, rather than the smell of blood, we inhaled the fragrance of roses and the boxwood hedges," said Bank.

Once deployed, the Jedburghs were equipped with all manner of small arms, as well as bazookas, heavy machine guns, and jeeps. Because their insertions had to be clandestine, parachute drops were made at low altitudes, thus reducing the time in the air when the parachutist would be most vulnerable to ground fire. Jumps were made from 500 to 600 feet as opposed to the more common 1,200-foot jumps made by regular airborne units. Additionally, the Jedburghs were not equipped with emergency reserve parachutes as they would have been useless at such low altitudes.

Although a few Jedburghs had been jump-trained by their former services, most had not. Consequently, a special "crash" course in parachute operations and parachute-handling skills was held at the Ringway airfield near Manchester, England. There the students underwent a rigorous program conducted by British airborne instructors. Before the Jedburgh hopefuls could move on to the next stage of training, they had to complete three jumps—one daylight jump and two at night.

During Operation Market Garden, the Allied invasion of Holland in September 1944, Jedburgh teams deployed with each of the airborne divisions. Working closely with senior American and British commanders on the ground, the Jedburghs conducted civil affairs suboperations and unconventional warfare missions in support of the overall operation. The missions were conducted in similar fashion to the roles played today by twenty-first-century special operations forces (Army Green Berets, Delta Force commandos, and Navy SEALs) during large-scale airborne and air assault operations. But the *primary* responsibility of Jedburghs during Market Garden was the collection of battlefield intelligence about the Germans from in-place resistance forces.

Nearly 300 Jedburgh operatives were sent to the European continent over the course of the war. They included 83 Americans, 93 British, 103 French, and a handful of men from the Netherlands, Belgium, and Canada. The Jedburghs also carried out more than 100 operations in Europe between the Normandy landings and VE Day—93 in France and 8 in Holland.

> One of the best known of the American-led Jedburghs was the team led by William Egan Colby (a future director of the CIA) that was code-named Bruce. Colby, then a major, was code-named Berkshire. He commanded two free French commandos, Jacques Favel (code-named Galway) and Louis Giry (code-named Piastre).

The Jedburghs suffered 50 casualties in Europe: 19 were killed in action, 2 died of wounds while in enemy hands, 2 were executed by the Nazis, and the remainder were either wounded in action or injured during their parachute jump.

With the surrender of Germany, some of the Jedburghs were transferred to Burma, where they saw action against the Japanese. Twelve were killed in the Far East.

CHAPTER 18

PARACHUTE-TRAINED COVERT OPERATIVES

Americans have always had an ambivalent attitude toward intelligence. When they feel threatened, they want a lot of it, and when they don't, they regard the whole thing as somewhat immoral.

—U.S. Army Lt. Gen. Vernon A. Walters, former deputy director of the CIA, in *Silent Missions*, 1978

Although the American intelligence community traces its lineage back to the early spooks, spies, and double agents of the American Revolution, no centrally controlled federal intelligence organization existed until just before the beginning of America's involvement in World War II in 1941. A permanent intelligence agency did not appear until 1947, two years after the close of hostilities.

As previously mentioned, when America entered World War II in 1941, the only centrally controlled U.S. intelligence entity was former U.S. Army officer William J. "Wild Bill" Donovan's Office of the Coordinator of Information (COI), which had only been established four months prior. Previous intelligence and counter-intelligence efforts had fallen under the respective domains of the Departments of Navy and War (usually by Army and Navy attachés stationed overseas) and the Federal Bureau of Investigation (FBI). But those efforts suffered from poor coordination, a duplication of services, and sometimes rabid organizational rivalries. Covert action operations requiring special insertions were rare, and parachute insertion was still in its infancy when the COI was created.

On June 13, 1942, the COI was redesignated the Office of Strategic Services (OSS), often referred to as the direct predecessor of the Central Intelligence Agency (CIA). During the war, the OSS proved to be an effective government entity responsible for intelligence collection, counterintelligence, and covert operations, the latter often requiring its operatives to be parachute-qualified for special clandestine insertions (see Chapter 17).

However, the OSS was dissolved in October 1945, and its services were transferred to other government entities. A short-lived Central Intelligence Group (CIG) was established in January 1946. On September 18, 1947, the National Security Act was passed, which reorganized America's defenses and established, among other things, a separate U.S. Air Force and CIA.

THE TWENTY-FIRST-CENTURY CIA

Today the CIA is an enormous federal bureaucracy, employing an estimated 12,000 to 14,000 analysts, administrators, scientists, technicians, and field officers. Because of their covert-operations duties, an unknown number of field officers are required to be parachute qualified.

For most of its existence, the CIA has been comprised of four primary directorates: the Directorate of Administration, the Directorate of Intelligence, the Directorate of Operations, and the Directorate of Science and Technology. However, in June 2001, the Directorate of Administration was abolished and its functions were transferred to a few separate offices. The Directorate of Operations is responsible for training parachutists (when needed) and coordinating CIA parachute jumps and/or the CIA's participation in military airborne operations.

Candidates for membership into the clandestine or operations side of the CIA (the Directorate of Operations) must first undergo a rigorous application and selection process. Those who pass the selection phase are sent to Camp Peary, Virginia (near the historic town of Williamsburg). At Camp Peary—also known as "the Farm"—field officer candidates learn all manner of Agency tradecraft techniques that will enable them to complete their given missions, moving in and out of their operational areas safely and successfully.

The tradecraft taught at Peary includes methods of infiltration and exfiltration, hand-to-hand combat techniques, the effective use of weapons and weapons of opportunity (ice picks, ballpoint pens, credit cards, and so on), explosives, and special radios and other communications gear. Field officer candidates also learn how to pick locks, write secret messages, and master the art of covert photography. For some of Camp Peary's attendees, training in how to handle a parachute during covert operations—especially at night—is essential.

PARACHUTE TRAINING

The specialized airborne training conducted at Camp Peary is a closely held secret, as it must be for security's sake. Nevertheless, former Agency insiders—usually disgruntled employees—occasionally pull back a portion of the veil.

Philip Burnett Franklin Agee, a former Latin America-based case officer, resigned from the CIA in 1969 and became one of its most outspoken, controversial critics. In 1975, Agee wrote what would become his best-selling expose of the Agency, *Inside The Company: CIA Diary*. The book covered a variety of topics, primarily his angry musings about how "huge and sinister" the organization was during his time as a field officer. But he also touched on secret parachute training at Camp Peary.

"Infiltration by air requires black overflights for which the Agency has unmarked long- and short-range aircraft including the versatile Helio Courier [a small single-engine airplane] that can be used in infil-exfil operations with landings as well as parachute drops," wrote Agee. "Restricted areas of Camp Peary along the York River are used for maritime training and other parts of the base serve as landing-sites and drop zones."

Although the CIA does sometimes train its own parachutists "in house," most parachuting CIA officers have been jump-trained at Fort Benning, Georgia, during previous military service. Others, such as Col. Jeffery Bearor, have served as CIA operations officers while detached from one of the branches of the U.S. armed forces. Bearor, an active-duty Marine Corps officer, has made jumps while working with the Agency's Counterterrorism Center. But in his words, "It is only one of several means of operational delivery available" to CIA officers and detached personnel. Other methods of operational delivery might include insertion by small inflatable boat, fishing trawler, or other watercraft; helicopter; fixed-wing aircraft, automobile or other land vehicle; or simply humping-in on foot.

"TONY POE"

The CIA has always attracted men and women with unique talents and a sense of adventure. Some of the most adventuresome adrenaline junkies to work for the Agency have been drawn from the ranks of America's military airborne forces. One of those airborne warriors, Anthony "Tony Poe" Poshepny, was among the first graduates of the CIA's then-new training facility at Camp Peary in the early 1950s. During World War II, Poshepny joined the Marines and served as a member of the Corps' 2nd Battalion, 1st Parachute Regiment (see Chapter 14).

"Tony's outstanding boot camp performance and physical ability led to his selection for the elite para-Marines," wrote University of Georgia professor William M. Leary in *The Death of a Legend* for the Air America Association (Poshepny died on June 27, 2003). "Following jump school, he [Poshepny] joined the Second Parachute Battalion, commanded by Victor 'Brute' Krulak. Tony served with the parachute raiders in the Southwest Pacific until the special units were broken up." (Actually, Poshepny was a member of the Marine "parachutists," not "parachute raiders." Although Marine parachutists and Marine Raiders fought side by side during the Guadalcanal campaign of 1942, they were altogether different in terms of organization and training.)

Poshepny would go on to have a distinguished career as an operations officer in the CIA, serving in Korea, Taiwan, Laos, and Thailand, among other locations throughout the world. While in Thailand, Poshepny worked closely with Thai government, military, and police officials. He organized the program that eventually became the Border Patrol Police, and he established the Police Parachute Training School in Hua Hin.

LAWRENCE N. "SUPER JEW" FREEDMAN

One of the most storied, albeit little known, paratroopers to work for the CIA was Lawrence N. Freedman, a former Army Special Forces soldier who was killed in 1992 while working for the Agency in Somalia.

A native Philadelphian, Freedman had a boyhood reputation as a tough kid and was a natural athlete who excelled in diving and gymnastics. At 13, he attempted to rob a service station with a bow and arrow not so much for the money, but for the adrenaline rush. He attended Kansas State University in the late 1950s. There he quickly developed a reputation as a motorcycle-riding lady's man, a notorious flirt, a leader among his male peers, and something of a larger-than-life "superman" with whom no sane man wanted to tangle. Freedman thrived in the spotlight, and antics such as climbing buildings from balcony railings from one floor to the next earned him a moniker he would proudly carry with him for the rest of his life—"Super Jew."

A colorful character indeed, in 1965 Freedman enlisted in the U.S. Army and volunteered for airborne and Special Forces training. After earning his jump wings and his green beret, he was shipped to Vietnam where time and again he distinguished himself under fire. When the war ended, he remained in service but chafed under the yoke of inactivity. In 1978, he joined the Army's newly formed counterterrorist group, Operational Detachment-D, better known as Delta Force (see Chapter 11). With Delta Force—also known as the D-Boys—he honed his proficiency in hand-to-hand combat, marksmanship, and battlefield medicine.

Freedman's "Super Jew" nickname also became something of a source of affection and respect from his fellow D-Boys. Freedman recognized it and milked it for everything it was worth.

"In some ways, Lawrence N. Freedman was an unlikely candidate for the career he chose," wrote journalist Ted Gup in a 1997 article, "Star Agents," for *The Washington Post*. "Born into a devoutly Jewish home in Philadelphia, he brazenly declared himself 'SuperJew,' a nickname used by his colleagues in Delta Force, the elite counter-terrorist unit headquartered at Fort Bragg, N.C. His sister even made him a Superman-like cape with the Hebrew letter for 'S' that he wore at parties. On Friday evenings he would sometimes say the blessing over the Sabbath candles, but he could also be as obscene and profane as anyone on base."

In 1980, Freedman, still serving in Delta Force, was directly involved in the ill-fated attempt to rescue the 81 Americans held hostage by Iranian terrorists in Teheran. He left the Force in October 1982.

After Delta, according to Gup in *The Book of Honor*, Freedman's military record became somewhat "murky," and the mystery continued years after his death. "Only weeks after leaving Delta, Pentagon records note he was an 'infantry man (special project),'" wrote Gup. "A year later, he became a 'special projects team member.' None of those operations have come to light."

Beginning in 1984, Freedman served as a training instructor for the Army's fledgling counterterrorist commando forces. By 1986, he had attained the rank of Sergeant Major. But "Super Jew" was a combat soldier at heart and he was ready to get back into the fight.

He briefly considered working as a mercenary for the Mossad Le Aliyah Beth or simply MOSSAD, Israel's secret intelligence service. Instead, he applied to the U.S. Drug Enforcement Administration (DEA). Freedman was in perfect physical condition—running and lifting weights every day, but, being nearly 50 years old, the DEA wasn't interested.

Freedman then joined the CIA. He had worked with Agency officers on previous joint operations between the CIA and the Army, and he saw it as a way to get back into fieldwork. With the CIA, he served as a member of the Agency's newly established Counterterrorism Center.

On December 23, 1992, while operating with the CIA in Somalia, Freedman's luck ran out. He was killed as the jeep he was driving hit a land mine.

In death, the U.S. government officially described him to the media as "a civilian employee of the Department of Defense." But for his service to the nation, Director of Central Intelligence Robert M. Gates awarded him a posthumous Intelligence Star for exceptional service. According to the citation, Freedman was so awarded for his "superior performance under hazardous combat conditions with the Central Intelligence Agency."

Freedman also earned an anonymous "star" on the CIA's Wall of Honor and in the Agency's Book of Honor, both in the main lobby of the George Bush Center for Intelligence (CIA headquarters) in Langley, Virginia.

His life deeds were also remembered by his fellow paratroopers and Special Forces soldiers. Following his burial at Arlington National Cemetery, a call for contributions was made for an addition to the Special Warfare Museum at Fort Bragg, North Carolina. The addition will be known as the Sergeant First Class Lawrence "Super Jew" Freedman Memorial Theater.

AFTERWORD

As I pen the final chapters of this book, it seems wholly appropriate that Mars—the mythical Roman god of war—is closer to the earth than it has been in 60,000 years. It is still some 35 million miles away, but in the clear predawn darkness the rusty red planet can be seen with the naked eye. In fact, not since before the end of the Neanderthals have the two worlds—Earth and Mars—been so close.

Contemplating the fantastic history of American parachute forces and the future of airborne warfare, I watch the so-called war god blazing in the southwestern sky. From the point where I am standing in central South Carolina, Mars is positioned in the exact same sky where the pioneering men of the parachute test platoon first leapt 63 years ago—this very day—over Fort Benning, Georgia. And it is the same sky where nearly all America's airborne soldiers have since earned the title paratrooper, or died trying.

As Mars looks down upon me from that sky, American soldiers, sailors, airmen, and Marines—many wearing silver or gold parachute wings—are either holding the line or seeking out America's enemies in the current war against terror: a strange, shadowy war that has been raging for nearly two years. And it is not only in Afghanistan and Iraq where America's airborne warriors are fighting, winning, and sometimes dying. U.S. paratroopers are currently deployed throughout the world, often involved in dramatic operations and performing heroic deeds that—because of the clandestine nature of this war—may never be discussed outside their operational circles.

Like James A. Michener in his best-selling book *The Bridges at Toko-Ri*, I ask rhetorically, "Where do we get such men?" Then I remember my own experiences as a young airborne hopeful, not much more than a kid. I recall that sweltering summer at Fort Benning. That first exhausting day where the "black hats" ran us and dropped us for push-ups over and over again in an attempt to weed out those unwilling to stay the course. The face of that huge offensive lineman from a Midwestern university who, gasping for breath, struggled to his feet, conceded he'd "had enough," and quit. The frenzied pace of the next two weeks. Morning inspections. Endless deep knee bends. Hitting. Rolling. Leaping from towers. More push-ups. More deep knee bends. The sweat stinging our eyes as the Georgia sun burned our faces. Standing in awe as a tight formation of mature, heavily muscled Army Rangers ran by.

Then there was the heady combination of fear and exhilaration as we boarded the aircraft in week three. I jumped out of a C-123 and a C-130, both high-performance, propeller-driven transport planes, as well as a C-141, a much larger jet aircraft. In the C-130, I was the first man out the door. Consequently, I stood in the open door frame for several seconds, trying in vain to control my shaking legs as we neared the airspace over the drop zone.

Then above the deafening, rushing torrent of prop blast and high-altitude winds, I heard the jumpmaster's command, "Go!" and felt his hard slap on my thigh.

I hurled myself up and out into that brief whirling, roaring space between aircraft and Earth. "One thousand! Two thousand! Three thousand! Four thous ..." A quick jerk, and I was swinging beneath a fully blossomed canopy.

The world was suddenly silent again. The aircraft was droning away in the distance, and for the first time I could hear my breathing, my racing pulse, and the wind rattling the canopy panels above me. Below, parallel to, and above me were other parachutists, hundreds of them. A few were coming too close to others. Then quickly tugging on their risers, the jumpers slipped away from one another.

The earth below seemed flatter than usual, broad and as unforgivingly hard as granite.

A distant, single plume of colored smoke rose from the ground signaling the direction the wind was blowing. I reached up and pulled my parachute risers as hard as I could toward my chest and began turning into that wind, hoping to lessen the speed at which I would make contact with the earth.

As my eyes became level with the horizon, I brought my feet and knees together and braced for a "good" landing.

Wham! The force with which I hit the ground is impossible to articulate. Let's just say it was similar to that which would be felt by two fully padded football players running full steam into one another. Nevertheless, my training kicked in and my body instinctively tumbled properly on impact. I was down, alive, and uninjured.

Adrenaline pulsing through me, I made a fist and punched my harness-release mechanism, quickly clambered to my feet, and began gathering up my chute. Other jumpers dropped nearby and began the same procedure. Several hundred yards away, the "black hats" were barking unintelligible instructions through megaphones. "If only Mom and Dad could see me now," I thought. "If only the entire world could see me."

My fellow paratroopers and I endured those weeks at Benning for two primary reasons: the privilege of wearing a pair of thumb-size silver wings and earning what was to us a sacred title—paratrooper. For me, it was a feeling eclipsed only by my earning the title Marine—a similar feeling, I'm sure, for those who have earned the titles Ranger, Green Beret, or SEAL.

(Author's collection)

Cpl. W. Thomas Smith Jr., U.S. Marine Corps, in the early 1980s.

But there is another often unspoken reason young warriors become airborne. It is the fact that if war comes to their nation, they want to be the first to fight, and they want to fight shoulder to shoulder with the best in the war-fighting business. Though I felt those things as a young man,

I could not then offer a definitive reason why. Only looking back objectively can I say that it *seemed* to be a combination of a passionate sense of patriotism, a desire for adventure, a measure of physical courage beyond what most people are imbued with, and, of course, the risk and fear of death. It is an odd sense of control and empowerment: a coming to grips with the fact that there are some things worse than death, and that the risk of death somehow gives us inner strength.

It doesn't mean that we are not afraid: There can be no real courage without fear. But there is an empowering quality in fear and risk, particularly when we discover the inner means by which we can perform well despite our fears.

U.S. Army Lt. Col. Dave Grossman described this quality as the "dark power of atrocity." In his book *On Killing*, Grossman described how he, in fact, was empowered by death. "The first time I saw a soldier plummet to his death in a parachute jump it took years to sort out my emotions," said Grossman. "Part of me was horrified at this soldier's death, but as I watched him fight his tangled reserve chute all the way down another part of me was filled with pride. His death validated and affirmed all that I believe about paratroopers, who stare death in the face daily. That brave, doomed soldier became a living sacrifice to the spirit of the airborne."

Today, American paratroopers empowered by their own sense of patriotism, adventure, courage, and Grossman's "dark power of atrocity" continue to be in the first wave of the fight we are currently taking to the enemy. Perhaps they are further heartened by the nighttime presence of Mars, the god of war. Perhaps they view Mars as an omen, preferably a positive one.

Omen or not, America and the free world can take heart in the knowledge that the descendents of those magnificent "devils in baggy pants" are the ones doing battle with those who seek to wipe us and our way of life from the face of the earth.

Semper Fidelis,
W. Thomas Smith Jr.
August 16, 2003

PROCLAMATION OF NATIONAL AIRBORNE DAY BY THE PRESIDENT OF THE UNITED STATES

AUGUST 16, 2002

The history of Airborne forces began after World War I, when Brigadier General William Mitchell first conceived the idea of parachuting troops into combat. Eventually, under the leadership of Major William Lee at Fort Benning, Georgia, members of the Parachute Test Platoon pioneered methods of combat jumping in 1940. In November 1942, members of the 2nd Battalion, 503rd Parachute Infantry Regiment [see the sidebar at the end of the appendix], conducted America's first combat jump, leaping from a C-47 aircraft behind enemy lines in North Africa. This strategy revolutionized combat and established Airborne forces as a key component of our military.

During World War II, Airborne tactics were critical to the success of important missions, including the D-Day invasion at Normandy, the Battle of the Bulge, the invasion of Southern France, and many others. In Korea and Vietnam, Airborne soldiers played a critical combat role, as well as in later conflicts and peacekeeping operations, including Panama, Grenada, Desert Storm, Haiti, Somalia, and the Balkans. Most recently, Airborne forces were vital to liberating the people of Afghan-istan from the repressive and violent Taliban regime; and these soldiers continue to serve proudly around the world in the global coalition against terrorism.

The elite Airborne ranks include prestigious groups such as the 82nd Airborne Division, "America's Guard of Honor," and the "Screaming Eagles" of the 101st Airborne Division (Air Assault). Airborne forces have also been represented in the former 11th, 13th, and 17th Airborne Divisions and numerous other Airborne, glider and air assault units and regiments. Paratroopers in the Army's XVIII Airborne Corps, the 75th Infantry (Ranger) Regiment and other Special Forces units conduct swift and effective operations in defense of peace and freedom.

Airborne combat continues to be driven by the bravery and daring spirit of sky soldiers. Often called into action with little notice, these forces have earned an enduring reputation for dedication, excellence, and honor. As we face the challenges of a new era, I encourage all people to recognize the contributions of these courageous soldiers to our Nation and the world.

NOW, THEREFORE, I, GEORGE W. BUSH, President of the United States of America, by virtue of the authority vested in me by the Constitution and laws of the United States, do hereby proclaim August 16, 2002, as National Airborne Day. As we commemorate the first official Army parachute jump on August 16, 1940, I encourage all Americans to join me in honoring the thousands of soldiers, past and present, who have served in an Airborne capacity. I call upon all citizens to observe this day with appropriate programs, ceremonies, and activities.

IN WITNESS WHEREOF, I have hereunto set my hand this fourteenth day of August, in the year of our Lord two thousand two, and of the Independence of the United States of America the two hundred and twenty-seventh.

GEORGE W. BUSH

APPENDIX A: PROCLAMATION OF NATIONAL AIRBORNE DAY

Though the president contends it was the 2nd Battalion, 503rd Parachute Infantry Regiment that made the first combat jump; some histories state that the first combat jump was made by the 509th Parachute Infantry Battalion. Both the 2nd *Battalion* of the 503rd Parachute *Regiment* and the 509th Parachute Infantry *Battalion* were one in the same. The confusion stems from the fact that both the first-ever combat jump and the numerical redesignation of the 509th Battalion from the 2nd Battalion of the 503rd Regiment took place within weeks of one another. Either way, it was indeed the battalion in question that held both designations and made the first combat jump.

The first "National Airborne Day" was held exactly 62 years to the day after the first jump was made by the U.S. Army's "parachute test platoon," exactly 60 years to the day after the redesignation of the 101st Infantry Division to an airborne division, and exactly 42 years to the day after U.S. Air Force Capt. Joseph W. Kittinger Jr. made the highest-altitude parachute jump in history.

APPENDIX B

INTERESTING AIRBORNE "FIRSTS" AND FACTS

- The patron saint of paratroopers is Saint Michael. In the Judeo-Christian tradition, Michael is the archangel who led an angelic army loyal to God in the heavenly war against the devil and his followers.
- The first American leader to articulate the value of dropping armed men from the sky was Benjamin Franklin in 1784.
- The first American leader to propose parachuting armed men into combat was U.S. Army Air Corps Gen. William P. "Billy" Mitchell on October 17, 1918.
- The first American unit to be considered for airborne operations was the 1st Infantry Division—the "Big Red One"—on October 17, 1918. The 1st never did become an airborne division. To this day, it remains a regular infantry division, and it is considered one of the finest combat units in the world.
- Before the title *paratrooper* was adopted by the U.S. Army, a proposal was made by the Army Air Corps to refer to parachute soldiers as "air grenadiers."
- The "father of United States airborne" is Maj. Gen. William Carey "Bill" Lee.

- The first American military unit to supply men for airborne service was the 29th Infantry Regiment.
- The first American parachute unit was the U.S. Army's "parachute test platoon," established on June 26, 1940. The platoon made its first jump on August 16, 1940.
- The first American airborne instructors were parachute riggers from the U.S. Army Air Corps (the predecessor organization to the U.S. Air Force).
- The first American airborne officer to parachute from an airplane was 1st Lt. William T. Ryder of the "parachute test platoon."
- The first American airborne-enlisted soldier to parachute from an airplane was Pvt. William N. "Red" King, also known as "the Spartan," of the "parachute test platoon."
- The first paratrooper to yell "Geronimo!" while jumping from an airplane was U.S. Army Pvt. Aubrey Eberhardt of the "parachute test platoon" over Fort Benning, Georgia, August 1940.
- The first combat-ready American airborne force was the U.S. Army's 501st Parachute Battalion, established in November 1940. The 501st was formed from the "parachute test platoon."
- The first American soldiers to wear "jump wings" were the paratroopers of the Army's 501st Parachute Battalion. The wings were presented to the 501st on March 15, 1941.
- The lowest-altitude mass tactical parachute jump was conducted by the U.S. Army's 509th Parachute Infantry in June 1942. The jump, conducted at 143 feet above the earth's surface, was part of a large-scale training exercise over England. German *Fallschirmjäger* (paratroopers) made the lowest-altitude mass "combat" jump—250 feet—over Crete the previous year. In July 1944, the Pacific island of Noemfoor was the site of the lowest-altitude mass combat jump by American paratroopers. There the 1st Battalion, 503rd Parachute Infantry Regiment, conducted a 400-foot combat jump. However, inaccurate altimeter readings led two of the transport pilots to inadvertently drop two plane loads of sky soldiers at an astonishing 175 feet above the earth's surface.

- Just prior to and during World War II, U.S. Marines earned their jump wings at the Parachute Training Schools at Lakehurst, New Jersey; New River, North Carolina; Camp Elliot, California; and Camp Gillespie, California.

- The first American airborne force to engage in combat against an armed enemy was the U.S. Marine Corps' 1st Parachute Regiment. The action was fought on the Pacific island of Gavutu against the Japanese in August 1942. However, the Marines did not jump into the fight; they landed from the sea in classic Marine fashion.

- The unofficial "father of Marine airborne" is Lt. Col. Robert H. Williams.

- The first American airborne force to parachute into combat was the U.S. Army's 509th Parachute Infantry Battalion (previously designated as the 2nd Battalion of the 503rd Parachute Infantry Regiment). Paratroopers of the 509th, an independent battalion, jumped from a C-47 transport aircraft behind enemy lines in North Africa on November 8, 1942.

- The first civilian war correspondent to jump into action was reporter John H. "Jack" Thompson—also known as "Beaver" Thompson—of the *Chicago Tribune*. On November 15, 1942, Thompson jumped with Lt. Col. Edson Duncan Raff's 509th Parachute Infantry Battalion over Youks-les-Bains, Algeria.

- The first American airborne force to parachute into combat in the Pacific was the U.S. Army's 503rd (Parachute Infantry) Regimental Combat Team (RCT). On September 5, 1943, the 503rd RCT jumped over the Japanese-held Markham Valley on New Guinea. Aside from its tactical success, the jump proved to senior American military planners that vertical envelopment operations were viable.

- The first American paratrooper to win the Congressional Medal of Honor was Cpl. Paul B. Huff of the 509th Parachute Infantry Battalion. Huff won the award for "conspicuous gallantry and intrepidity at risk of life above and beyond the call of duty, in action on 8 February 1944, near Carano, Italy."

- The first American paratrooper to land in German-occupied France on D-day—June 6, 1944—was Capt. Frank L. Lilly, a pathfinder attached to the 101st Airborne Division. Lilly jumped just after midnight at exactly 12:15 A.M.

- Among the Marines who participated in the famous flag-raising on Iwo Jima's Mount Suribachi in 1945 were three Marine Corps parachutists. Sgt. Henry O. Hansen assisted in the raising of the first small flag. Cpls. Ira H. Hayes and Harlon H. Block were among the immortal six men who raised the second, larger flag. The second flag-raising was captured on film by Associated Press photographer Joe Rosenthal.

- The only large-scale American parachute assault during the Vietnam War was conducted by the U.S. Army's independent 173rd Airborne Brigade. The drop was made on February 22, 1967, during Operation Junction City.

- The first Marine Corps unit in history to make a "combat" jump was the 1st Force Reconnaissance Company during the Vietnam War. In fact, 1st Force Recon made the Corps' first three jumps. The first was a Recon team of 12 Marines lead by Capt. Jerome Paull on June 14, 1966. The second was a nine-man team lead by Gun. Sgt. Walter Webb on September 5, 1967. The third was a six-man team led by 1st Lt. Wayne Rollings on November 17, 1969.

- U.S. paratroopers receive their coveted silver parachute wings after successfully completing five parachute jumps or one combat jump.

- U.S. paratroopers from all branches of service receive their basic parachute training at Fort Benning, Georgia. However, the decades-old tradition of sailors attending Army jump school may soon be coming to an end. As of this writing, according to Naval Reserve Lt. Cmdr. Mark Divine, SEALs are scheduled to begin parachute training in house.

- Although the numbers of U.S. Air Force personnel who train for ground combat are far fewer than the numbers of U.S. Army soldiers who do so, the Air Force's Combat Controllers are usually the first men on the ground during any large-scale Army Airborne operation. The reason is that the airmen are responsible for setting up the drop zone.

- Although they undergo parachute familiarization training, American military pilots are not required to attend basic parachute training.

AIRBORNE CREED

Author's note: Two versions of the American Airborne Creed (also known as the Airborne Soldier's Creed or the Paratrooper's Creed) have been written. Both follow, with the terms and expressions used in the earliest published version of the creed noted parenthetically.

AIRBORNE CREED (1)

I volunteered as a parachutist (an airborne soldier), fully realizing the hazard of my chosen service and by my thoughts and actions will always uphold the prestige, honor and high esprit de corps of parachute troops (the airborne).

I realize that a parachutist (airborne soldier) is not merely a soldier who arrives by parachute to fight, but is an elite shock trooper and that his country expects him to march farther and faster, to fight harder, to be more self-reliant than any other soldier (man). Parachutists of all allied armies belong to this great brotherhood.

I shall never fail my fellow comrades by shirking any duty or training, but will always keep myself mentally and physically fit and shoulder my full share of the task, whatever it may be.

I shall always accord my superiors fullest loyalty and I will always bear in mind the sacred trust I have in the lives of the men I will accompany (lead) in to battle (combat).

I shall show other soldiers by my military courtesy, neatness of dress and care of my weapons and equipment that I am a picked and well trained soldier.

I shall endeavor always to reflect the high standards of training and morale of parachute troops.

I shall respect the abilities of my enemies, I will fight fairly and with all my might, surrender is not in my creed.

I shall display a high degree of initiative and will fight on to my objective and mission, though I be the lone survivor.

I shall prove my ability as a fighting man against the enemy on the field of battle, not by quarreling with my comrades in arms or by bragging about my deeds (which needlessly arouses jealousy and resentment against airborne troops).

I shall always realize that battles are won by an army fighting as a team, that I fight first and blaze the path into battle for others to follow and carry the battle on.

I belong to the finest unit in the world (Army). By my (appearance,) actions and (battlefield) deeds alone, I speak for my fighting ability. I will strive to uphold the honor and prestige of my outfit, making my country proud of me and the unit to which I belong (serve).

(This version of the Airborne Creed is excerpted from "US Army Infantry School Guide for Airborne Students," June 1993, author anonymous.)

AIRBORNE CREED (2)

I am an airborne Trooper! A paratrooper!

I jump by parachute from any plane in flight.

I volunteered to do it, knowing well the hazards of my choice.

I serve in a mighty airborne force—famed for deeds in war—renowned for readiness in peace. It is my pledge to uphold its honor and prestige in all I am—in all I do.

I am an elite trooper—a sky trooper—a shock trooper—a spearhead trooper.

I blaze the way to far-flung goals—behind, before, above the foe's front line.

I know that I may have to fight without support for days on end.

Therefore, I keep mind and body always fit to do my part in any airborne task.

I am self-reliant and unafraid. I shoot true, and march fast and far.

I fight hard and excel in every art and artifice in war.

I never fail a fellow trooper.

I cherish as a sacred trust the lives of men with whom I serve.

Leaders have my fullest loyalty, and those I lead never find me lacking.

I have pride in the airborne! I never let it down!

In peace, I do not shirk the dullest duty nor protest the toughest training.

My weapons and equipment are always combat ready. I am neat of dress—military in courtesy—proper in conduct and behavior.

In battle, I fear no foe's ability, nor underestimate his prowess, power and guile. I fight him with all my might and skill—ever alert to evade capture or escape a trap.

I never surrender, though I be the last.

My goal in peace or war is to succeed in any mission of the day—or die, if need be, in the try.

I belong to a proud and glorious team—the airborne, the Army, my Country.

I am its chosen pride to fight where others may not go—to serve them well until the final victory.

I am a trooper of the sky! I am my Nation's best! In peace and war I never fail.

Anywhere, anytime, in anything—I am AIRBORNE!

(This version of the Airborne Creed is excerpted from the book Airborne: A Guided Tour of an Airborne Task Force *by Tom Clancy. It is also found on the official website of the U.S. Army Infantry, Fort Benning, Georgia, at www.benning.army.mil/airborne/content/history.htm. There is no published attribution for this particular version of the Airborne Creed, but it is widely attributed to Michael Meister in other sources.)*

THE PARACHUTE RIGGERS' PLEDGE

I will pack every parachute as though I am to jump with it myself and will stand ready to jump with any parachute I have certified.

I will remember always that another human life is as dear as my own.

I will never pass over any defect, nor neglect any repair, no matter how small, as I know that omissions and mistakes in the rigging of a parachute may cost a life.

I will never sign my name to a parachute inspection or packing certificate unless I have personally performed or directly supervised every step, and am entirely satisfied with all the work.

I will keep always a wholehearted respect for my vocation, regarding it as a high profession rather than a day-to-day task, and will keep in mind constantly my grave responsibility.

I will be sure always.

PARACHUTIST BADGES OF AMERICAN AIRBORNE FORCES

PARACHUTIST

The signature emblem of American airborne forces is the familiar "silver wings" badge worn by graduates—from all branches of service—of the U.S. Army airborne school. Officially approved for wear on March 10, 1941, the badge was designed by Cpt. William Pelham "Bill" Yarborough of the U.S. Army's 501st Parachute Battalion (Yarborough would rise to the rank of lieutenant general). Five days after the badge was approved, paratroopers of the 501st pinned them over their left breast pockets, becoming the first soldiers in American military history to wear jump wings.

The badge is today—just as it was then—comprised of an open silver parachute centered over a pair of inwardly curving silver wings.

Senior officers and noncommissioned officers in both the Army and Air Force are often seen wearing the traditional jump wings with a star or a star-and-laurel wreath above the parachute canopy. Both the star and the star-and-laurel wreath—approved for wear on January 24, 1950—signify a higher degree of airborne qualification and experience. A star fixed above the badge indicates the wearer is a senior parachutist. The star-and-laurel wreath indicates a master parachutist.

The official qualification degree requirements are as follows.

Basic Parachutist

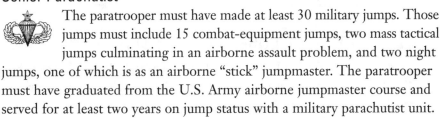

Any soldier, sailor, airman, or Marine who has "satisfactorily completed all of the prescribed proficiency tests while assigned or attached to an airborne unit or the Airborne Department of the Infantry School" is qualified to wear the wings of a basic parachutist. To qualify, an individual must have completed five military parachute jumps from an airplane or participated in at least one combat parachute jump.

Senior Parachutist

The paratrooper must have made at least 30 military jumps. Those jumps must include 15 combat-equipment jumps, two mass tactical jumps culminating in an airborne assault problem, and two night jumps, one of which is as an airborne "stick" jumpmaster. The paratrooper must have graduated from the U.S. Army airborne jumpmaster course and served for at least two years on jump status with a military parachutist unit.

Master Parachutist

The paratrooper must have made 65 military jumps. Those jumps must include 25 combat-equipment jumps; 5 mass tactical jumps "culminating in an airborne assault problem with a unit equivalent to a battalion or larger, a separate company/battery, or organic staff of a regiment size or larger"; and 4 night jumps, one of which is as an airborne "stick" jumpmaster. The paratrooper must have graduated from the U.S. Army airborne jumpmaster course and served for at least three years on jump status with a military parachutist unit.

Combat Parachutist

Tiny bronze stars superimposed on the basic, senior, or master parachutist badge indicate that the wearer has jumped into combat.

 One tiny bronze star centered on the parachute just below the canopy signifies one combat jump.

 Two tiny bronze stars mounted on each wing signify two combat jumps.

 Three tiny bronze stars, one centered on the parachute just below the canopy and two on each wing, signify three combat jumps.

 Four tiny bronze stars, two of which are mounted on each wing, signify four combat jumps.

A slightly larger gold star centered on the parachute just below the canopy signifies five combat jumps.

NAVY AND MARINE CORPS PARACHUTIST

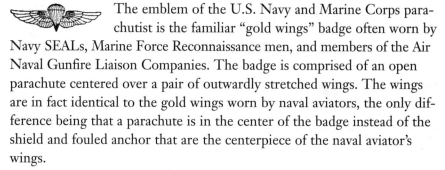 The emblem of the U.S. Navy and Marine Corps parachutist is the familiar "gold wings" badge often worn by Navy SEALs, Marine Force Reconnaissance men, and members of the Air Naval Gunfire Liaison Companies. The badge is comprised of an open parachute centered over a pair of outwardly stretched wings. The wings are in fact identical to the gold wings worn by naval aviators, the only difference being that a parachute is in the center of the badge instead of the shield and fouled anchor that are the centerpiece of the naval aviator's wings.

Before winning the coveted gold wings, sailors and Marines must first attend the U.S. Army airborne training "jump" school—or make one combat jump—and win their "basic parachutist" badge. Then they must make five additional "qualifying" jumps with a Navy or Marine Corps unit whose mission includes parachute jumping. A common misconception is that five additional jumps are all that is required beyond jump school, but the five must meet certain requirements (night, equipment, varying altitudes, and so on). The gold wings are worn in lieu of the silver wings. The Navy and Marine Corps parachutist badge was adopted on July 12, 1963.

MILITARY FREE-FALL PARACHUTIST

The most recently designed and officially authorized badge of airborne forces is the silver dagger-and-wings emblem of military free-fall parachutists. The badge is comprised of a Fairbairn-Sykes commando knife that is centered—blade up—over a pair of outwardly stretched, downwardly sloping wings. Also in the center is a small, arched "tab." Rising above the dagger and wings is an open ram-air parachute.

The commando knife is symbolic of special operations forces. The badge is one of several models used by U.S. Army Rangers and operatives of the Office of Strategic Services (the predecessor organization of the modern Central Intelligence Agency) during World War II. The arched tab represents the shoulder tabs worn by Rangers and other special operations forces. The wings are a symbol of flight and airborne forces, and the ram-air parachute symbolizes free-falling parachutists.

A prototype of the badge was designed in 1983 by Sgt. First Class Gregory A. Dailey of the 5th Special Forces Group. The final design—including a star-and-wreath addition for free-fall jumpmasters—was later developed by Gen. Wayne A. Downing and a civilian historian with the Special Forces Association, James Phillips. The badge was initially approved for wear by qualified free-fall parachutists assigned to the U.S. Army's Special Operations Command (and subordinate elements) on October 1, 1994. Unrestricted wear was approved on July 7, 1997.

The military free-fall badge is awarded at two levels: basic and jumpmaster.

Before winning the basic free-fall badge, paratroopers must accomplish one of two tasks. They must complete a military free-fall training program approved by the U.S. Army's John F. Kennedy Special Warfare Center and School at Fort Bragg, North Carolina, or they must make at least one military free-fall "combat" jump. To receive a jumpmaster badge, paratroopers must complete a military free-fall program for jumpmasters approved by the Kennedy Special Warfare Center.

PARACHUTE RIGGER

The silver parachute rigger badge is comprised of a pair of extended wings with an open parachute in the center. Emblazoned across the parachute lines is a tab with the engraved title "rigger."

The first parachute rigger badge was designed by U.S. Army Maj. Thomas R. Cross of the 11th Airborne Division in 1948. The badge, which was made of cloth, was comprised of an open parachute with a single wing extended on the right. In time, another wing was added and the title "rigger" was emblazoned across the parachute lines in bold red letters. Though rigger badges have been worn unofficially for years, the current silver, metal parachute rigger badge was officially approved for wear on June 9, 1986.

Before winning the parachute rigger badge, soldiers must first successfully complete jump school at Fort Benning, Georgia. This is followed by a required course of instruction for parachute riggers offered by the Aerial Delivery and Field Services Department at the U.S. Army Quartermaster Center and School in Fort Lee, Virginia.

GLIDER

Though no longer awarded, as gliderborne infantry no longer exists, the "silver wings" badge of gliderborne forces was similar in design to the basic parachutist badge. The wings were slightly different, and instead of a parachute, the badge's central piece was the frontal view of a glider.

The badge was authorized for wear on June 2, 1944, just four days before glider troops—and their parachuting brothers—were to spearhead the famous Invasion of Normandy.

Those authorized to wear the badge had to have completed the required course of instruction for gliderborne warfare or made at least one combat glider assault. Additionally, glider soldiers had to have been assigned or attached to a gliderborne or airborne unit.

PATHFINDER

 Though most pathfinders are first and foremost experienced paratroopers, a soldier does not have to be airborne qualified to become a pathfinder. Nevertheless, the path-finder badge is listed among airborne badges because the role of the American path-finder is inextricably connected to the overall mission of U.S. airborne forces.

The unique U.S. Army Pathfinder badge is comprised of a gold "sinister" wing attached to a gold torch with red and gray flames. The wing is symbolic of flight and airborne forces, whereas the torch represents guidance in darkness, which is the basic responsibility of a pathfinder. The badge was originally a felt patch approved for wear on May 22, 1964. The patch was replaced with the current metal and enamel badge on October 11, 1968. The pathfinder badge is awarded to soldiers who complete the U.S. Army's pathfinder training program at Fort Benning, Georgia.

THE BERET: A SYMBOL OF AIRBORNE FORCES

The beret, a distinctive form of military headdress for most American airborne soldiers, first appeared in the form of a bonnet that was worn by Scottish Highland warriors in the seventeenth century. Soon thereafter a continental variation of the bonnet—the beret—appeared in France and Spain.

In the 1920s, British armored forces began wearing berets as a practical alternative to their "stiff khaki service-dress caps." Such caps had to be worn backward or be removed completely while working inside a tank in order to sight the vehicle's main gun. Soon, the beret became a symbol of tank crews worldwide.

During World War II, the wearing of berets expanded to several units within the British army, and varying colors distinguished one unit from another. For instance, the crack British airborne forces wore the now-famous maroon beret, the British Special Air Service (SAS) commandos wore khaki berets, and Royal Marines and British army commandos wore green berets.

The beret was first worn by American troops in 1943, when British Airborne Gen. Sir Frederick A. M. Browning authorized the presentation of maroon berets to paratroopers of the 509th

Parachute Infantry Regiment for their stellar service. The American paratroopers proudly wore their jaunty British berets, but the U.S. Army did not grant authorization for official use.

A few years after the war, the U.S. Marine Corps briefly experimented with green and blue berets, but Corps' leaders concluded that berets looked too "foreign" and "feminine" for leathernecks.

In 1953, a handful of "special warfare" soldiers within the Army began unofficially wearing berets. The soldiers were members of a newly formed counterinsurgency organization known as Special Forces, soon to be known affectionately as the Green Berets.

On October 12, 1961, President John F. Kennedy visited Fort Bragg, North Carolina. There he was greeted by Brig. Gen. William Pelham "Bill" Yarborough and his Special Forces men, all of whom at Yarborough's direction were wearing green berets. Yarborough, one of the "founding fathers" of both American airborne and special operations forces, had previously designed the famous silver parachute wings and would become one of the earliest proponents of airborne soldiers wearing red berets.

"Those [the berets] are nice," the president remarked. "How do you like the green beret?"

Yarborough replied, "They're fine, sir. We've wanted them a long time."

Green berets for Special Forces were approved later that day.

During the Vietnam War, berets of varying colors—mostly shades of green, black, blue, and red—were worn by certain units and individuals in the Army, Navy, and Air Force, sometimes without official authorization.

In the early post–Vietnam War years, Army commanders were encouraged to make "morale-enhancing uniform distinctions" in an attempt to boost the waning esprit de corps in an army demoralized by the strategic loss in Southeast Asia and the American public's distaste for all things military. As a result, the wearing of berets increased, particularly in tank units and armored cavalry regiments. In both cases, soldiers began donning the traditional black beret worn decades earlier by British armored forces.

In 1973, paratroopers in the 82nd Airborne Division began wearing the maroon beret. Soon thereafter soldiers in the 101st began sporting a short-lived light blue beret. Other units—nonairborne—began donning olive green, light green, and red berets. Two years later, the Department of the Army authorized the wearing of black berets by all Army Rangers.

By 1979, the wearing of colored berets had become so widespread that Army leadership halted all use without official authorization. The Rangers were allowed to keep their black versions, the Special Forces retained their green berets, and all paratroopers were permitted to don maroon berets.

For the next two decades, berets in the U.S. Army were a symbol of elite forces, all of which were comprised of airborne-qualified soldiers.

In October 2000, Army Chief of Staff Gen. Eric Shinseki created a firestorm of controversy—particularly within the Army special operations and airborne communities—when he announced that the black beret would become standard Army issue for all soldiers the following year. Shinseki believed that such a move would instill pride and foster an attitude of excellence throughout the Army.

Ordinary soldiers with no desire to enter the world of special operations were thrilled. Rangers, Special Forces soldiers, and paratroopers were shocked, as were many airborne-trained veterans.

"This is the dumbest decision the Army has made since Custer's last stand," said Jim Grimshaw, a retired Army officer and president of the U.S. Army Ranger Association, during a December 2000 interview. "This is a treasured symbol you should have to earn versus just giving it away."

Today all soldiers in the U.S. Army rate black berets. Army Special Forces rate green, Army Rangers rate tan (khaki), and Army airborne units rate red (or maroon).

In the Air Force, only Combat Controllers and Pararescuemen (both airborne qualified) rate maroon berets. Air Force Security Police (the Air Force's version of military police) rate dark blue berets.

Marines and sailors, however, do not wear berets, even those who are airborne qualified.

AIRBORNE DEMONSTRATION TEAMS

The U.S. Army, Navy, and Air Force all maintain parachute demonstration teams. The Army team is known as the Golden Knights, the Navy team is known as the Leap Frogs, and the Air Force team is known as the STARS.

The oldest team is the Golden Knights, who trace their lineage back to 1959 when Brig. Gen. Joseph Stillwell, who was serving as Chief of Staff of the XVIII Airborne Corps, established the Strategic Army Corps Parachute Team. On June 1, 1961, the team became the United States Army Parachute Team. The following year the parachute team was officially renamed the Golden Knights, the title reflecting both the gold medals team jumpers had won and their "conquest of the skies."

The Leap Frogs trace their lineage back to 1969. At that time, Navy SEALs and former Navy frogmen volunteered to perform during air shows. The team was then known as the U.S. Navy UDT/SEAL Exhibition Parachute Team. The team's demonstration jumps were so successful in promoting the Navy and its recruiting efforts that in 1974 the chief of naval operations ordered the establishment of a permanent Navy parachute demonstration team. The team became officially known as the U.S. Navy Parachute Team Leap Frogs, a tribute to the fact that the vast majority of the team's jumpers have always been SEALs and/or their frogmen forebears.

In 1996, the Air Force established the parachute demonstration team the STARS—an acronym for Special Tactics and Rescue Specialists. Unlike the Army and Navy teams, jumping with the STARS is not a permanent duty assignment. STARS parachutists are all full-time Combat Controllers or Pararescuemen who take the time to perform for the public. Theoretically, these airmen may jump for show one day and be fighting enemy forces the next.

In addition to these three famous teams, other lesser-known "unit" parachute demonstration teams exist throughout the U.S. armed forces.

APPENDIX H

BIBLIOGRAPHY

"1st Infantry Division History." Cantigny First Division Foundation website, 2000–2001. http://www.rrmtf.org/firstdivision/

"101st Airborne Division (Air Assault)." CNN.com Special Report—War in Iraq, 2003. http://www.cnn.com.

"173rd Airborne Brigade." CNN.com Special Report—War in Iraq, 2003. http://www.cnn.com.

"504th Parachute Infantry." 504th Parachute Infantry Regiment website, 2003. http://bragg.army.mil.

A1C William H. Pitsenbarger website, 2003. www.angelfire.com/mo2/Mudsoldiers/Pitsenbarger.html.

Abbott, Donald E. "A Condensed History of the 503rd Parachute Regimental Combat Team (The 503rd Parachute Regimental Combat Team Heritage Battalion Online)." The Corregidor Historic Society, 1997. corregidor.org/503_abbott/503.htm.

"A Brief History of the 82nd Airborne Division." 82nd Airborne Division website, July 17, 2003. bragg.army.mil/www-82DV/.

"Airborne Soldier's Creed." *The Bayonet*, May 16, 1946.

Airborne and Special Operations Insignia. Quartermaster Museum, U.S. Army Quartermaster Corps website, March 25, 2001. http://www.qmmuseum.lee.army.mil/airborne.

Agee, Philip. *Inside the Company: CIA Diary.* New York, NY: Farrar Straus & Giroux, 1975.Ambrose, Stephen E. *Band of Brothers: E Company, 506th Regiment, 101st Airborne from Normandy to Hitler's Eagle's Nest.* New York: Simon & Schuster, 1992.

Anderson, Rich. "The United States Army in World War II." Military History Online website, 2000. militaryhistoryonline.com/wwii/usarmy/infantry.aspx.

The Army Almanac: A Book of Facts Concerning the Army of the United States. Washington, DC: U.S. Government Printing Office, 1950.

"Army Jump School: Not Just a Training Course for Soldiers." About.com, 2003.

"A Quick Look at 82nd Airborne Division Training." 82nd Airborne Division website, 2003. bragg.army.mil/www-82dv/Training.htm.

Astor, Gerald. *June 6, 1944—The Voices of D-Day.* New York: Dell, 1994.

Atkinson, Rick. *Crusade—The Untold Story of the Persian Gulf War.* New York: Houghton Mifflin, 1993.

"Bald Eagle: The U.S.A.'s National Symbol." American Eagle Foundation website, 2003.

Bank, Aaron. *From OSS to Green Berets: The Birth of Special Forces.* Novato, CA: Presidio Press, 1986.

Barris, Ted. "What ties a day to history? I now know the June 6, 1944, invasion largely succeeded because of the trust between soldiers." *The Globe and Mail,* June 6, 2003.

Bass, Jack, and Marilyn W. Thompson. *Ol' Strom: An Unauthorized Biography of Strom Thurmond.* Marietta, GA: Longstreet Press, 1998.

Bentley, Stewart. "Of Market-Garden and Melanie: 'The Dutch Resistance and the OSS.'" Central Intelligence Agency Center for the Study of Intelligence website, Spring 1998. cia.gov/csi/studies/spring98/index.html.

Billings, Linwood W. "The Tunisian Task Force." Historical Test Archive website, 1990–2003. historicaltextarchive.com

Blair, Clay. *Ridgway's Paratroopers—The American Airborne in World War II.* Garden City, NY: The Dial Press, 1985.

Bolger, Daniel P. *Americans at War, 1975–1986, an Era of Violent Peace.* Novato, CA: Presidio Press, 1988.

Bowden, Mark. "Blackhawk Down (the *Philadelphia Inquirer* series)." *The Philadelphia Inquirer*, November 16, 1997—February 2, 1998.

Broder, Jonathon. "The army of the right." (An interview with author Thomas E. Ricks.) Salon.com, January 1998. salon.com/news/1998/01/06news.html.

Brown, Arthur. "The Jedburghs: A Short History." April 1991. freespace.virgin.net/arthur.brown2/index.htm.

Burgett, Donald R. *Currahee! A Screaming Eagle at Normandy.* New York: Presidio Press, 1999.

Burns, Robert. "Assistant Army Secretary Sara Lister says she thinks 'the Army is much more connected to society than the Marines are.'" The Associated Press, November 14, 1997.

Burriss, Moffatt T. *Strike and Hold—A Memoir of the 82nd Airborne in World War II.* Washington, DC: Brassey's, 2000.

Bush, George W. National Airborne Day, 2002: A Proclamation by the President of the United States of America. Washington, DC: The White House, Office of the Press Secretary, August 16, 2002.

———. Transcript: [President George W.] Bush Announces End of Major Combat Operations in Iraq. Washington, DC: United States Department of State, Office of International Information Programs, May 1, 2003.

Calhoun, William C. "Bless 'em all." Brisbane, Australia: The 503rd Parachute Regimental Combat Team Heritage Battalion Online. The Corregidor Historic Society, 1999–2003. corregidor.org.

Carter, Phillip. "How Are Army Divisions Numbered?" March 28, 2003. slate.msn.com.

Carter, Ross S. *Those Devils in Baggy Pants*. Mattituck, NY: Amereon House, 1951.

Cerasini, Marc. *The Complete Idiot's Guide to the U.S. Special Ops Forces*. Indianapolis: Alpha Books, 2002.

Clancy, Tom. *Airborne: A Guided Tour of an Airborne Task Force*. New York: Berkley Publishing, 1997.

———. *Marine: A Guided Tour of a Marine Expeditionary Unit*. New York: Berkley Publishing, 1996.

Clark, William George, and William Aldis Wright. *The Unabridged William Shakespeare: A Complete Library of His Works*. Birmingham, Alabama: Sweetwater Press, 1997.

Cole, Ronald H. *Operation Urgent Fury: The Planning and Execution of Joint Operations in Grenada*. Washington, DC: Joint History Office, Office of the Chairman of the Joint Chiefs of Staff, 1997.

Collins, Thomas W. "173rd Airborne Brigade in Iraq." *Army*, June 2003.

Contemporary Authors Online. Gale Group Databases, 2003.

Cronkite, Walter. *A Reporter's Life*. New York: Alfred A. Knopf, 1997.

———. Foreword to *Silent Wings at War: Combat Gliders in World War II*, by John L. Lowden. Washington, DC: Smithsonian Institution Press, 1992.

"Currahee Mountain." *Georgia*, 2001.

Cunningham, H. S. "An open letter from the commanding general to the men of the 173rd Airborne Brigade." *Sky Soldier*, June 1, 1970.

Denger, Mark J. *Historic California Posts—A Brief History of the U.S. Marine Corps in San Diego*. Sacramento, CA: California Center for Military History, California State Military Department, The California State Military Museum, 2003.

Devlin, Gerard M. *Paratrooper! The Saga of U.S. Army and Marine Parachute and Glider Combat Troops during World War II*. New York: St. Martin's Press, 1979.

Dunnigan, James F. *The Perfect Soldier: Special Operations, Commandos, and the Future of U.S. Warfare*. New York: Citadel Press, 2003.

"Early U.S. Army Glider Training Program." National WWII Glider Pilots Association, Inc., website, 2003. ww2gp.org/training.htm.

Eisenhower, Dwight D. *Crusade in Europe*. Garden City, NY: Doubleday & Company, 1948.

Enkoji, M. S. "Black smoke jumpers' bittersweet past." *Sacramento Bee*, April 8, 2000.

"The Face of Battle." Washington, DC: Federation of American Scientists website, 2000. fas.org.

Fall, Bernard B. *Street Without Joy*. Mechanicsburg, PA: Stackpole Books, 1994.

Flanagan, Edward M. Jr. *Airborne—A Combat History of American Airborne Forces*. New York: Presidio Press, 2002.

———. *The Angels: A History of the 11th Airborne Division*. Novato, CA: Presidio Press, 1989.

———. *The Los Banos Raid: The 11th Airborne Jumps at Dawn*. Novato, CA: Presidio Press, 1986.

"For Men Only—Airborne U.S. Army." Fort Benning, GA: Airborne Recruiting brochure, circa 1950–1960.

Frisbee, John L. "The Longest Leap." *Air Force*, June 1985.

Frizzell, Art. Office of Strategic Services Operational Groups. 2003. ossog.org.

Fuentes, Gidget. "Starting Small, Corps Joins World Of Spec Ops." *Navy Times*, June 30, 2003.

Gabel, Kurt. *The Making of a Paratrooper: Airborne Training and Combat in World War II*. Lawrence, KS: University Press of Kansas, 1990.

Galvin, John R. *Air Assault: The Development of Airmobile Warfare*. New York: Hawthorne Books, 1969.

Gavin, James M. *On to Berlin: Battles of an Airborne Commander, 1943–1946.* New York: Viking Press, 1978.

Gawne, Jonathan. *Spearheading D-Day: American Special Units in Normandy.* Paris, France: Histoire & Collections, 1998.

"The 'G' stands for guts." Lubbock Online website, October 18, 2002. lubbockonline.com/silentwings2/pilot.shtml.

Grossman, Dave. *On Killing: The Psychological Cost of Learning to Kill in War and Society.* Boston: BackBay Books, 1996.

Gup, Ted. *The Book of Honor.* New York: Random House, 2000.

Hackworth, David H. *About Face: The Odyssey of an American Warrior.* New York: Touchstone, Simon & Schuster, 1989.

Halberstadt, Hans. *Airborne: Assault from the Sky.* Novato, CA: Presidio Press, 1988.

"Harold Raynsford Stark, Admiral, United States Navy." Arlington National Cemetery website, December 11, 1999. arlingtoncemetery.com/hrstark.htm.

"Henry L. Stimson." Nuclear Age Peace Foundation website, 2002. nuclearfiles.org.

"Historic World Leaders." Farmington Hills, MI: Gale Group Databases, 2003.

"History of the 11th Airborne Division, The Angels." Grunts.net, 1999–2000.

Hoffman, Jon T. *Silk Chutes and Hard Fighting: U.S. Marine Corps Parachute Units in World War II.* Washington, DC: History and Museums Division, Headquarters, U.S. Marine Corps, 1999.

"In Depth: Afghanistan 2003—Operation Athena: Canadian Units in Afghanistan." CBC News Online, Canadian Broadcasting Corporation, July 21, 2003. http://www.cbc.ca.

Kazmierski, Michael J. "United States Army Power Projection in the 21st Century: The Conventional Airborne Forces Must Be Modernized to Meet the Army Chief of Staff's Strategic Force Requirements and the Nation's Future Threats." 2003. geocities.com/equipmentshop/airborne52.htm.

"King Philip's War: The Causes." Pilgrim Hall Museum website, July 14, 1998. pilgrimhall.org/philipwar.htm.

Lanning, Michael Lee. *Blood Warriors: American Military Elites*. New York: Ballantine Books, 2002.

Lanning, Michael Lee, and Ray William Stubbe. *Inside Force Recon: Recon Marines in Vietnam*. New York: Ivy Books, 1989.

Leckie, Robert. *Warfare*. New York: Harper & Row, 1970.

"Lewis Hyde Brereton, Lieutenant General, United States Air Force." Arlington National Cemetery website, December 3, 2001. arlingtoncemetery.com/brereton.htm.

"Little Rock Central High School National Historic Site—We Shall Overcome, Historic Places of the Civil Rights Movement." Little Rock, Arkansas, National Park Service website, October 15, 2003. www.cr.nps.gov/nr/travel/civilrights/ak1.htm.

Lowden, John L. *Silent Wings at War: Combat Gliders in World War II*. Washington, DC: Smithsonian Institution Press, 1992.

MacFarquhar, Neil. "U.S. Commander Confirms Search for 2 Top Targets Is Over." *The New York Times*, July 22, 2003.

Manchester, William. *American Caesar: Douglas MacArthur, 1880–1964*. Canada: Little Brown & Company, 1978.

Matloff, Maurice. *American Military History—Army Historical Series*. Washington, DC: Office of the Chief of Military History, United States Army, 1969.

"MC-130E Combat Talon I." GlobalSecurity.org, 2003.

McGowan, Sam. "Liberating Los Baños—As Allied forces reclaimed the Philippines, a number of prisons were liberated, including a civilian internment camp on the island of Luzon." *World War II*, January 1998.

McKenzie, John. *On Time On Target: The World War II Memoir of a Paratrooper in the 82nd Airborne*. Novato, CA: Presidio Press, 2000.

Mitchell, Brian. *Women in the Military*. Washington, DC: Regnery, 1998.

Moore, Byrle. "Maroon Berets Symbolize the Army Melting Pot." Sacramento: *Grizzly*, May 2000.

Moskin, J. Robert. *The U.S. Marine Corps Story*. New York: McGraw Hill, 1982.

Mrazek, James. *History of the 13th Airborne Division*. The Drop Zone Virtual Museum website, 2002. thedropzone.org/units/13thhistory.html

Mullen, Frank X. Jr. "Reno veterans fight to keep black beret an elite symbol." *Reno Gazette-Journal*, December 3, 2000.

Murphy, Edward F. *Dak To: The 173rd Airborne Brigade in South Vietnam's Central Highlands, June–November 1967*. Novato, CA: Presidio Press, 1993.

Murphy, Jack. *History of the U.S. Marines*. Greenwich, CT: Bison Books, 1984.

"Naval Special Warfare Center—Basic Underwater Demolition/SEAL (BUD/S) Training." U.S. Navy SEALs website, 2003. sealchallenge.navy.mil/seal/default.asp.

Nofi, Albert A. *Marine Corps Book of Lists: A Definitive Compendium of Marine Corps Facts, Feats, and Traditions*. Philadelphia: Combined Books, 1997.

O'Donnell, Patrick K. *Into The Rising Sun: In Their Own Words, World War II's Pacific Veterans Reveal the Heart of Combat*. New York: Free Press/ Simon & Schuster, 2002.

"Operation Market Garden." Wikipedia website, 2003. wikipedia.org

Oxford Essential Dictionary of the U.S. Military. New York: Oxford University Press, 2001.

Parrish, Thomas. *The Simon & Schuster Encyclopedia of World War II*. New York: Simon & Schuster, 1978.

Partridge, Wayne. "Army hopes test will put men, women on equal training ground." *Columbus Ledger-Enquirer*, April 26, 1998.

"Pentagon: Saddam's sons killed in raid." CNN.com, July 22, 2003.

Pushies, Fred J. *U.S. Air Force Special Ops*. Osceola, WI: MBI Publishing, 2000.

Quarrie, Bruce. *Airborne Assault: Parachute Forces in Action, 1940–91*. Great Britain: Patrick Stephens Limited, 1991.

"Ranger History." The Ranger Training Brigade website, 2003. benning.army.mil/rtb/HISTORY/rtb.htm.

Raum, Tom. "Bush Proclaims End to Saddam's Regime." Associated Press, July 23, 2003.

Richter, William, and Mark Cowen. *We Stand Alone Together: The Men of Easy Company*. New York: Dreamworks/Playtone, Home Box Office (HBO Video), Time Warner Entertainment Company, 2002.

Ringler, John M. "The Los Banos Raid." *Winds Aloft*, July–October, 1989.

Roche, James G. "Combat Controllers—The Cutting Edge of 21st Century Warfare." Secretary of the Air Force's remarks to the graduating class of Combat Controller School Class 02-04. Pope Air Force Base, NC: December 17, 2002.

Rogers, Patrick A. *Strong Men Armed: The Marine Corps 1st Force Recon Company*. Manchester, CT: The Accurate Rifle, 2000.

Sadler, Barry, and Robin Moore. "Ballad of the Green Berets." New York: RCA Victor, 1966.

Schreitmueller, Ginger. "Air Force 'STARS' take to the skies." *Aerotech News and Review*, May 12, 2000.

Seydel, Carie A. "Shoot, Move, Communicate." *Airman*, March 2002.

Shafritz, Jay M. *Words on War: Military Quotations from Ancient Times to the Present*. New York: Prentice Hall, 1990.

Shapiro, Milton J. *The Screaming Eagles: The 101st Airborne Division in World War II*. New York: Simon & Schuster, 1976.

Simmons, Thomas E. *Forgotten Heroes of World War II: Personal Accounts of Ordinary Soldiers*. Nashville: Cumberland House, 2002.

Slavin, Barbara, and Tom Squitieri. "Korea talks under way, but answers are elusive." *USA Today*, August 27, 2003.

Smith, Carl. *US Paratrooper 1941–45*. Great Britain: Osprey Publishing, 2000.

Smith, Michael S. *Bloody Ridge: The Battle That Saved Guadalcanal*. New York: Pocket Books, 2000.

Smith, S. E. *The United States Marine Corps in World War II: The One-volume History from Wake to Tsingtao—By Distinguished Marine Experts, Authors, and Newspapermen*. New York: Random House, 1969.

Smith, Stephen E. "WWII Mini-Series Portrays Local Retiree." *The Pilot*, 2001.

Smith, W. Thomas Jr. "An Old Warrior Sounds Off: General Westmoreland, commander of U.S. forces in Vietnam until 1968, talks of war and General Giap." *George*, November 1998.

———. *Encyclopedia of the Central Intelligence Agency*. New York: Facts On File, 2003.

———. "Waging War—A crash course in the war on terror, the possible expansion of that war into Iraq, and how we fight it." *Charleston City Paper*, December 18, 2002.

———. "Black berets under fire." *Palmetto Journal*, November 9, 2000.

Special Operations Forces Reference Manual (Version 2.1 Academic Year 99/00). Fort Leavenworth, KS: Army Command and General Staff College, 2000.

Stanton, Shelby L. *The Rise and Fall of an American Army: U.S. Ground Forces in Vietnam, 1965–1973*. Novato, CA: Presidio Press, 1985.

Straub, Bill. "Conflict with Iraq: 82nd Airborne and its famous exploits." Scripps Howard News Service, April 5, 2003.

Streit, Peggy. "What is courage." *The New York Times* magazine, November 24, 1963.

Strobel, Wallace C. "Ike with Paratroopers." Denison, TX: Eisenhower Birth-place State Historical Park website, 2003. eisenhowerbirth-place.org/troops.htm.

Stroud, Phil. "Air Force seeks re-trainees for special operations." Air Force News, Air Force Recruiting Service Public Affairs, August 12, 1997.

Sturkey, Marion F. *Warrior Culture of the U.S. Marines.* Greenwood, SC: Heritage Press International, 2002.

Summary of Vietnam Casualty Statistics, National Archives Combat Area Casualty File. Vietnam Wall website, November 1993. vietnamwall.org/pdf/casualty.pdf.

Thomas, Evan. *The Very Best Men—Four Who Dared: The Early Years of the CIA.* New York: Simon & Schuster, 1995.

Thompson, Leroy. *The All Americans: The 82nd Airborne.* Great Britain: David & Charles Publishers, 1988.

Thurmond, J. Strom. Letter (published) from Thurmond to J. F. Ouzts. *Greenwood Index-Journal*, September 14, 1944.

United States Special Operations Forces Posture Statement 2000. Washington, DC: Office of the Assistant Secretary of Defense, 2000. defenselink.mil/pubs/sof/index.html.

Updegraph, Charles L., Jr. "U.S. Marine Corps Special Units of World War II." Washington, DC: History and Museums Division, Headquarters, U.S. Marine Corps, 1977.

U.S. Airborne During World War II: Overview website. geocities.com/Pentagon/5340/18corps.

U.S. Army Airborne website. Fort Benning, GA: U.S. Army Infantry Homepage, 11th Infantry Regiment, 1st Battalion (Airborne), 507th Infantry website, January 21, 2003, benning.army.mil/airborne.

U.S. Army Field Manual 3-21.220 (57-220), Static Line Parachuting Techniques and Training. Fort Benning, GA: Headquarters, U.S. Army Infantry School, Department of the Army. February 2003.

Uschan, Michael V. *The Korean War.* San Diego: Lucent Books, 2001.

U.S. War Department. "Commendation: Members of Test Platoon, Parachute Troops and Air Infantry, United States Army. General Order No. 89, Section V." October 19, 1945.

Vietnam Studies: U.S. Army Special Forces 1961–1971. CMH Publication 90-23. Washington, DC: Department of the Army, 1989.

Vinch, Chuck. "History of the Beret in the U.S. Army." *Stars and Stripes*. October 29, 2000.

Warner, Ezra J. *Generals in Gray: Lives of the Confederate Commanders*. Baton Rouge: Louisiana State University Press, 1988.

Widner, James F. "Eric Sevareid." Radio News website, May 9, 2003. otr.com/news.html.

"William C. Lee." General William C. Lee Museum website, 2002. fatherofairborne.org

Wright, Robert K. "Joint Task Force South in Operation Just Cause— 20 December 1989—12 January 1990: Oral History Interview with Major General James H. Johnson, Jr., commanding general, 82nd Airborne Division (conducted at Fort Bragg, NC)." Washington, DC: U.S. Army Center of Military History, March 5, 1990.

Yardley, Doyle R. *Home Was Never Like This: The Yardley Diaries: A WWII American POW Perspective*. Evergreen, CO: Yardley Enterprises, 2002.

Young, Charles H. *Into the Valley: The Untold Story of USAAF Troop Carrier in World War II, From North Africa Through Europe*. Dallas, TX: PrintComm, 1995.

INDEX

INDEX

INDEX